About the Author

Joining the London Fire Brigade as a cadet at the tender age of sixteen, **DAVID PIKE** was destined to become very much an operational firefighter. Awarded the Queen's Commendation for Brave Conduct as a young fireman, he rose steadily through the ranks during his thirty-plus years' service within the LFB. He commanded one of London's busiest and most challenging fire stations, Brixton. Heavily committed to raising monies for fire service charities, he rowed himself into *The Guinness Book of Records* whilst attracting many thousands of pounds through his, and his companions', endeavours. He retired in senior rank from the Brigade in 1996. David now lives in Devon.

Austin Macauley publishes David's autobiography *Beyond the Flames* (2013), along with his previous histories of the London Fire Brigade, *London Firefighters* (2015) and *Fire-Floats and Fireboats* (2016).

David C. Pike

I WAS A LONDON FIREFIGHTER

Fire Brigade Stories

AUSTIN MACAULEY PUBLISHERS™
LONDON • CAMBRIDGE • NEW YORK • SHARJAH

A CIP catalogue record for this title is available from the British Library.

ISBN 978-1-52891-800-8 (paperback)
ISBN 978-1-52891-801-5 (eBook)

www.austinmacauley.com

First Published (2018)

Austin Macauley Publishers™ Ltd.
25 Canada Square
Canary Wharf
London
E14 5LQ

Dedication

To old firemen and former firefighters everywhere
and to today's men and women of the London Fire Brigade.

To Dave

to a namesake.

Good reading

Dave Pike

22/2 19

Acknowledgements

The London Fire Brigade

The Massey Shaw Education Trust

Michael Gilbey

Sian Griffiths

Kevin McDermott

Carol Newton

Nigel Saunders

Darren Shirley

Harry Simmons

Garry Warren

David Waterman

Paul Wood

Kevin Wright

My Dad – Charlie Pike

A special mention, and enormous thank you, to
Walter Stephenson (Austin Macauley) for having faith in
this book and working so hard to make it happen.

Contents

Foreword

THE LATEST WORK FROM the pen of former London fireman David Pike provides a fascinating mixture of real and fictitious stories from the London Fire Brigade ranging from Captain Eyre Massey Shaw, first Chief Officer of the Metropolitan Fire Brigade in 1866 to the recent horrific fire at Grenfell Tower. They shine a light on the heroism, dedication, selflessness and teamwork of the capital's fire service in addition to providing a rich insight into how today's firefighters – both male and female – and yesterday's firemen handle the mental and physical demands engendered by that most terrifying and unpredictable of all events, a fire.

Bravery and a sense of duty often go hand in hand, but underlying them and supporting them is a rigorous training regime, part of which I have been lucky enough to have witnessed for myself at the Fire Service College at Moreton-in-Marsh, in Gloucestershire. To a layperson it seems a hard enough task to squeeze through tortuous passages in a mock-up building in broad daylight, but to consider having to do it fully kitted up and wearing breathing apparatus, in total darkness and dense smoke, was almost unimaginable. In another demonstration, the effects of heat were amply demonstrated by placing some of us in a sealed room representing a ship's engine room and lighting a small fire in one corner. We were asked to see how long we could stay before having to evacuate and, with thick smoke rapidly descending from the ceiling, it cannot have been more than half a minute before we were forced to seek safety outside.

The most recent of the author's books, a history of London's firefloats and fireboats, includes the story of the service of the iconic

Massey Shaw fireboat. He was generous enough to donate all of the proceeds of that book towards her continued upkeep. He has kindly offered to do likewise with this work and once again I must thank him most warmly for such a magnanimous gesture which will mean so much to the supporters and volunteers of 'The Massey', as she is fondly known on the river Thames.

The 83-year old veteran fireboat again features here in the retelling of her involvement in the dramatic evacuation of Dunkirk in May 1940. She has returned to Dunkirk on several occasions since and, God willing, will do so again in 2020.

I wish the book well and hope that it will give pleasure to firefighters old and new as well as to the wider general public, who will learn more about the invaluable work of one of London's oldest and most respected emergency services – the London Fire Brigade.

Lord Greenway
Chairman, Massey Shaw Education Trust

Introduction

THIS BOOK IS NOT a definitive history of the London Fire Brigade. Neither is it a detailed record, although some of the accounts printed here are highly detailed. It is 'what it says on the tin': a collection of fire brigade stories; stories, which are either factual accounts or tales of fiction. They are narratives, yarns from a fire brigade I was proud to be a member of for over 30 years.

In putting this collection together I have been assisted by those of a similar ilk. None of these have viewed or still view their time in this foremost of UK fire brigades through rose-tinted glasses. We served, at various times, over the period of the last 60 years, some starting in the late 1950s, others serving into the 21st century. The aim of this book is to provide a flavour of those times through a combination of individual chronicles. Combined, they offer a valuable insight into the life, and role, of London's former firemen as well as an awareness of their modern counterparts, today's firefighters in London's Fire and Rescue Service.

The nature of the 'fireman's lot' has changed dramatically over the years. What hasn't? Today's firefighters would be hard pressed to recognise some of the practices of their forebears who, in turn, would most likely be equally bemused by the practices of those currently serving on the front line of the capital's blue-light services. So whilst the nature of fire has not changed, the manner in which it is tackled has, along with the way that many non-fire-related 999 emergency situations are dealt with today. This book highlights some of those changes through its true accounts; they are also woven into the fabric of the fictional storylines.

Kevin Wright was a former London fireman. He joined in 1969, rising to the heady heights of a Leading Fireman. He was congratulated for bravery not once but twice. Just an ordinary bloke doing an extraordinary job. He was once asked the question: 'How to put a fireman's lot into words?' He answered the question his way.

"You know that adrenaline rush which sees every one of your senses go into overdrive. That sees you kneeling on the landing outside that top floor flat, having run up all the stairs because the bloody fire lift doesn't work again! You paced yourself because you're carrying a 40 pound breathing apparatus set on your back whilst wearing full fire gear. But you will still need to use up precious seconds as you try to get your breath back.

You know that you must control both your breathing and that adrenaline. Your heart is beating like an express train. You need to control your breathing because the harder, and faster, you breathe the quicker the air in your air cylinder will run out and reduce your ability to fight this fire. The contents of your cylinder are the only thing keeping you alive in the conditions you are entering.

You know that the heat you felt when touching the door, with the back of your ungloved hand, means you're going to take a beating. You know, through experience and training, that this one might just 'flash over'. But you trust your experience, firefighting skills learnt from, and passed down, by your mentors – plus, of course, a certain amount of luck.

You know that as soon as you force your entry you will be flat on the floor. You're crawling along on your stomach due to the intense heat. The only way to move forward is slowly. Your body tries to compensate and adjust to the heat. It's getting hotter and hotter, your pulse is climbing higher and higher. The near one thousand degree heat at ceiling level will turn your sweat into superheated steam. Given a chance it will search you out. It will attack you and scald any part of your unprotected body it can find.

You know you will hear glass shattering. Fixtures and fittings falling where the heat has melted whatever held them in place. The high pressure jet of water that you're fighting this fire with is knocking things down like coconuts off a shy. It's throwing everything around like confetti, all adding to the crescendo in your ears.

You know you must search for any persons involved. The

neighbour said that there's nobody in, but you still must search, room by room, hoping all the time that the neighbour is right.

You know, as you carry out your smoke-induced blind search, that every time your hand touches something – a cushion, a child's toy – your heart will skip a beat. But you continue to search. Your heart has skipped a thousand beats over the years whilst carrying out such searches. You know what to expect; it will always be the way.

You know the noise of a fire as it consumes everything in its path. But you still jump and your heart beats so loudly that you can hear it in your head. It will feel as though it will burst through your chest as a light bulb explodes or a thousand and one everyday household items help to feed the fire.

You know as soon as you hit the fire with the water your already restricted visibility will disappear. The thick, black, evil smoke will drop. It drops down to floor level and the water spray that you are using will come back at you so hot it too will search you out and peel any unprotected skin it can find.

You know that the plaster on the walls and ceilings will hit you as you cool it and it shatters into thousands of pieces of all sizes. It will hinder your progress as it falls and forms more obstacles for you to negotiate. Your fire gear will be protecting you the best it can, but you know this wouldn't be the first time something has managed to penetrate it.

You will know you have taken that beating. As the adrenaline wears off you feel drained and exhausted as you exit the fire. The steam is coming off of you, head to toe, as if you are enveloped in your own personal fog.

You know that you have done your job and done it well. It's when those that you would follow anywhere say nothing but give you that special look. A look that speaks volumes and says more than a thousand words could ever say.

You know that others will still be here for a couple of hours, turning over and damping down, cutting away and ensuring that this fire is fully extinguished. You will eventually get back to the fire station, change the cylinder on your breathing apparatus set and hopefully get a shower, grab a cup of tea and a rest before you have to do it all over again.

You know that nobody makes you do it. That you love your job.

That you don't look for thanks or praise, and that there is no higher accolade than being part of that dedicated, professional, team.

You know that your body can only take so much, and to still to be doing this at sixty is not an option.

You know it's easier to fight the fire than to try and answer the question... what makes you do it?"

Eyre Massey Shaw

By David C. Pike*

EVERY STORY HAS A beginning: this happens to be ours. Captain Eyre Massey Shaw is considered by many to be the great-great grandfather of London's Fire Brigade. Shaw was appointed as the first Chief Officer of the Metropolitan Fire Brigade, which was founded in 1866. So it would be remiss not to include some words and images† of this iconic figure in our collection of fire brigade stories and to provide a glimpse of this eminent man of London society and his prodigious achievements in the early years of fire-fighting and later fire prevention.

Eyre Massey Shaw was born in Ireland in 1828 of a Scots-Irish family which had settled in Ireland in the seventeenth century. George Bernard Shaw, the playwright, was another member of the wider Shaw family. After attending Dr Coghlan's school in Dublin, Shaw studied at Trinity College and took his MA there in 1854. It was intended by his family that he should enter the Church. However, when the time came for him to take Holy Orders he couldn't face it and bolted to North America.

This is so unrepresentative of Shaw – to run away from something – that it deserves examination. Why should a serious-minded, intellectual type of man like Shaw refuse to enter a profession which seemed likely to prove congenial and where his family could secure

---

* All stories and articles are by David C. Pike unless otherwise stated.

† See the 'Photographic Section' starting on page 151.

him preferment? The answer might lie in family letters, but these, to my knowledge, do not exist. I can only speculate as to the true explanation.

Though the years of Shaw's childhood and early manhood may have been happy enough for him personally – as the third son of Bernard Robert Shaw of Monkstown Castle, he is unlikely to have suffered any material hardship – they were far from kind to Ireland as a whole. The years between 1840 and 1850 were the years of famine. It is believed that as many as eight million people died from starvation in Ireland or emigrated to avoid it; approximately half the population. Villages and towns were emptied and corpses lined the roadsides. The effect on a sensitive boy – perhaps when riding home from school through villages where death and disease had carried off half their inhabitants, where starving women shook their fists at anyone on a horse, or were even too apathetic to protest – must have been disturbing. He might even have doubted the benevolence of his Maker and the value of the Protestant Church for which he was intended.

Anyway, Shaw took ship to North America and stayed there for several months. One incident occurred during this time which is worthy of comment. While he was in New York, the hotel in which he was staying caught fire and the guests had to evacuate the building. There is little doubt that the incident made an indelible impression on Shaw. He returned home on the understanding that he might choose another career.

In 1855 a commission was obtained for him in the North Cork Rifles, a militia regiment, and he married a Portuguese lady from Lisbon. By 1859 he had risen to the rank of Captain and was the father of two children, but he had still to find a profession that suited him. In 1860 he left the Army to become Chief Constable and the Superintendent of Fire Services in Belfast and was at once a success. He quelled the riots between Sinn Feiners and Orangemen without forfeiting the respect of either party, and reorganised the Belfast Brigade which had been in very poor order. It was this latter achievement which led to his appointment to succeed James Braidwood who, as the first Superintendent of the London Fire Engine Establishment, was killed by a falling wall whilst directing his force of firefighters at a disastrous warehouse fire at Tooley Street in 1861.

The years from 1862 to 1865 were Shaw's years of apprenticeship when he acquired a detailed knowledge of every aspect of firefighting. The London Fire Engine Establishment was a small and vastly overworked force paid for by the insurance companies. It never numbered more than 130 men or 19 stations, but it was well trained and completely professional. Under its first Superintendent it had won considerable popularity, with a remarkable reputation for efficiency.

The Tooley Street fire, however, had persuaded the insurance companies (who ran the London Fire Engine Establishment) and London's public that the defence against fire should not be a matter for private enterprise. The Metropolitan Fire Brigade was established on 1 January 1866 and Captain Shaw was the natural choice as its first Chief Officer. The men from the London Fire Engine Establishment formed the core of the new Brigade, and added to them and their stations and equipment were the escapes and conductors of the Royal Society for the Protection of Life from Fire. Later, Shaw persuaded his employers, the Metropolitan Board of Works, to buy those fire engines of the London parishes which were in good working order.

The Brigade at this time was composed exclusively of seamen, from both the Royal and Merchant Navy, men who were used to irregular hours and living in confined quarters. Shaw was a stern but fair martinet, rising at 3 a.m. to drill and train his men when the streets were empty, but there was no doubt of his personal popularity. When men refer to a senior officer formally by name or rank it can imply a lack of acceptance, or even active dislike or disrespect; Shaw was universally known among his firemen as the "Skipper" or "the Long 'Un".

At a fire in the basement of a big warehouse in Upper Thames Street, a fireman was struggling to drag a hose towards the centre of the fire when dimly through the smoke he noticed someone behind him. The fireman suggested quickly, and coarsely, that the 'long' person behind him should give him a useful hand with the heavy hose instead of aimlessly standing about doing absolutely nothing. The person in question, Shaw, merely told a fireman with him to take up the hose as suggested. There were no further repercussions following this incident. This story contrasts nicely with that of a subsequent London Chief Officer who, very early in his Brigade career, arrived at a fire and angrily demanded of the officer in charge why the firemen were not formed up on parade and awaiting his orders. It is not known what the officer said in reply but I imagine his expression would have been sufficient indication that London firefighters don't wait to be told what to do at a fire.

Perhaps a further clue to Shaw's personality lies in the care he showed for his men's safety at fires. Warehouses at that time presented a particular risk. They were commonly built of brick with unprotected steel or iron girders to support the floors and roof. In a fierce fire the girders would expand with the heat and push out the walls of the building. The floors, laden with goods – many which could absorb large quantities of the water used to fight the blaze – added significantly to the fire loading, which in turn frequently caused floors to collapse in a fire. A fireman directing a hose through a lower window from the street was particularly exposed to danger from falling brickwork. Shaw took the greatest pains to see that his men were posted in positions where they would be safe.

On one occasion in the 1880s, at a very big fire at the King and Queen Granaries, Shaw was superintending firefighting operations when there was a crash of brickwork. The huge walls, bulging under the weight of swollen maize and tons of water, looked as if they were going to collapse. One of the firemen who was directing a jet from the centre of an escape ladder dropped his hose, slid down the escape, and started to run. Shaw caught him by the arm as he ran. "Don't run," he told him, "you run into danger. Go and pick up your hose and carry on. I'll tell you when to run." The fireman looked at the bulging walls, looked at his Chief Officer, who stood quietly on the very spot where the walls would crash if they did collapse, picked up the nozzle and resumed his work. The walls did collapse, but not until three days later.

Finally, Shaw backed his men on every occasion when they made representations for improvements in their pay and conditions. For three shillings a day when he joined, a man was required to remain continuously on duty, fully dressed in uniform, boots, belt and axe. If he took off his boots, he was liable to be fined the best part of a day's pay. Leave was allowed for a few hours during the day with the Station Officer's agreement, but beyond this, or after 10 p.m., Shaw's personal permission was necessary. When recruiting was poor and men fell ill, firemen might be on duty for six days at a time, never shifting out of their clothes.

In 1884 the position at last improved. Station officers could grant leave for 24 hours; District Officers could grant leave for 48 hours. However, this was a special privilege, not a right, and the firemen were still otherwise employed on continuous duty. The strain on the firemen was enormous. Shaw could ensure that few died on active duty – there were, in fact, only ten deaths in the 30 years he was Chief Officer – but he could not prevent the breakdown in health and early retirement into which many were forced.

It is difficult to estimate how much these conditions arose from public penny-pinching (the Metropolitan Board of Works ran the Brigade on a very cheap shoestring) and how much from the defects in Shaw's own character. There is a modern tendency to look for feet of clay on every idol and Shaw had his faults. If nothing else, he had some of the defects of his many virtues. His powers of leadership almost certainly surpassed those of any other fireman in the world at that time, but he seems to have been quite unable to secure the backing of any elected body or committee with whom he had dealings.

He was an aristocrat by birth and an autocrat by nature. He expected implicit obedience from his subordinates. He never forgot for a single moment that he was a gentleman and on the friendliest terms with Royalty. When Shaw was injured at a fire in 1883, which left him with a permanent limp – he collected several injuries in the courses of his firefighting career – the Prince of Wales, a close personal friend, together with other members of the Royal family, drove in open carriages to the Brigade's headquarters at Southwark, where Shaw was convalescing, through streets lined with cheering Londoners. There can be very few people who belonged to quite so many London clubs as Shaw. Besides the Carlton and Pratt's there were at least five others. He was very much a member of London Society.

Shaw was a character to admire rather than to love. Throughout his life, apart from the single lapse when he preferred flight to

America to Holy Orders, it seems doubtful that he ever flinched from the path of duty even in the full glare of publicity. He wrote of a fireman's work: "If he wants to do it well, he must show moral as well as physical courage; in short, he must harden his heart and act as if no one were looking on."

I have a suspicion that Shaw may have enjoyed disdaining public approval and flexing his moral muscles. It would probably have served his own interest, and those of the Fire Brigade, better if he had on occasion showed that he cared even a little what other people thought and felt. One would have thought, for example, that when the Metropolitan Board of Works gave way to the London County Council in 1889 he would have used his immense influence and personal authority, combined with his great popularity amongst the general public, to have persuaded the Fire Brigade Committee to expand the Brigade and improve working conditions for firemen. The financial restrictions which had bedevilled the Metropolitan Board of Works had disappeared; money could be found quite easily. Instead, matters went from bad to worse.

Two years after the London County Council was formed, Shaw abruptly retired. It is difficult to know exactly why. The Committee Clerk was notably discreet, and nothing of the true facts was allowed to infiltrate the minutes. The Committee, as a whole, was genuinely surprised and expressed their pain to see him go. They may also have secretly been relieved. He had become an institution, and institutions can be obstacles to evolution. But he departed with the Committee's thanks, an inscribed marble clock from Queen Victoria, a fine silver tea service from the insurance companies and a knighthood.

He became Managing Director of the Palatine Insurance Company and Chairman of the Metropolitan Electricity Board. He was even appointed Deputy Lieutenant of Middlesex. But these are peripheral to his real achievement. He was the creator in his own time of the finest fire brigade in the world, and when he died in 1908, his legs amputated and approaching eighty years old, this was remembered by the thousands who followed his funeral cortège from Pimlico to Highgate Cemetery where he lies buried with his wife and children.

Shaw remained a potent influence in the London Fire Brigade

right up until the late 1990s. His memory is perpetuated in the fireboat bearing his name. The Massey Shaw showed some of his indomitable courage in 1940 off the beaches of Dunkirk, but his was the moral fervour which makes firefighting in the London Fire Brigade more than a way of earning one's livelihood. Even until more recent times the brigade brought with it membership of one of the most tightly-knit, morally-motivated groups of men in the world.

I am none too sure what the ghost of Sir Eyre Massey Shaw would make of the policies and practices of today's London Fire Brigade. His was a growing London. Fires were far more frequent and gave rise to genuine public concern. He worked during a period of growth with more firemen being employed and more fire stations built. Today's Brigade is a very different 'kettle of fish'. Recent reductions in the number of fires have led to consequential reductions in both staff and fire stations. (Ten London stations were closed in 2014.) The new brigade has a privatised control room, 'out-sourced' training regimes and even a for-profit offshoot, LFB Enterprises Ltd. LFB Enterprises provides a range of community safety, fire-related products and training tailored for organisations. It is a fact that Shaw was none too fond of the fledgling London County Council. He was a man of his time; today is in the now. Whilst many former London Fire Brigade staff find might find themselves in the same boat as he – unsure and occasionally ill at ease with this rapidly changing world – it is a world in which the modern London Fire Brigade must contend. With its first ever female Commissioner (Chief Officer) appointed in 2017, despite the fiscal challenges she faces, the Brigade continues to move forward. As with Shaw, it will take the passage of history to see what progress is actually made.

(Fact)

A Fire-Float Went to War

WHEN THE LONDON FIRE-FLOAT Massey Shaw first left her river moorings for Dunkirk, she had only ever been to sea once before. That was on her maiden journey from the Isle of Wight to the Thames in 1935, after being constructed at the John Samuel White boatyard at a cost of £18,000. Following her final fitting out at Greenwich she was placed into operational service with the London Fire Brigade that summer.

Massey Shaw was never intended to be a sea-going vessel. She had, until the time of Dunkirk, been stationed at the Blackfriars river station, adjacent to Blackfriars Bridge in London. Her two massive 8-cylinder, 160 hp diesel engines had more than enough power to propel her up and down the Thames at 12 knots. However, they were principally intended to operate her 3,000 gallon-per-minute centrifugal pumps to put out fires along London's river front.

She had been named after Captain Eyre Massey Shaw (1828–1908) who, at the age of thirty, was the first Chief Officer of the Metropolitan Fire Brigade. Her first major operational test was, literally, an ordeal by fire. An eight-storey riverside warehouse, Colonial Wharf, containing rubber products, and located in Wapping High Street, burned for four days from 27 September 1935. It had required 60 fire engines and three fire-floats to contain the blaze. This was the first major incident, and test, for the new fire-float and one where she greatly assisted land crews, who were hampered by very difficult access. The Massey Shaw's single monitor threw vast quantities of water high into the inferno, thus allowing the land crews to regroup and prevent the fire from spreading to adjoining warehouses.

However, that was not to be her most noticeable service

achievement. Shortly after the start of World War II, the London Fire Brigade volunteer fire-float crew of the Massey Shaw would perform heroically as they joined the fleet of "Little Ships" that evacuated British soldiers from the beaches of Dunkirk in Northern France. Navy sailors, volunteers with their small craft and London firemen all worked side by side to rescue members of the British Expeditionary Force trapped by the German Army on the French beaches.

On May 29 and 30, 1940 the Massey Shaw's crew had seen tugs coming down the river towing strings of small boats, yachts, lifeboats and even dinghies. Then they heard that their destination was Dunkirk and that the Massey Shaw was to follow them from her mooring at Blackfriars. Her volunteer crew of 13 was chosen and with a formal send-off they departed from the Brigade Headquarters river station by the Albert Embankment in Lambeth.

Thirteen was more than her normal crew complement because they had expected to spend several days fighting fires off the French coast without relief. A river pilot took them to Greenwich and another onto Ramsgate. Her sparkling brass-work and fittings were covered with grey paint on the way. A young Royal Naval Sub-Lieutenant came aboard to take command of the Massey Shaw. He carried nothing more than his steel helmet and a chart to show him how to navigate through the minefields across the channel from North Goodwin Lightship to Bray Dunes, the beach where they were to pick up Allied troops.

The Massey Shaw did not even possess a ship's compass, but the firemen had bought one hastily from a chandlery in Blackfriars. There was no time to swing and correct it, which made it rather unreliable since the large steel hull of the fire-float caused a massive deviation. As a result, despite the excellent landmark of smoke from Dunkirk's burning oil tanks, they were well outside the swept channel when they got to the French coast. But the boat's shallow draft enabled them to cross the hazardous sandbanks without grounding.

The fires ashore were what the Massey Shaw's firemen crew were used to, but the bursts of high-explosive shells, bombs and anti-aircraft fire were a new experience. As they steamed parallel to the beach, they saw columns of men wading out in the shallows, waiting to be picked up by a host of small boats. Late that afternoon, they anchored off Bray Dunes.

They used a light skiff, picked up at Ramsgate Harbour, to go ashore and collect the first of the men. Most of the soldiers were non-swimmers and, at first, too many of them tried to get aboard so they swamped and sank the skiff. There were many other small boats operating from the beach, but each of them already had its own ship to fill. After many attempts to find a suitable way of ferrying soldiers to the Massey Shaw a line was made fast to a derelict lorry and a small boat was used to ferry altogether 40 of a company of Royal Engineers aboard the Massey Shaw.

The young Royal naval officer, having spent most of the day in the water between the fire-float and the beach, then safely navigated her back to Ramsgate where they arrived next morning. They escaped major damage despite an attack by a German bomber, which had spotted the Massey Shaw's phosphorescent wake, but whose bombs missed by a boat's length.

The crew of the Massey Shaw re-fuelled hastily, got some food and left for another trip. Some of the exhausted firemen were replaced by naval ratings and they brought a Lewis gun on-board as a defence against air attack, although this was never used. Another RN officer, this time a Royal Naval Volunteer Reserve Lieutenant, came aboard to command the ship and they brought two stokers to take care of the engines plus a beach party, commanded by a second young naval officer, to handle the embarkation on the other side. They also took a 30-foot ship's lifeboat in tow as a tender.

At 11 p.m. they arrived and anchored off Bray Dunes in ten feet of water with their prow facing the shore. The fires of Dunkirk gave them enough light to work by and the thick blanket of smoke provided some cover from air attack. But the shelling from German guns was relentless. The two naval officers set a splendid example of calm and the beach party rowed ashore, fixing a line to maintain contact with the fireboat. After four or five journeys, the Massey Shaw was full once more with troops pressed together in the cabin and standing shoulder-to-shoulder on deck. Her load of nearly 100 men was transferred to a troopship at anchor in the channel and she returned to be re-loaded. This was only possible after some engine trouble that the naval stokers, who were unused to the Massey Shaw's machinery, eventually managed to overcome.

Stretcher cases now began to arrive; these were hard to handle and transfer to the troopship. The Massey Shaw crew made about five journeys from the beach to a paddle steamer and it was estimated that they embarked 500 men in this way. As dawn broke, the troopship was full and left for England. The Massey Shaw returned to the beach and started loading again. At this point, on a falling tide, the boat began to bump on the sands and was in danger of damaging her propellers but, with the engines throbbing at full power, the crew just managed to get back into deep water. At 3.30 a.m. she was the last boat to leave that part of the beach. Halfway across the channel, the naval skipper began to have doubts about the compass, but then, to his relief, they came across a drifter towing two small boats packed with troops. They followed the drifter into Ramsgate where they arrived at 8.00 a.m. on Sunday 2 June, landing 30 or 40 more soldiers.

The Massey Shaw returned to Dunkirk again the next evening with a London Fire Brigade crew. This time they went to the jetty off Dunkirk harbour. It was difficult for soldiers to board her from the towering jetty and she came away empty. After returning to Ramsgate, she was ordered back to London. Off Margate the Emile de Champs, a French ship, which had sailed to England from Dunkirk laden with troops the previous night, was passing her at a distance of 200 yards when it struck a mine and sank almost immediately. The Massey Shaw picked up 40 men, all severely injured, and took them back to Ramsgate.

Early on Wednesday 5 June, she finally returned to London. As she came up the River Thames she was cheered as she passed each fire station. Finally, the wives and families of all those on board were waiting at the Lambeth Headquarters when the boat docked at the Lambeth river station to great jubilation. The crew were given a splendid reception at the Headquarters station.

Footnotes

Sub-Officer A. J. May was subsequently awarded the Royal Navy's Distinguished Service Medal, a rare honour for any civilian. Two of the Massey Shaw's firemen, Henry Ray and Edmond Wright, were also mentioned in the Royal Navy's account of the evacuation and both awarded the King's Commendation for Gallantry.

In August 1941 the National Fire Service was created and the London Fire Brigade became a Region of the NFS. The term fire-float was changed to fireboat, as it remains today.

(Fact)

The Case of the Peculiar Out-Duty...

NOTHING WAS WORKING OUT for Olly as he had intended. A recently qualified 'Proto' breathing apparatus (BA) fireman, he served at a busy inner London fire station. In fact, Olly was one of the very first to undertake the Brigade's extended and improved breathing apparatus courses, something which had been introduced in the summer of 1960 in the wake of the death of two London firemen at the Smithfield Meat Market fire in 1958. The two men had entered a smoke-filled basement in BA and never came back out alive.

Now not only was Olly working a night duty on All Hallows eve, when he had hoped to take his wife and two young children to the special evening family service at his local church, but he was to miss the special mess supper too. His request for a night's leave had been declined. Olly's name had been entered on the roll call board as riding BA on the back of the pump when he had wandered into work at around 5.30 p.m. However, when his name was called out at the 6.00 p.m. roll call it had nothing to do with riding the pump. He was ordered to 'stand-by' for the watch at the dock-side fire station on the far side of the Division. He wouldn't get to enjoy the quarterly mess dinner, something all the watch chipped in for and which the talented mess manager was busily preparing when Olly passed the kitchen, carrying his kitbag, on his way out of the station to perform this unwelcome out-duty.

It was a Sunday night. One free of normal evening work routines. There was something of a festive mood across the watch: an anticipation of the special meal, with laughs shared and a glass of beer enjoyed with their dinner. Beer was something the guvnor only allowed at these infrequent events.

Olly crossed the station yard and placed the kitbag, with his black fire helmet tied on top, in the side-car of his trusty motorcycle combination. As he was preparing to depart there was relief on the faces of other firemen on the watch that they had avoided the unfortunate out-duty. It was all the luck of the draw. Olly's name was simply next up on the rota.

Olly was an extremely likeable man. He had been keen to learn. He listened to what he was told by the more senior hands. Now in his third year, he was also a respected member of the watch. He had a couple of decent BA fires under his belt. Even so, the 'old sweats' would still much prefer to cough up lumps of soot rather than put on a 'sissy' BA set at a fire unless they were ordered to do so by their Station Officer, who was simply called 'Guvnor'.

The guvnor ran a tight ship. Although not an overly friendly man, he was not considered a harsh taskmaster, rather someone who was both firm and fair. More importantly, he was thought of as a first class fire officer. On the fire-ground his word was law. His operational judgement was considered sound and highly regarded by rank and file. Now, much to Olly's amazement, his guvnor strolled over to him as he prepared to kick-start his motorbike.

"Take care, old son," said his Station Officer. "That station can have some surprises if you are not careful."

With that the Station Officer turned around, walked back into the station and was gone. His words played on Olly's mind as he navigated his way across the Division on the almost deserted Sunday evening streets. The 'old man' – not that Olly would ever say that in ear-shot of his guvnor – had never spoken to him before when he had done an out-duty. In fact, he did not say much to Olly at all, unless it was to bark an order at a fire or to shout an instruction on the station's drill ground.

Moving closer to the river, the buildings started to change in appearance, reflecting the former use of the area. The once busy general warehouses and wharves had fallen on hard times in recent years. But the cobbled side streets gave the place a timeless quality. One where the Victorian workers, who once filled the streets, would have felt right at home had their spirits returned to pay a visit. Something Olly thought was a strange thing to think of. Even as a churchgoing man, he firmly believed that once you're dead, you're dead.

The autumn river mist was thickening. It was sweeping into the surrounding narrow streets. It gave everything a surreal feel. One might even be forgiven for thinking it was all a tad spooky – if one were that way inclined. Olly was glad he was not heading over to Whitechapel; the thought of Jack the Ripper stalking similar streets gave him a sudden shiver.

Then in the distance light shone out onto the street. It was the light from the open appliance room of his stand-by fire station. It was one of many such London stations that had no rear entrance. Everything had to pass through the appliance room to get into the rear, rather claustrophobic, yard. This was where he could park his motorcycle combination.

As he drew nearer both sets of doors were wide open. Olly assumed that the station had had a 'shout'. Not many station crews would delay their turn-out by stopping to shut the appliance doors before proceeding onto an emergency call, despite the fact that they were required to do just that. Clearly this was one such station. What Olly had not expected to see was the unfamiliar fire engine, a pump, standing there in the station!

Parking his bike in the rear yard he walked back towards the appliance room. He had ridden his bike wearing his fire-gear, exchanging only his fire helmet for his favourite leather crash hat and flying goggles, something he always wore whenever riding his beloved motorcycle. He immediately noticed something strange about the fire engine, something he had not noticed before.

"Bloody 'ell," he thought, "they must really be scraping the bottom of the barrel for spare appliances these days." The engine was red enough and it carried all the requisite ladders, but it could easily have come from a museum. He walked past it and into the station watchroom situated in one corner of the appliance room. It was where the three-man crew stood in complete silence. They all had the look of 'old' hands, each in their late 40s. None looked overjoyed to see him arrive.

"I am here to stand by for the watch," said Olly.

"They're out and have picked up a job down the road," said the Sub Officer.

The other two firemen did not give Olly a second glance; one of them looked strangely familiar.

"That's a crap machine you have been given," commented Olly, hoping to lighten the mood. He failed.

"It will do us," said the Sub.

Olly gave up on the conversation but could not help feeling a distinct chill. He put this down to riding his motorbike to this station in his fire tunic. He looked over at the watchroom desk. The station log book lay open on the top of the desk. He noticed that nobody from the crew had booked on duty in the watchroom nor had they booked in the peculiar-looking London Fire Brigade pump at the station as required. Not wishing to make a fuss, he made a note on the watchroom message pad stating what time he had arrived at the station, 6.45 p.m., together with the station name he had come from. Any further attempt by Olly at conversation was interrupted by the old, breathless, man who came running into the station. The old man saw the others standing in the watchroom and rushed in. He started speaking before he got through the door. In fact, he was shouting more than speaking and to no one in particular.

"There's lots of smoke coming from the warehouse around the corner."

The only one to respond was the Sub Officer. "Calm down, old chap, we are on our way. You," – meaning Olly – "ride with us".

Olly had ridden his motorbike wearing his belt and axe so putting his fire helmet on he found himself sitting on the rear of the pump as the engine roared into life. The driver seemed to know where to go without a word being said. Certainly the old man had not given a precise address. The fire engine turned left out of the station and within a short distance turned right into a riverside alley. Even to Olly it was clear that they had a working job on their hands. Thick, billowing, brown smoke was coming from the upper loophole openings of a warehouse. Inside the warehouse the sound of burning timber, crackling angrily, could be clearly heard whilst above the five-storey building, reflected in the swirling mist, was an angry red and orange glow.

Olly had expected the Sub Officer to reach for the appliance radio, to send a priority message requesting immediate reinforcements. But there was no radio.

"Some bloody spare appliance this is," thought Olly.

Instead, the Sub Officer turned to the driver and told him to find a public call box and make a 'fire-flash' call (a fireman's 999 call) and 'make pumps six'. Jumping down from the engine the Sub Officer kicked open the locked side entrance door. Inside there was a short landing which led directly onto the wooden internal staircase that gave access to the upper floors. Further along the hallway another staircase led down to the sub-basement.

"Right you two; get your sets on and have peek downstairs. I am going to have a quick shufti up above."

With that, and seemingly impervious to the thick acrid smoke, the Sub Officer made his way up the flight of stairs. Even before he was halfway up he disappeared, lost to view in the churning smoke. The next thing that Olly noticed was that the Proto breathing apparatus set he was using was not like the one he had trained on or used back at his own station. His was the Mark V Proto set. What he was now throwing over his shoulder was the BA set that preceded it. It had a leather and canvas harness. But in all other respects he was familiar with it and how to start it up. Which was just as well as his "oppo" was looking as though he had no intention of waiting for Olly. Olly recalled the words of his BA instructor who said that steady, slow-hand clapping was once the distress signal if BA men ever got into difficulties. Olly thought that a useful thing to remember right now.

As the pair entered the warehouse the smoke got thicker. Even with their battery-operated CEAG lamps turned on, the visibility was almost non-existent. Using the open wooden staircase the pair headed down into the sub-basement. As they reached the floor a sudden violent rumble somewhere overhead seemed to shake the building to its very core. They felt the vibrations rise up through their fire boots. Next followed a loud whoosh as escaping hot gases and fierce flames exploded through the roof into the night sky.

The upper floors started to collapse, one on top of the other. The deafening sound filled their heads as tons of falling masonry, and other debris, came crashing down. Olly made a dive to his left. His BA colleague dived to the right. Everything went black followed by an unexpected stillness. Shaken, but uninjured, Olly found himself trapped in a small alcove. A half-lit, barred window, just below the ceiling, was level with the outside pavement. The entrance to the room blocked by a wall of debris. Then something broke the dust filled silence. He listened intently, then he heard it again. It was coming from the other side of the fallen debris. It was the unmistakable sound of slow regular hand clapping. Clap…clap…clap.

Back at the fire station the pump-escape and pump had returned from the false alarm at the far end of the station's ground. It was whilst they were reversing into their respective bays that the Station Officer walked into the watchroom and discovered the old man sitting in the dutyman's chair. He was still trying to regain his composure after all that evening's excitement.

"What are you doing here?" demanded the officer.

"I came to report the fire" said the old man, clearly offended by the officer's attitude.

"What bloody fire?" insisted the officer.

"The one that your other engine is attending," shouted back the old man, now irritated that his act of civic duty was being questioned in such an aggressive fashion.

By now the dutyman had entered the watchroom and passed the Station Officer Olly's note which he had found on the watchroom desk.

"Book us back," said the officer, "and ask Control why they sent a stand-by appliance here to cover our station."

The dutyman did as instructed. He looked bemused as he informed his guvnor that no stand-by machine had been sent into the station. The Station Officer looked menacingly at the old man.

"Now you tell me exactly what happened and what you saw."

Which the old man did. Reiterating his tale, adding that he was surprised that the firemen never asked him exactly where the fire was. He added that one of the firemen took off a motorcycle helmet, put on a fireman's helmet before he got on the fire engine. It was then that Olly's kitbag was noticed in the corner of the watchroom.

"Search the whole station," demanded the Station Officer.

The two crews quickly completed their task – "Nothing, Guv." – as they ran back to the watchroom to report. "No one here except this old bloke," commented the Sub Officer.

"Exactly where was this fire?" asked the Station Officer, now in a far more conciliatory tone.

"The warehouse in Druids Alley, just around the corner," said the old man.

"Put the bells down dutyman, we're going," ordered the officer.

The Station Officer made pumps ten, turntable ladders two even before he got down from the pump. The upper floors of the warehouse were totally ablaze. Olly had managed to smash a pane of glass but could only reach high enough to stick his hand through the jagged opening to attract attention. No one noticed him at first, there too much going on. The attack on the fire was gathering pace, with each additional fire engine crew adding to the overall weight of attack. Finally two of the pump-escape's crew noticed the hand sticking out of the broken window. They worked feverishly to prise away the stout iron window bars. Removing two gave sufficient space for Olly to be lifted up and out, but not with him wearing his breathing apparatus set. Taking a deep breath of the life-giving oxygen, he lifted the set over his head and dropped it to the floor. The men hauled Olly to safety.

Olly's first words were not, "Thank you," but, "Get the others out, they are still inside."

"What others?" said one of his rescuers. "We were the first two fire engines here. There was no one else around! That old bloke must have got it wrong and just saw you run round here on your own."

Olly was too confused and shocked to argue. But to his credit the Leading Fireman, who helped Olly out of the sub-basement, passed the comments on to a senior officer. That was when the 'mire' hit the fan. A full roll call was ordered but no one was found to be missing or unaccounted for.

With the first of that night's reliefs ordered and in place Olly returned, on the pump, to the station some hours later. No sooner had he stepped off the engine than he was ordered by the Station Officer into the watchroom to be interviewed by a senior officer from the Divisional HQ. An Assistant Divisional Officer sat in the dutyman's chair. The officer was both senior in rank and in his length of service. His fire tunic smelt of the acrid smoke from the warehouse blaze where he had just come from. He had a brusque and off-hand reputation on the fire-ground and was known to be fond of using the odd expletive to those who were slow to react to his commands. But all Olly saw was a more human side of this man's character.

"I have already spoken with the old gentleman who gave the 'running call', son," said the senior officer. "I just need to hear your side of the story."

So Olly told him – everything, from beginning to end; from his arrival and the strange looking pump, right up to his rescue from the cellar. It was whilst the senior officer was on the phone to the control room that Olly noticed the small memorial plaque on the watchroom wall. It recorded the deaths of a Sub Officer and one fireman on the night of 31 October 1949 whilst standing by covering the station. Olly felt he had nothing to lose so asked the senior officer what had happened.

"Their pump stood by here, as the plaque says. They picked up a call to a fire in Druids Alley. It was well alight when they arrived. Whilst the Sub went up the stairs to investigate the extent of the fire the floor collapsed and he was killed outright. The driver who ran for the phone box went the wrong way. By the time he got back there was nothing he could do. The other lone fireman had gone down in the basement in BA hoping to locate the Sub Officer. He became trapped by fallen debris. It was impossible for anyone to reach him although the driver said he heard the man's regular slow hand-clapping for help. But no one can be certain what the driver actually heard. The trapped fireman's oxygen eventually ran out and his body was recovered the following day. It was said that it was the deaths of his mates which led the driver to take his own life."

"Why is his name not recorded here?" asked Olly.

"He was your guvnor's elder brother and it was his wish not to have the name added," replied the ADO.

"So what now?" asked Olly.

"Nothing," said the man behind the desk as he closed his notebook. "My report will say you responded to the running call whilst the station's two machines were attending the false alarm. You acted in the finest traditions of the service and no more will be said about it. Understand?"

But Olly didn't understand. So much went through Olly's head as he lay on his bed, unable to sleep.

The new day brought him no new cheer. At the change of watch he got back on his motorbike to return to his base station. However, he could not return without one last look at the scene of the previous night's happenings. All the reliefs had now departed. The alley was deserted. The warehouse was a smouldering ruin. The overpowering smell of burnt wood and debris filled his nostrils as he parked his motorcycle at the end of the eerily quiet turning. He looked around and saw the street level window, its missing iron bars indicating the place he had been pulled to safety.

He knew what had happened. It was imprinted in his brain. But he needed to see if the old leather-harnessed Proto set still lay on the floor where he left it. However, the sub-basement was more akin to a swimming pool, filled with the thousands upon thousands of gallons of water used to contain and then extinguish the fire. But he looked in anyway, drawing ever closer to the opening. It was deathly silent... or so he thought.

It was then he heard a sound. Then he heard it again. Olly's heart started pounding as he turned an ashen white. He knew that noise. He had heard it before. It was unmistakable. It was the sound of someone clapping their hands together; slowly, repeatedly. Clap... clap... clap...

As Olly stood the clapping became even louder. The clamour filled his head as he ran towards his motorbike. Even his bike's powerful engine noise could not silence the rhythmic sound. Its regular distress signal followed Olly as he drove away at speed through those narrow, deserted streets...

(Fiction)

Starting in West Ham

By Michael Gilbey

APART FROM MY TIME as a GPO telegram boy straight after I left school, my entire career was spent in the fire service. I joined the West Ham fire brigade three days before my 18th birthday. It was not legal, but rules could be more easily bent in those days. I retired 42 years later. I believe that I may have been the longest-serving member of the fire service at that time. The latter years of my very enjoyable service were in a non-operational role. This was due to both my age and failing eyesight. But with so many years under my belt I gathered up a wealth of knowledge about the service, including its remarkable history.

I had joined West Ham in the early 1960s but was later transferred into the London Fire Brigade. West Ham was one of many brigades absorbed into an enlarged Brigade in 1965 following the creation of the Greater London Council (GLC). So much of my initial service education came from the senior West Ham firemen. Quite a number of them had joined after the end of World War II; they, in turn, learned from the wizened firemen of their day. Many of London's fire stations still exist, stations originally built in the 19th century – a time when fire engines were either horse-drawn steamer pumps or escape carts, the firemen on the rear clinging to the sides.

One of my earliest lessons was to learn some of the fire service jargon. Every organisation has its own lingo; the fire service, it seemed, had more than its fair share. So in the fire service if a piece of equipment becomes defective, be it large or small, it is described as being 'off the run'. Conversely, equipment that is fit for use is deemed to be 'on the run'. Often the defective equipment had a label tied onto it with just the letters 'OTR'. This phrase originates from the fire service of the 1800s, when horse-drawn vehicles dominated the scene.

By the mid-1800s, as today, everything was designed for a speedy turnout from the fire station. The longer the delay, the greater the chance of loss of life from fire or its effects. The horses were kept in the fire station stables, normally located immediately to the rear of the appliance room. The appliance was where the 'steamer' and escape cart stood in readiness, the steamer with a constantly lit boiler. Stable doors were normally spring-loaded. They could be opened mechanically or by pulling on a rope. When the station call-out alarm sounded, the stable doors would open and the trained horses knew exactly what to do. They trotted, unaided, from their stable into the appliance room to stand alongside the shafts of the steamer and/or the escape cart. Suspended above their heads, and fixed in an opened-out position in a cradle, was the harness which would be swiftly lowered onto the horses, the rear of the harness being already attached to the engine being pulled. A rope and pulley system allowed the harnesses to be lowered onto the horses and fitted by means of quick attachment buckles. Counterweights and springs would then lift the cradle back towards the ceiling so as not to delay the turn-out.

To assist the engines to rapidly depart station the floor where it stood was sloped. This helped overcome the initial inertia of getting the engine moving. With the brake released the engine would roll forward under its own weight, which assisted the horses to leave the station at some speed. The sloped floor was known as the 'run'. When the steamer was fired up and ready it was said to be 'on the run'. It is recorded that from the time of receiving a call the horses could be out of the stables, harnessed and out of the station in less than two minutes. Some even claimed this could even be as quick as 30 seconds.

The pumps on these 'steamers' were piston-powered. They operated in a similar way to the pistons on a steam train. The disadvantage was that this caused the water to squirt out of the jets in a pulsating movement, plus the pistons could not pump against the branches (jets) when closed. So a large sealed metal dome was fitted to these pumps to absorb extra water from the pistons and help smooth out pulsations in the jet. Today's fire engines use centrifugal pumps. There no pistons: these pumps are fitted with an internal spinning disc known as an impeller. This allows water to flow at an even pressure at all times even if the branch is open or closed.

The first fireman's tunic I wore was the traditional 'Melton' design. It was a design which had been around since before the turn of the 20th century. Tunics are vastly different today. Our fire helmets were black and made of cork, whilst our leggings, also black, only covered our legs, leaving the backsides of our work overalls exposed to the elements! Today's firefighters' helmets are completely enclosed and fitted with a protective visors; some have built-in communications equipment. My original fire boots were made of strong leather with non-ferrous and spark-proof nails in the heels. Comfortable as they were, they offered little protection against penetrative chemicals and water. Later, these were replaced by strong rubber boots with reinforced toecaps and a metal plate: this protected against stepping on nails and other sharp debris but rubbed my heels raw.

My first fire engine was similar to fire engines stationed around London generally. One was called a pump-escape. It carried the 50-foot wheeled wooden escape ladder and was considered the rescue appliance. Its ladder was mounted on two large carriage wheels and weighed about one ton. It was a very robust ladder, one that was in frequent use on the fire-ground back then. However, due to a number of factors – not least the cost of maintenance and replacement problems – it was necessary to replace this ladder in the mid-1980s by a 13.5 metre (45 foot) aluminium 'Lacon' ladder. The pump-escapes were re-designated 'pump-ladders'. My other fire engine was the 'pump'. This carried a 30-foot ladder and breathing apparatus, and was considered the workhorse of the Brigade.

Despite popular misconceptions a fireman's (now firefighters') job is far more than just squirting water at a fire. It remains a very technical job: one that requires considerable knowledge of various subjects, since a firefighter is expected to deal with a range of hazards and resolve many emergency situations besides fires.

I was stationed at Plaistow Fire Station in those early years. It was one of the three stations in the former West Ham Fire Brigade. The area covered by this station was extensive in both its area and the types of risks it contained. The old station, originally built in 1932 under the former West Ham Fire Brigade, is now gone. It was replaced by the new modern station standing on the same site. With the closure of Silverton Fire Station in 2014 that station's fire-ground is now mainly covered by Plaistow. The area was once a mixture of profuse old terraced housing, heavy industry and shipping in the Royal group of docks. Even the former, famous, West Ham United football stadium was protected by this fire station. The infamous Ronan Point, which collapsed during 1968, was located on this station's ground too. Its appliances were the first to reach the scene of this high-rise disaster.

The East End of London is well-known for its community spirit. However, I once attended an incident where I witnessed a far more intolerant attitude by some individuals to a fellow human being. Nowadays people realise that firefighters have a multi-faceted rescue role. But in those early years people tended to think of 'firemen' dealing only with fires. We did, of course, attend a whole range of incidents which were not fire-related. Generally, they come under the heading of special services; they still do today. Attending and releasing people shut in lifts is but one example. There are many different lift installers across London, each with a variation in the lift design, yet having to comply with a comprehensive set of uniform safety rules and standards.

So whilst cinema and television disaster movies love to show lifts plunging at high speed down a lift shaft, it rarely ever happens in real life. One of the many safety features built into lifts are special lift brakes, which spring out, gripping the guides and wedging the lift stationary in the shaft. This occurs if the speed of travel increases above a predetermined limit, such as in the unlikely event, of a lift cable breaking. I attended many lift incidents in my career, too many to recall, sometimes several calls in a shift. But one individual occasion remains embedded in my mind.

In the early 1970s we received a call to a lift incident about 8 a.m. On arrival at the tower block we heard the voice of a boy calling out for help in a lift car. The lift had stopped between the ground and first floor. It soon became apparent that the boy had been delivering the morning newspapers on the various floors when the lift stopped on his way down and out. He was now worried at being reprimanded for being late for school. A small crowd of residents, entering the building, had gathered in the lobby waiting to use the lift. It was explained to them that once we got the boy out the lift would remain out of service until the lift engineer had inspected the lift and would, hopefully, reinstate it.

The first thing we attempted was to return the lift to the ground floor using the 'Fireman's Switch'. All tall buildings have a lift with a special circuit built into them for fire brigade use in the event of fires. The switch is inside a locked box, operated by a key carried on the fire appliance. Once the switch is actuated the floor buttons within the lift car and the landing call buttons become inoperable. If the lift is going up it will continue to the next floor and stop, then without the doors opening it will return to the ground floor without stopping at any intermediate floors. If the lift is travelling downwards it will continue to do so until it reaches the ground floor. Once there the lift doors open, allowing the fire service to take control of the lift. The landing call buttons remain inoperative. However, on this occasion the lift refused to move.

The accepted Brigade lift procedure entails part of the crew going to the floor above where the lift is stationary whilst the remainder proceed to the lift motor room; this is normally at the top of the building and is kept locked. A standard key that, again, is carried allows access to the motor room. Additionally, appliances carry special lift 'spoon' keys. They are long metal, specially shaped, keys which pass through similarly shaped slots in the outer lift door. The keys release the safety mechanism which keeps the outer landing doors closed unless a lift is at that particular floor. With the outer doors open it is possible for crews to communicate, via the lift shaft, to the other members of the crew working in the motor room. In the motor room the crew must first turn off the electrical supply to the lift motor. They then use a brake-release lever to disengage the cable drum's brake. This brake is applied whenever the lift is not moving. With the brake released, but controlled, the other firefighter turns a winding wheel to raise or lower the lift to the required floor level. It can be a slow process.

Although you would think it easier to lower the lift than to raise it, the reverse is actually true. This is due to the heavy counter-weights attached to the lift cables, the weights being heavier than a fully occupied lift. However, on this day we had another problem as the lift door on the first floor would not open when we inserted the 'spoon' key! It had to be lowered which meant winding the heavy counterweights up. It was much harder and slower than normal. Now with the lift door open in the ground floor lobby we could hear the young lad clearly. He was getting increasingly anxious about being late for school, but none too worried about his enforced confinement. We reassured him there was no problem and the small crowd in the lobby joined in to give him calls of reassurance. The small crowd also talked amongst themselves, saying how brave the young boy was being.

Finally, with the lift car lowered and level with the floor we oper-ated the mechanical switch that allowed the inner door to open. As the door opened it revealed the lad and the sympathetic murmurings from the small crowd suddenly stopped. The boy, despite his East End accent, was not white – a fact which turned a few of the crowds' sympathies into instant verbal disdain. Aggressive and intimidating comments followed. It was my officer-in-charge who put a reassur-ing arm around the youngster's shoulder and escorted him through the crowd. Once outside he gave the youngster a pep talk and told him he had done nothing wrong. He also gave him the fire station's private telephone number in case his school queried his lateness so someone at the fire station would confirm his story.

Although forty years have elapsed since that snapshot of life at the time, on the positive side there were only a few ignorant indi-viduals in that small crowd whose racism instantly reversed their previous sympathetic values. I like to think, if a similar incident occurred today, such unpleasant comments would never be made. I recall feeling angry at those racist comments at the time: the blink-ered view of a few individuals. I could not help but think how much of life they were missing due to their narrow, self-imposed view. But the Brigade back then was far from perfect. Individuals within it harboured similar, albeit, minority views.

Television dramas and action films tend to portray a firefighter's job as something of a heroic occupation: a profession tinged with a hint of glamour as they dash around in their fire engines with their flashing warning lights and sirens sounding. The truth is often far removed from the perceived aura presented by film directors and producers. The image normally seen by the public is of a passing fire appliance when on its way to an emergency call. To the fire-fighter the journey to an incident is "dead time"; their task will only begin on arrival. The quicker they can safely arrive, the quicker they can render assistance to whoever is in need of their help. I always remember the advice given me by an 'old timer', a fireman who had been through the London Blitz back when I started my career. He told me never to forget that every time "the bells go down", someone out there is shouting for help and you are one of those, in that moment of time, who can help them.

As their career progresses, a firefighter faces many and varied types of incident. Fires will include the large, small and mundane. Many will involve people. Occasionally the results are harrowing. Firefighters will rescue the living or recover the dead. Road traffic accidents, people trapped in lifts, animals in trouble: the list of permutations is very lengthy indeed. It is by a combination of skill and knowledge, gained through both experience and constant training, that firefighters are able to tackle incidents no matter how daunting they may seem. It is only when watching firefighters in action that the public might get a chance glimpse of them demon-strating these skills and knowledge. Sadly, most of the time it goes unnoticed and infrequently recorded in the national press!

I attended many testing and tragic incidents in my career. One of the most demanding and vexing was the Moorgate Under-ground train disaster. Incidents such as Moorgate, due to their size or complexity, require close inter-service co-operation. Deemed 'major incidents', they are too large for the local crews, or even just for one service to deal with. Also work at such an incident requires both hard physical and mental exertion. The first phase may require the short concentrated effort of a sprinter to undertake initial rescues and save life. As the situation develops, the firefighter needs the stamina-challenging effort of a marathon runner. At such protracted events no fire crew can be expected to maintain such an effort for the entire length of a shift, although frequently they have to be ordered away from an incident, so determined are they to see it through to the end. To overcome this problem relief crews from around the Brigade area are brought in phases to work three- to four-hour stints before they too are relieved by other firefighters.

One tragic incident I will always remembered occurred in Star Lane, in Canning Town, around 1967. It occurred in a four-storey tenement block that has since been demolished. This particular evening I was riding the pump-escape. When more than one fire appliance was ordered to a fire it was always the pump-escape that led the way from the station. The prime purpose of this fire engine, with.its 50 foot escape ladder, was rescue. The follow-up appliance would deal with water supplies and tackling the blaze. As an incident is dealt with, and wound down, the pump-escape is the first appliance to be released from the scene. I liked, and trusted, the escape ladder. It was large and heavy and normally required four firemen to manhandle and manoeuvre it. It was very dependable and could take almost unlimited punishment at an incident.

We arrived at the Star Lane fire at night. We could see volumes of noxious smoke billowing from an open window on the third floor. You can guarantee at any serious fire that a lethal cocktail of gases and heat will be produced. Our training meant we did not need instructions on what to do. We knew our part in the team, our individual roles and what was required of us. Slipping the escape ladder made a crashing sound as the weight borne by the carriage wheels hit the ground. With one fireman on each wheel and two guiding it we wheeled the ladder across the road at speed. Using the ladder's momentum, we mounted the kerb-stone and pushed the ladder onto the pavement. A small communal area lay between the front of the building and the pavement. It was protected by a waist-high wooden picket fence supported at intervals by upright concrete posts. The entrance to the flats had similar concrete posts, either side, making the gap too narrow to push the escape ladder through. We were left only one option: making our own entrance through the fence. The weight and strength of the escape ladder made it an idea tool for the job. It was used as a battering ram as we attacked the boundary fence. After a couple of charges the fence gave way and we wheeled the escape ladder towards the building. The ladder was swiftly extended to the third floor window. By now it was not necessary use the escape ladder as colleagues, from our pump and wearing breathing apparatus, had managed to gain entrance to the flat via a door on a landing. But as you can never be certain how a fire situation will develop when you first arrive, two points of entry are always better than one.

Whilst all this activity was taking place the officer in charge sent his priority assistance message from the appliance radio. 'Priority' messages are short and decisive. His message was: "Make pumps four, persons reported." This meant that two further fire appliances were urgently required and that there was reason to believe that people were involved or trapped in the fire. Ambulance and Police control rooms are contacted by direct line and they order an ambulance and the police to the incident. A senior fire officer would also be mobilised. This activity is helpful to the officer in charge of an incident as it relieves them of additional concerns and allows them to concentrate on the situation in hand.

Leaving the escape ladder in situ, I had made my way around the front and up to the flat. On the staircase I was passed by two colleagues rushing down. Each was carrying a small unconscious child. As I reached the flat's doorway a fireman wearing breathing apparatus emerged with a third unconscious child. He thrust the child into my arms. Without exchanging words I knew that he would already be exhausted – exhausted from searching by touch, in the smoke and darkness of the apartment, for anyone in the oven-like temperatures. As I ran down the stairs holding the child in one arm I administered mouth-to-mouth resuscitation and carried out cardiac massage. On reaching the street I hurried to the awaiting ambulance. As I carried the unconscious child onto the back of the ambulance the scene was like something out of 'bedlam'.

The other two children were already on board, as were their parents. The parents were extremely distressed, both shouting and screaming in shock and fearful for their children's lives. All three children remained unconscious. The ambulance attendant was already attempting to resuscitate one child which left the child I was holding and another still needing urgent attention. Neither I nor the ambulance attendant knew if the parents were injured. Both were hysterical which meant they were alive and so a lesser priority. The ambulance attendant could only do one thing at a time, his priority being the three children. It was when a Catholic priest put his head around the rear door and asked if he could help. I told him to get aboard and with that the back doors of the ambulance were closed and we sped off towards Queen Mary's Hospital.

I asked the priest to give cardiac and mouth-to-mouth resuscitation to the third child. He said that unfortunately he was not trained in first aid. I felt for the third child's pulse but could feel none. I gave the child a controlled thump on the chest in an attempt to induce the heart to start beating. I quickly demonstrated to the priest how to administer nose and mouth aid and breathe air into the child's lungs whilst at the same time using his two fingers to pump the little person's heart. (A child's heart beats much faster than an adult's, making a need for much faster although gentler pressure.) The priest immediately took to his new-found skills but the journey to the hospital was a traumatic one. The route had a considerable number of sharp bends which, combined with the speed of the ambulance, threw us all from side to the other. The constant anxious cries of the distressed parents only added to the harrowing ordeal of the journey.

We arrived at Queen Mary's Hospital and were hurried into the Accident and Emergency area, by-passing other patients awaiting treatment. We were led directly into the treatment room. The ambulance crew, via their control room, had advised the hospital of the dire situation and the A&E team had cleared the emergency treatment rooms to await our arrival. I handed over my child to the waiting doctors and nurses. My role came to an end. I suddenly felt like a fish out of water. I was left standing in the patient waiting area in my firegear, smelling of smoke. About 10 minutes later a doctor returned, his face already telling its own sad story even before he explained that all three children had died. I assumed their small lungs could not cope with the lethal cocktail of fire fumes. Their age ranges must have been about from one year to four or five years old. It was their tender young ages that made their loss all the more tragic. I never saw the parents again. There was nothing else left to do but find myself a cup of tea in the hospital café and to telephone my control room so as to make arrangements to transport me back to my fire station.

As to the Catholic priest, who had rendered assistance that night, I never heard of him again. I never knew his name, where he came from, or what happened to him afterwards. I only know, in that short journey to the hospital, we shared a common purpose, trying to save the lives of those children. We moved like two ships passing in the night.

I recall this incident because it is the type of thing that firefighters experience away from the public's gaze. There were no 'pats on the back' or medals afterwards. But such incidents leave an inner satisfaction of knowing you have done the best that you're trained for. As for me being in the ambulance? It was the way the dice fell that night. Had the circumstances been different, it would have been another colleague in that ambulance doing the same thing.

After 42 years in the fire service I retired. It is not easy to calculate how many thousands of incidents I attended during that time. The only common factor between all of them is no two incidents were ever the same. To me most would appear mundane, but to those who were assisted by our crews, these were situations they would probably remember for the rest of their lives. What to me was a 'small' fire, in fire service terminology, is often something of a disaster to those needing help. Some of those incidents were unfortunately tragic, but rather than dwell on the sorrow that such incidents entail, I am rather proud to think there are a number of people walking around today that would not be here except for the part I played as a well-trained team member in saving their lives.

None of us really know what our epitaph will be, but if I had to choose my own it would simply say, "I was a London firefighter". Those words say more than volumes ever can.

(Fact)

Yesteryear's Fires: Bishopsgate Goods Depot

IN THE FINAL MONTHS of the London County Council's London Fire Brigade, on 4 December 1964, the Brigade faced its biggest challenge in terms of a post-WWII blaze. In fact the fire at the Bishopsgate goods depot, located by Commercial Street, E1 and on the eastern side of Shoreditch High Street, was one of the biggest peacetime fires in Britain. It caused five million pounds' worth of damage and killed two customs officers working at the site. This massive fire also stretched the resources of the then London Fire Brigade to the full.

Although classified as a 40 pump fire, at its height more than 45 pumping appliances, 10 turntable ladders and 13 other specialist fire engines attended, with 235 London firemen fighting this conflagration. The blaze travelled at an astonishing speed and quickly engulfed the huge British Rail depot. The depot, with its main building of two and three floors, covered an area of approximately 350ft (107 metres) and was some 600ft (183 metres) in depth.

Bishopsgate Goods Depot had started life as Bishopsgate Station. It had opened in 1840 as a passenger terminal providing a passenger route between London, Ipswich, Norwich and Colchester. The station had closed to passenger traffic in 1875. It reopened six years later as Bishopsgate Goods yard, a major freight station serving the eastern ports of England.

The premises had been constructed in two stages. The main portion being completed around 1880 and the remainder finished about 1914. The depot mostly had brick load-bearing external walls and the floors were supported internally by unprotected cast-iron columns at the first and second floors and by a brick arch construction at the ground floor.

Bishopsgate's main buildings continued through ground floor arches, under the marshalling yard, and ended in a fruit bank platform at main rail level which was covered by a canopy. The whole of the depot was connected by open staircases. Floors were also connected by lifts and various hoists. The main building, which formed a vast cube in one undivided cell, measured over 10.5 million cubic feet (300,000 cubic metres).

By the twentieth century the depot was used for the handling and storage of the wide variety of commodities transported by the then British Railways. On the day of the fire the occupancy of the depot was as follows.

The ground floor (main railway line level) consisted of general storage and handling of goods (including drinking/potable spirits in the 'vulnerable (at risk) arches'), plus mess rooms and offices. Some arches, which faced the public street, were let as shops.

The first floor housed loading banks with railway lines between, vehicle roadways and ancillary offices. Storage at this level was contained on the loading banks, inside railway wagons and road vehicles in the cage store. This store also contained undelivered goods. It was some 15–17ft long, 8–9ft wide and 8ft high (5 metres x 3metres x 2.5 metres). It was constructed on a wooden frame; the lower part was of sheet steel, the upper portion of expanded metal lined with hardboard and cardboard. The top was covered by a tarpaulin. Entry into the cage was via a double door.

The second floor was a warehouse floor. At the eastern end of which was a large partitioned area which formed an HM Customs cage. At the time of the fire the two unfortunate HM Customs and Excise Officers were on duty in a customs office at the northeast corner of this floor.

The depot contained various rolling stock and road trailers on the night of 3 December, comprising 112 British railway wagons (average 2.5 tons gross content weight), 17 continental ferry wagons (between eight to ten tons content weight), 140 three to six ton road trailers. These were located throughout the first floor. The rail wagons contained various goods, including fruit, machinery, biscuits, surplus clothing and general goods. The warehouse and customs cage contained large quantities of general merchandise and included plastic articles, toys, etc.; bales of carpets; synthetic fabrics and furs in cartons; baskets; leather handbags and glassware.

The first 999 call to the Lambeth headquarters fire brigade control room on that Friday morning was at 6.20 a.m, from a passer-by dialling from an exchange telephone. They reported a fire at the 'Bishopsgate Goods Depot.' Four minutes later, a second call was received by exchange telephone to a fire in the vicinity of the Goods Depot, Bishopsgate. A further six calls were received by the Lambeth control room, the last being received at 6.58 a.m.

The initial attendance came from Shoreditch and Whitechapel fire stations. The new state-of-the-art basement control room at Lambeth had only just been refurbished and modernised. This was to be its first major test by fire, literally. The Brigade Control officers now dispatched the Capital's fire engines via teleprinters, something that had been introduced in 1963 across all the LFB fire stations and the four Divisional headquarters.

Shoreditch turned out from its brand new fire station, located in Shoreditch High Street, having recently vacated its former Victorian-built fire station in Tabernacle Street. The fire appliances ordered in response to that first call were Shoreditch's pump-escape and pump, and the pump and a turntable ladder from Whitechapel. As those appliances arrived at the incident, and on receipt of the second call at 6.24 a.m., the pump-escape from Whitechapel was sent.

Fire cover in the City of London was changing. On 6 November 1963, the LCC's Fire Brigade Committee had agreed a report on the City's revised fire cover. A new Barbican station was to replace both Redcross Street and Bishopsgate; a new station, which would replace both Whitefriars and Cannon Street, was also to be built in Upper Thames Street. Construction of the new Barbican was commissioned around the same time as the Shoreditch station, but planning and land acquisition issues meant it was not possible to start the proposed new Upper Thames Street station. The Redcross Street fire station was closed in February 1964 but its PE and personnel were transferred, temporarily, to Cannon Street while retaining their station identity of B33.

It had been expected that the new Barbican station would open before the new Shoreditch but in the event Shoreditch opened first on 4 November 1964. Clerkenwell's Emergency Tender (ET) moved to Shoreditch on 6 November, and B Divisional HQ was relocated from Clerkenwell the day after. It had been determined that Bishopsgate fire station would be closed in advance of Barbican opening. It closed on 10 November 1964, its appliances being relocated to the new Shoreditch as a second (or B) pump and its PE temporarily to Clerkenwell, again as second pump.

When those first appliances from Shoreditch arrived at the entrance to the Bishopsgate Depot at Shoreditch High Street, the Station Officer in charge saw vast quantities of smoke issuing from the windows on the first and second floors. As the appliances drove along the road, smoke was seen to be issuing from all the first floor windows and, to a lesser degree, from the windows on the second floor. The first appliances had pulled up adjacent to the canopied loading bank and the Station Officer made his way, on foot, to the loading bank and entered the building.

With considerable difficulty he managed to progress about 25 yards into the building, parallel in direction to Bethnal Green Road. He saw in front of him, and to his left, a wall of fire with the smoke apparently emanating from the Shoreditch High Street end of the building. He was unable to see across the cavernous depot floor area, to the Quaker Street side of the building, because of the high volumes of thick dense black smoke. Upon returning outside, and only five minutes after the first call was made, he gave instructions that a priority message be sent to Brigade Control, making 'pumps ten'. He then got his crews to get two jets to work into the building and near to the loading platform. The internal British Rail hydrant was set into for their initial water supplies.

As the pump from Whitechapel arrived, and drove up Wheeler Street Hill to the Shoreditch High Street entrance, its Station Officer saw that fire had spread throughout the building and that beyond the front bank loading platform the depot was well alight for as far as he could see. He also noticed that BR depot staff were attempting to tackle the fire with a jet of water and working from an internal hydrant in front of the depot offices.

Shoreditch's Station Officer, having given instructions for the positioning of the first two jets, quickly returned to the gate by which he had entered and was met by a Security Officer. He was told that lighted embers were falling from the first floor to the ground floor by way of an open lift shaft. The crews of the initial reinforcing appliances were instructed to deal with the falling brands and a jet was got to work on the first floor.

The pump-escape from Cannon Street arrived at 6.30 a.m. It had a Station Officer in charge. He immediately gave instructions to his crew to supply water to the pump from Whitechapel. He saw that the whole building, including the roof, appeared to be well alight. Drums of liquid were bursting and the walls at the Commercial Street side of the building were beginning to crack. The combined efforts of the crews of the two appliances from Whitechapel and Cannon Street enabled three jets to be quickly got to work on the fire from the front loading bank.

Shoreditch's Station Officer had meanwhile returned to his own crews, who had by now got one jet to work and were laying out their second, when there was a loud explosion. The Station Officer noted it came from second floor and in a position that appeared to be to his front and to the left. This first explosion was followed by a number of minor ones, also apparently coming from the second floor. He made 'pumps 20'.

Immediately following the explosions, fire spread at great speed along the lines of the goods wagons and loading platforms on the first floor and in the warehouse on the floor above. It spread so quickly that the crews had to break their hose connections and move both appliances to prevent them from becoming involved in the fire. As it was, the appliances were severely blistered but their operational performance was not impaired. Both were able to play an extremely useful part in the subsequent firefighting.

As the appliances were being repositioned, fire broke through the roof of the building and a further assistance message was sent, making turntable ladders three.

Divisional Officer Fredrick (Fred) Lapthorn was the senior officer in charge of the B Division. He arrived together with the reinforcing appliances at around 6.30 a.m. He was quickly joined by the duty Assistant Division Officer, ADO Lloyd. Fred Lapthorn went to Wheeler Street Hill side of Bishopsgate whilst the ADO took the

Bethnal Green Road side of the building. As he got to Bethnal Green Road he saw fire through the windows on both the first and second floors for about 300 feet on that side of the building. ADO Lloyd returned to the Shoreditch High Street end at first floor level to see that about four-fifths of the first and second floors were a mass of fire; fire which was spreading rapidly towards the loading bank.

At 6.36 a.m. DO Lapthorn sent an informative message which gave, in graphic but brief details, a picture of the dire situation: a message which told that the vast building was very well alight. Seven minutes later he made 'pumps 30, turntable ladders 5'. At this point both DO Lapthorn and ADO Lloyd realised that the situation within the building was rapidly becoming untenable for their firemen and all crews were withdrawn to positions outside the building.

At about 6.45 a.m., the first of a series many major wall collapses occurred on the Bethnal Green Road side of the building. The debris completely obstructed the inclined road. Fortunately, there were no personnel or appliances at work on the inclined road. There were, however, appliances, including two turntable ladders, and personnel at work in Bethnal Green Road. Urgent steps had to be taken to move the appliances to safety. This was accomplished only minutes before a further major collapse on this side of the building partially obstructed Bethnal Green Road.

With the Brigade's principal officers arriving from the Lambeth headquarters and its major control unit set up, the duty Assistant Chief Officer first took charge before Deputy Chief Cunningham took command. From this time onwards it became apparent that all firefighting would have to be carried out from the perimeter of the building. Further requests for reinforcements were sent. Pumps were made '40' and the turntable ladders increased to ten. Additionally, ten radial branches were also urgently required.

Firefighting was seriously hampered by the strong north-westerly wind. The adjacent property in Quaker Street, on the south side of the fire, was menaced, both by radiated heat and by a large quantity of flying embers. A number of fires broke out but these were successfully dealt with and no serious damage occurred. The firemen's jets were concentrated at Wheeler Street with the object both of stopping the spread of fire along the south side of the goods depot and protecting the property in Quaker Street. The turntable ladders were positioned at vantage points on both sides of the building and these were as soon reinforced by the arrival of the radial branches.

Further jets were got to work at the main rail entrance to the depot and as the fire was contained these jets were worked progressively into the building. However, great care was required owing to the very dangerous condition of the structure of the building. At the height of fire-fighting operations 21 jets and 14 radial branches were at work.

One and half hours after the first call the danger of any further spread of fire had been overcome. By 10.29 a.m. a 'stop' message was sent to Brigade Control indicating that the fire was under control. Crews remained in attendance, cooling down the debris, over the next 36 hours to ensure that there was no re-occurrence of fire.

Shoreditch's Station Officer twice made enquiries in the early stages of the fire as to whether any persons were in the building. On the first occasion he was informed by a British Railways policeman that he "did not know". Shortly afterwards, and in response to the same request, he was shown by a security officer a group of employees who were in no apparent danger. The first indication that persons might be involved was given to the Brigade's Control Unit staff and the officer-in-charge caused a message to be sent to all senior officers over the walkie-talkie network at 7.13 a.m. The message indicated that information has been received that two customs officers were resident at the Sclater Street end of the building.

There was confusion as to whether the men had left the building before the fire and gone home. It was learned that there had been three HM Customs Officers in the building the previous night, one of whom had left at about 3.00 a.m. By the time of the first indication that there was a possibility that the men were missing, the fire had involved the whole of the building and the portion of the building housing the customs office had already collapsed. It was impossible at that stage to enter and search the building. As soon as conditions allowed – and despite the quantity of debris and the instability of the structure – a search of the building was commenced. At 12.20 p.m. the two customs officers, both fatally injured, were located in the debris and in a position some 200ft distant from their office. Firemen removed the men's bodies.

London Fire Brigade 'relief' crews remained on site until the early evening of December 12, eight days after the fire started, and when the incident was finally closed down.

Footnotes

1. The destruction of all material evidence by the fire made it impossible to decide the probable cause of the fire. The Goods yard and depot was rendered unusable. Over the next 40 years, the site became derelict. It was made safe by a major demolition project in 2003–4.
2. Some difficulties were experienced in obtaining enough water during the early stages of the fire. These were quickly overcome as reinforcing crews got to work. Despite the very large volumes of water used in fighting the fire there was no shortage.
3. Although this fire was apparently first seen by railway employees to be in the 'returns cage' on No. 3 bank, it was considered by the Brigade's Fire Prevention officers that the fire could not developed and have spread in the way it did if the fire had originated in this position. What was considered more probable is that the fire started on the warehouse floor above and the ignition in the 'returns cage' resulted from burning debris falling from the floor above, either by burning through the floorboards or by falling down the adjacent hoist shaft and ricocheting into the cage.
4. At an early stage, while BR employees were tackling the fire, there were reports of 'flashes of flame'. These may have been caused by the ignition of cartons containing numerous books of matches (240 per book) or cartons containing plastic aerosols of hair lacquer. Further explosions were also reported at both the track level and in the warehouse and were attributed to the bursting, due to heat, of drums of oil and numerous other containers.

The sequence of the 'make-up' assistance messages:

0620	Time of call. (Six further calls received.)
0625	Make Pumps 10
0629	Make Pumps 20
0630	Make TL's 3
0643	Make Pumps 30, TL's 5
0657	Make Pumps 40
0700	Make Turntable Ladders 10. 10 addition radial branched required
1029	Stop message sent.

Stations attending:

Code	Station	Supplied	Comments
A1*	Manchester Square	P TL	
A3*	Camden Town	PE P	
A4	Euston	PE P TL ET	
A5	Soho	P TL	
A7*	Knightsbridge	HLL	
A10	Kensington	P	
A14	West Hampstead	TL	
B20*	Clerkenwell	PE P P	Bishopgate's former PE
B21	Islington	PE	
B23*	Kingsland	PE TL	
B26	Bethnal Green	PE P	
B27	Shoreditch	PE P ET P	Bishopgate's former P
B28*	Brunswick Road	TL	
B29*	Burdett Road	PE P	
B30	Whitechapel	PE P TL	
B31	Shadwell	PE P	
B35*	Cannon Street	PE TL	plus B33 Redcross Street PE at B35
B36*	Whitefriars	PE P	
B37	Holloway	PE P	
C40	New Cross	TL	
C42	Deptford	PE P	

C43	East Greenwich	P	
C49	Lee Green	HLL	
D60	Clapham	P	ordered to Lambeth to collect the radial branches from the ET
D61	Lambeth	PE P CU	
D62*	Southwark	PE P	
D63	Dockhead	PE P	
D65	Peckham	PE P	
D66	Brixton	P	
D70	Wandsworth	TL	
'B' DHQ	BACV – Shoreditch		
'C' DHQ	BACV – New Cross		

Plus the Auxiliary Fire Service pumps from Euston, Belsize, Kingsland, Whitechapel and Greenwich.

Key:
PE   Pump-Escape
P   Pump
TL   Turntable Ladder
ET   Emergency Tender
HLL Hose-Laying Lorry
CU   Control Unit
*   Fire stations since closed

(Fact)

The London Fire Chief Who Never Was

Mr Sidney Gompertz Gamble, Second Officer of the London Fire Brigade

FOR WHATEVER REASON THE London County Council (LCC) authorities passed over Sidney Gamble whenever the matter of his possible appointment to the Brigade's Chief Officer post came before them. It bemused many, both in the service and beyond it – not least Sidney Gamble himself, although he never commented upon his disappointment at non-selection, publicly at least. Gamble just got on with his job of guiding the Brigade, and the various men actually appointed to the position of Chief Officer. Gamble's CV was truly impressive, far more so than some of those to whom he reported.

Gamble was not a Londoner. He was born in Grantham, Lincoln-shire on 20 September 1854. As a child he was weaned on firefight-ing. He was the eldest son of Alderman Gamble, who was both a supporter and activist in the Volunteer Fire Brigade of the town. In his boyhood days Gamble attended many fires in the borough. At the age of only 19 he became the Deputy Superintendent of the Borough of Grantham Fire Brigade. Gamble had qualified as an architect and surveyor and was, prior to his appointment to the Metropolitan Fire Brigade, the Borough Surveyor of Grantham as well as the Chief of Grantham's Fire Brigade.

When it came to being appointed Chief – or not being appointed in Gamble's case – this highly competent man appears to have been just plain 'unlucky'. He was either 'in the wrong place at the wrong time' or 'tarred with the same brush'. Both phrases seemed to haunt the unfortunate Gamble when it came to securing the position of London's Chief Fire Officer: a position that can justifiably argued was his for the asking.

Gamble, aged 38, arrived at the then Metropolitan Fire Brigade headquarters in Southwark Bridge Road in February 1892, a year after the first Chief Officer, Captain Massey Shaw (at that time Sir Massey Shaw) retired. Officer appointments to the Brigade were made by the LCC's General Purposes Committee. It was they who appointed Gamble as the Brigade's 'second' officer (deputy Chief). Their choice of another Army officer to replace Shaw was rejected when presented to the full Council. Instead, they chose Mr J. Sexton Simonds who had been Shaw's deputy. His five reign came to an acrimonious end due to some 'dodgy' dealings on his part. Asked to resign, Simonds refused; so the LCC sacked him, paying him a gratuity of £1650.

Sadly, Gamble paid the price of his former Chief's money-making scheme. So incensed were the LCC over Simonds' behaviour that they refused to consider any serving member of the London Brigade for the vacant Chief's post, even though Gamble was in effect 'minding the shop' whilst a new Chief Officer was being sought. In the end, Captain Wells (RN) was appointed in November 1896. This looked to be a wise choice until the Queen Victoria Street fire in which nine people died.

On June 9, 1902 a waste paper basket caught fire in a workshop on the top floor of a city building. It was a premises owned by the General Electrical Company. With the spiral wooden staircase quickly ablaze, 13 typists and packers, all girls, were trapped. The Brigade's regular escape ladders, at 50 feet, were too short to reach the upper floors. As a result some of the young women jumped to their deaths rather than be consumed by the fire. There was a public outcry, fuelled by erroneous reports in the newspapers. The *Daily Mail* declared that "Captain Wells must go".

Calling of the fire brigade had been delayed, and when they arrived heroic efforts were made to save the trapped people. Station Officer West, from the Watling Street station lowered himself down from the roof on a telegraph cable and saved two lives. Two more were saved using the 'long ladder', a 75 foot wheeled escape dispatched from the Southwark headquarters. However, eight young woman – along with a young man, who had tried to help – perished in the blaze.

At the subsequent Coroners Inquiry, held at the City of London's Guildhall, the Brigade was exonerated. Despite the jury's unanimous findings, however, the LCC and the MFB came under steady attack. The finger of blame was pointed at Captain Wells who was accused of being hostile to change; this, despite Wells designing and introducing a radically improved fire-float. Hook ladders were introduced into the Brigade as a direct result of that fire, an introduction that saved many lives in the years that followed. Station Officer West was awarded the MFB's Silver Medal, the equivalent of the fireman's VC.

But the toll told on Captain Wells and he resigned the following year. Once more the Brigade and the London insurance companies, who held Gamble in considerable esteem, lauded praise on him and cheered for him to take over. The LCC had other ideas and again bypassed Gamble, appointing yet another external 'officer and gentleman'.

The LCC's appointee was James de Courcy Hamilton, a Captain in the Royal Navy. He is widely credited with being a Rear Admiral but Captain Hamilton was only promoted to rear-admiral on the retired list in 1910, which was a year after he had left the Brigade to run the Army and Navy Stores. Hamilton may well have looked the part of a Chief Officer, but it was widely considered that he knew little of fire brigade matters when he started; his knowledge was said to have little increased by the time he left. It was left to Gamble, and the Brigade's Superintendents, to look after the Brigade and to drive it forward.

Hamilton is credited with increasing the number of the Brigade's motorised appliances. (The Brigade only had one motor steamer when he was appointed.) However, it was Gamble that remained the power behind the throne and the real force for change. In 1904 the name of the brigade changed to the London Fire Brigade, a name that it still retains today. London's first horse-drawn turntable ladder was introduced in 1905.

Gamble was 55 when in 1909 the LCC General Purposes Committee was seeking to appoint yet other new Chief. Once again they selected an outsider and yet again their decision was overturned by the full Council. Gamble clearly did not have friends in high places. They had selected Commander C V de Morney Cowper (RN)* but, with their selection overturned, Mr Gamble would appear before the Board for a final time.

It was clear that the LCC Committee members were taking no chances on an ordinary fireman like Gamble. Everybody who knew anything about the internal organisation of the London Fire Brigade thought that, this time, the Fire Brigade Committee would see fit to glance at the man in their service who was experienced, fit and, in every way, most suitable for the job. Mr Gamble was considered the Brigade's most eligible candidate by its rank and file. He had years of experience of fighting fires and he was an enthusiastic fireman in theory and practice. He was brave to a fault, always ready to lead his men at the fiercest and dangerous point. If he was to be found at a fire it would be in the danger zone and where the flames were most intense.

However, Lieutenant Commander Sampson Sladen, aged 41, who had joined the Metropolitan Fire Brigade in 1899 as a direct entry officer and was the Brigade's Third Officer, pipped Gamble to the post. Ironically, Sladen was so certain that Gamble had got the job that he warmly congratulated Gamble before being called back before the Committee and told of his appointment as the new Chief Officer.

Throughout his career, Sladen was judged to be a 'committee man' and again Gamble was left to mind the shop. Sladen was never able to obtain the full confidence of his officers or his men, his loyalty siding with the LCC and not the Brigade. It was an issue that ultimately led to his resignation in 1918, after the War. Sladen did not give support to the much needed improvement in firemen's conditions which the now active Fire Brigades Union were pursuing.

The First World War had an immediate impact on the Brigade. Almost a third of its strength was depleted. Some firemen and

---

* Cowper died on 28th June 1918 when his ship was sunk by torpedo fired by a German submarine 130 miles from Cape Vilano off the coast of western Spain.

officers, who were reservists, were recalled to their colours. Others left the Brigade and volunteered to fight at the front. So short of men was the Brigade that its force was supplemented by the London Rifle Volunteers.

Gamble, now 60, took a major operational role, a role he never shirked when responding to the air attacks upon London. The first of these came in September 1915. Enemy attacks on London caused 224 fires and other incidents, all attended by the London Fire Brigade. Thankfully, only a few bombing attacks resulted in major fires. That said, 138 persons were rescued, for which members of the Brigade were awarded three King's Police Medals, one Silver Medal and 43 Commendations. Thirteen members of the brigade received injuries, from which three died – Firemen J. S. Green, C. A. Henley (both decorated posthumously) and A. H. Vidler – while three more were invalided from the brigade. One of those seriously injured was Gamble, although the exact details are not known. However, his injury would led to him being invalided out of the service.

In the 1917 New Year's Honours, the same list that 'Temp Major Morris' was award the Military Cross, Sidney Gamble and Arthur Dyer, both Divisional Officers in the Brigade, were awarded the Kings Police Medal (KPM). Deputy S. G. Gamble was medically retired on the February 22, 1918. Gamble was aged 64 and had completed 26 years' service.

"POLICE MEDALS and FIRE BRIGADE 1917
Announced in *The Times* February 13, 1917.
SERVICE AT HOME AND ABROAD.
His Majesty has been graciously pleased to award the King's Police Medal to the following officers of Police Forces and Fire Brigades in the United Kingdom, the Empire of India, and his Majesty's Dominions beyond the Seas:–
FIRE BRIGADE.
SIDNEY GOMPERTZ GAMBLE. Divi. Officer. London Fire Brigade. Second officer of brigade since 1892. Has displayed exceptional zeal, courage and ability. Frequently injured on duty."

Gamble had served all his 26 years as the deputy chief of the Brigade. He remains the longest served deputy Chief Officer in its history.

Would things have been different under his command; who knows? What is beyond doubt, given the endorsements and comments of London's rank and file and other fire service professional of the time, is that Gamble was a consummate leaders of his men and tour de force as a firefighter. He remains the Chief Officer that London never had.

In retirement Gamble published a book: *A Practical Treatise on Outbreaks of Fire; Being a systematic study of their causes and means of prevention* (1926). The life of Gamble, in his latter years, remains rather a mystery, although he was a regular attendee at the LFB 'Roundtreads' retirees' annual reunions, according to their records.

(Fact)

The OXO building incident, SE1

THE COMBINED AGE OF the six-man fire engine crew came to a staggering 107 years of operational service – although Alfie, with his meagre five years in, didn't add much to those totals. He was the new kid on the block, but he was far from a rookie: six years serving in the 3rd Battalion of the Parachute Regiment had seen to that. Unlike his fellow Emergency Tender (ET) companions, whose war service had seen two of them serving in the LFB whilst the others were either too young to fight or had been working in a reserved occupation, Alfie had first seen action in Suez, then Malaya. Sir Gerald Templer, the High Commissioner in colonial Malaya, had told his troops: "The hard core of armed communists in this country are fanatics and must be, and will be, exterminated." Alfie had taken life with his bare hands, whereas the others had only been involved in saving it. To look at Alfie, with his handsome, smiling face and deceptively athletic frame, you would never think so. It was only his haircut, still in his preferred military style of very short back and sides, that would give the keen observer any clue to his former life.

Les and Ken were the Watch's two senior hands. In fact they were the eldest two on the whole station. Only months separated both their ages and length of service – although Ken, as he would occasionally remind Les, was the more senior of the two. He had finished his training at the Brigade's recruit training school, then at Lambeth, whilst Les was only halfway through his. The pair had, over the intervening years, become the closest of friends and were a formidable duo on all things pertaining to the ET. There were things that separated the two men. Ken was a brigade driver, now only ever driving his beloved ET and Les wasn't. Each had been winners in

Brigade level competitions. Ken had excelled in both the pump-escape and pump competitions whilst Les had shined at volley ball, representing the Brigade at National and International levels.

They differed in other ways too. Les was partial to a drink and could be found on his night duties down in the headquarters' canteen with a pint in one hand and 'a short' in easy reach of the other. The thread veins in Les's nose let it be known that he enjoyed his liquid suppers more than was actually good for him. That said, Les was never found wanting on the fire-ground. One or two bursts of 100% oxygen straight from a cylinder en route to a call immediately cleared his head. Ken, on the other hand, would only ever be found with a mug of tea in the mess room, which was Ken's domain. He was the watch mess manager and woe betide anyone who was foolish enough to leave his galley kitchen in an untidy state. At morning stand-easy Ken was like a mother hen, fussing over the crusty cheese and onion rolls that he carefully laid out on the two large but battered enamel trays which had been on the station inventory ever since it had first opened in 1937. Lastly, Ken had never had a day's sick in his career, whereas Les took his 'lay-ins' very seriously. Never too many, never too few and certainly not any when he was actually feeling unwell.

Despite the watch being one of the largest in the Brigade, under-manning meant it had been below its authorised strength for months. Recent retirements on the watch had seen two ET men head off into the sunset and the promotion of their Leading Fireman to another station had left the watch short of both ET qualified firemen and officers. That is when Teddy joined the watch. Already a Leading Fireman, he had been transferred in from Greenwich where, until the previous week, he had been happily riding their ET. To say he was not delighted about his enforced move would have been an understatement, but he wasn't the type to take it out on his new-found colleagues.

The other two ET regulars on the watch were Butch and Tom. Butch had come from Croydon Fire Bridge in 1965 when the Greater London Council was formed and the enlarged London Fire Brigade was created. Posted into Lambeth, for months, he went round still wearing his old Croydon Fire Brigade cap badge despite instructions to the contrary. Finally, a visit by the Divisional Commander and an almighty bollocking saw him putting the new GLC-LFB badge in his cap. So now he didn't wear his cap at all. As for the Croydon badge, well that became his belt buckle on the leather belt he used to hold up his fireman's black leggings. Tom had originated from Somerset, his broad West Country accent standing out on a watch where most were London born and bred.

There was one other ET 'hand'. Enter Freddy Floyd. Freddy was actually a 'floatie', serving on the Firebrace fireboat moored at Lambeth's river station – one of the Brigade's two fireboat stations. A former Royal Navy gunner during the Second World War, Freddy had served for the past twenty years at Clerkenwell, mostly riding its ET. Now in the latter part of his career, Freddy wanted a quieter life and to get back on the water. He had put in for a transfer to the fireboat and got it. His ET qualification meant he was the first choice for any stand-by on the land station's ET, something that never pleased the watch's young river service trained firemen who had to take Freddy's place on the fireboat!

Southwark fire station's volley ball court was tucked away behind the drill tower on the far side of the Victorian buildings that were used as the recruits' accommodation block. It was as far away from the fire station as you could get on the once Metropolitan Fire Brigade headquarters site. Because you could not hear the station call bells from there, a special call bell had been installed by the GPO so that the summons of a fire call could be heard by the fireman when playing volley ball. For some unfortunate residents, living on the other side of the boundary wall, it summoned them too in the dead of night when the dutyman forgot to isolate the volley ball court call bell.

For now, however, their extended lunchtime game was in full swing. It had been allowed as a lunchtime 'shout' had taken up forty minutes of their one-hour lunch break. The warm day and the strenuous game meant that the six firemen, the leading fireman and the guvnor had all built up quite a head of steam. They were sweating freely and patches of sweat stained their uniform shirts.

The fire call bells rang simultaneously at Southwark and Lambeth fire stations and an alarm sounded at the Divisional Headquarters located at Clapham. In fact the sound to be heard at Clapham was a warbler, but it all meant the same thing: a fire call.

The singular feature that made Stamford Wharf, owned by the Union Cold Storage Company, stand out from the surrounding riverside warehouses was the iconic Oxo Tower. Back in 1927, the Liebig Extract of Meat Company, which made Oxo, had built a new wharf. Its reinforced concrete structure was built on the site of the former GPO power station. But in its heyday the wharf was the largest site in Britain for the importing of meat. When erected it was the second tallest building in London: a nine-storey, reinforced concrete building with river-facing exterior cranes. These days its zenith was over; however, it was still a busy cold store along with the nearby Chambers Wharf in Bermondsey and, more recently, the Nine Elms Cold store erected in Vauxhall.

Today, however, something else was making the Upper Ground wharf stand out. It was the over-powering aroma of ammonia leaking from its condenser room. That, and the flood of warehouse workers cascading out every exit into the narrow Bargehouse Street that ran alongside the River Thames. Most had streaming eyes, many were coughing and spluttering. Some never even made it out into the street; overcome, they lay inside the loading bay doors that fronted onto Upper Ground.

The scene when Southwark's pump-escape and pump arrived was one of chaos, something that Southwark's guvnor was no stranger to. Already eyes were smarting as two firemen from the pump's crew and one from the PE donned the three Proto breathing apparatus sets carried on the pump. The guvnor was wearing his fire helmet at his customary trademark rakish angle but the look of concentration on his face told a different story. With five cold stores on his station's or the first take's grounds, he was well aware that the main risks in the use of ammonia, as a refrigerant, were associated with its toxicity and flammability. He knew that ammonia gas can be ignited in relatively high concentrations and an ammonia explosion could cause structural damage to a building. However, he drew some comfort from the fact that the gas is difficult to ignite and so combustion can be prevented by relatively simple precautions. His pressing priority was that every second counted after an accidental exposure to ammonia refrigerant. He had given his watch station lectures about how to treat exposed individuals and the importance of proper medical treatment for ammonia exposure. The cold store maintained emergency safety showers and eye-wash stations, so individuals exposed to liquid ammonia or a very heavy concentration of ammonia vapour may flush the affected parts immediately with copious amounts of water. But these were all located inside the wharf, not out here in the street! The guvnor recalled from his own lecture notes that the flushing of the affected parts must be performed continuously for at least 15 minutes after exposure to minimise injury – injury that could involve his own crew now.

He was well aware that when ammonia enters the body (as a result of breathing, swallowing or skin contact) it reacts with water to produce ammonium hydroxide, a chemical that is corrosive and damages cells in the body on contact. Nevertheless, he ordered his BA crew into the wharf. Aware too, now, were his three firemen. Wearing their Proto sets they had moved forward to rescue two workers who had collapsed inside of the ground floor delivery doors. Immediately the chemical started to react with their body sweat. What started as mere tingling quickly moved onto discomfort and then graduated to actual pain. The ammonia vapour found the greatest concentrations of sweat under their arms and, in particular, around their groins.

Southwark's guvnor made pumps six, breathing apparatus required. He also requested a third ET with full protective clothing, plus four ambulances to attend. He knew his best chance of minimising further injury to his own crews, and to others, was the swift arrival of Lambeth's ET crew.

As said, ammonia is corrosive...very. The severity of the health effects depends on the path of exposure, its dose and the duration of that exposure. Exposure to high concentrations of ammonia in air causes immediate burning of the eyes, nose, throat and respiratory tract. In serious leaks it can result in blindness, lung damage or even death. Inhalation of lower concentrations can cause coughing, and nose and throat irritation, symptoms exhibited by many of those making their way out to the street. But those by the engines knew this; they were feeling the mild effects standing some 50 feet away from the wharf.

With his pump parked upwind, Southwark's guvnor gave short, curt, but precise instructions to his crew whilst secretly worrying what effects the concentrations of ammonia were having on his

BA crew inside the wharf. The pump driver had 'dropped' the water tank, a hydrant was being set in and the pump's hose-reel jets, on minimal pressure, were being used by his remaining crew to apply water spray to the faces of some of the worst affected cold-store workers in the street. Four galvanised two gallon buckets, from Southwark's two machines, had been filled with water so others could splash their faces and, in particular, rinse stinging eyes. The guvnor had instructed that the PE's large applicator be set into the pump with orders to douse the BA crew upon their exit from the wharf, if needed. It was.

The BA crew were staggering, rather than walking, out of the wharf's loading bay; carrying one casualty, they were leading the other who was clearly unable to see. She looked in considerable distress. The physical discomfort experienced by the BA wearers was intense. The corrosive effect of the gas appeared to be eating into their privates and burning at any exposed skin. The guvnor instructed his BA team to walk into the large applicator's vast cone of water spray, undress, and then undress the casualties. BA sets, fire gear, firemen's overalls and civvy clothes soon cluttered the ground as the five stood or lay in the neutralising effects of the water spray in their underpants and with the woman in her pants and bra. For one member of Southwark's crew it proved more embarrassing than for the others as he never wore underwear!

The street was filling with emergency vehicles. An ambulance crew moved into the water spray, to assist with the casualties, and were immediately drenched. Ken had positioned Lambeth's ET behind Southwark's pump. Teddy, Les, Butch and Alfie had rigged in Draeger full protective gas-tight suits on route. Now Tom and Ken, acting as the dressers, helped the four whilst connecting the full face masks to their oxygen 'Proto' sets. Normal practice dictated that two would enter the building and two remain outside to act as safety crew. But not today, as the cold store senior engineer had informed Southwark's Station Officer that one of his engineers was missing. The man had gone to shut down the isolation valves in the condenser room and had not returned. The senior engineer also said that to stop the leak the isolation valves must be shut down.

Les was pleased they still didn't have to wear the old Delta gas-tight suits which the one-piece Draeger suit had now replaced.

Both were gas-tight and gave the wearer full body protection, but the Draeger was easier to work in. Les also happened to know the cold store's general layout. He had attended many familiarisation visits, plus a couple of exercises, over the years. However, this was no exercise. The people around him were suffering. Les recalled the words of his wise old former Station Officer. He was a pre-war LFB officer who had led his crews with such distinction during the London Blitz. He himself had been awarded a gallantry medal, and received a badly scared back, after a burning beam had fallen on him during a hazardous and daring rescue at the height of an air-raid. The fireman standing next to him had been killed outright but he had saved two others. He had given his medal to the parents of the dead fireman; he was that type of man. So whenever any of the watch had moaned about going on visits to familiarise themselves with a potential risk, the 'old man' had always said: "Time spent in reconnaissance is rarely wasted." The 'old man' never spoke a truer word, thought Les as he listened to the briefing from the senior engineer.

It was agreed that Les and Butch would shut down the isolation valves whilst Teddy and Alfie searched for the missing engineer. This was Alfie's first full body protection job. He had only ever worn the gas-tight suits on his ET course and during station training. He was not overly keen on the full face either, much preferring the rubber Proto mouthpiece between his lips. On the upside, though, he could talk to Teddy without taking the mouthpiece out – a practice that was frowned upon but nevertheless a common trait with BA firemen.

The temperatures in the cold store came in three levels. They ranged from minus 18°C to minus 30°C over its nine floors. The condenser room was located on the third floor. Whilst the common areas and staircase were not refrigerated, the place was either cold, very cold or freezing. The pliable rubberised gas-tight suits stiffened immediately as soon as the two teams of two walked into the building. They found the lower floors were packed with timbers pallets, some piled high with frozen goods, others waiting to be loaded. The rapid evacuation of the building had left forklift trucks abandoned and the thick insulated individual cold store doors ajar. The freezing air spilling out into those areas normally not so cold. Eighty people worked at the warehouses, employed in a variety of shifts. Not all had got out when the alarm was raised; the engineer certainly hadn't.

Les led the way to the condenser room floor. Power to the lifts, and elsewhere, had been shut down after the alarm had sounded. Only the emergency battery lighting illuminated the wharf's escape routes and its emergency exits and even that was dim. The place was in near darkness with hardly a window to be found on any of the nine floors. The four were reliant on the beams of light from their individual spark-proof 'CEAG' lamps, lamps that could safely be used in an explosive atmosphere. Despite their ability to do so no one spoke. They just followed Les up the stairs to the third floor at a steady pace.

The vapour cloud coming through the third floor lobby doors hugged the ceiling. It continued up into the stairwell. It would rise to the highest level before filling the upper floors and filtering back down again if left unventilated. Passing through the outer lobby double doors the four men came across two other sets of doors; one was marked 'Plant/Condenser Room', the other led into the cold store. What little light there was on the stairwell failed to follow them as they passed through the outer doors. They walked into total darkness, four shafts of narrow torchlight their only illumination to work by. Les was the first to speak.

"We'll find the valves and shut them down, Teddy and Alfie, find the engineer. He will be in here if he is anywhere."

Divided into their pairs, they moved deeper into the plant room, an area about 30ft by 40ft. Above their heads, and shrouded in an ammonia mist, their torch beams picked out the array of pipework and control valves.

"We need isolation valves 'One and Two'," Butch reminded Les, but Les didn't need reminding and kept his mouth shut as they started their search.

Looking around the floor space was easier. Teddy's and Alfie's beams of light cut through the gloom. By the far right-hand wall stood a cabinet of switches, various dials – and a man lying unconscious on the floor.

"Found him," shouted Teddy, not expecting a reply. He didn't get one as the other pair went from valve to valve carefully inspecting each ID tag, looking for numbers one and two.

A scientist would tell you ammonia dissolves readily in water to form ammonium hydroxide, an alkaline solution. Whilst the concentration of aqueous ammonia solutions used in the home is typically around 5% to 10%, here in the cold store the solution was around 25% or more and was corrosive. Anhydrous ammonia reacts with moisture in the body's mucous membranes to produce ammonium hydroxide. Exposure to ammonium hydroxide results in corrosive injury to the mucous membranes of the eyes, lungs, and gastrointestinal tract as well as to the skin. The engineer was laying on his back; the light from the men's 'CEAG' lamps showed him to be in a bad way.

Trying to find a pulse whilst wearing Draeger rubber gloves is practically impossible, but Alfie tried anyway. He felt nothing. Moving as close as possible to the injured man's face Alfie looked for the faintest sign of life, like the man's exhaled breath condensing on the surface of his facemask. Nothing. Alfie had seen the Royal Army Medical Corps at work, close up and personal, in Malaya. He knew a bit about battlefield first aid.

"Check his airway," said Alfie. "Shine your torch in his mouth, Teddy. His windpipe looks burned and his airway is likely to close up completely. He has little chance unless we do something and do it quickly."

Alfie recalled something he had seen a medic do once. "What I have I got to lose?" he thought. "He is going to die if I don't do something." Alfie looked round and saw what he was looking for. He ran towards it. By the workbench drawer he found a bit of plastic tubing, about the diameter of a common garden hose. Cutting off a nine-inch section, he rushed back to the man.

"Teddy, hold his head back and open his mouth wide while I stick this down his throat."

Teddy held the man's head steady. Already nasty blisters were covering his neck and exposed face. Holding the man's tongue forward with a finger, Alfie inserted the tube into the man's mouth and slid it down the back of the man's inflamed and swollen throat.

"Right you bastard, breathe," said Alfie as he moved up to behind the man's head, his knees touching the man's shoulders. He started Holger Nielsen resuscitation. "You pump his heart, Teddy, when

I've got his arms outstretched," said Alfie, committed to getting the man breathing again.

After what seemed an age, but in reality was only a matter of minutes, the injured man made a gurgling noise before producing a convulsive spluttering cough. Although the man was unconscious, Teddy felt the air being exhaled when Alfie compressed the man's chest. He also felt the movement of breath when Alfie stopped the resuscitation.

"He's breathing, Alfie. We've got to get him out of here and bloody fast."

Calling to Les and Butch, Teddy and Alfie took the man out, half carrying, half dragging him back towards the staircase. Speed was of the essence. Whilst supporting his upper body they carried, in fact yanked, the unconscious engineer backwards down the staircase, one on either side of him, their rapid progress marked by the man's boots bumping on each step during their descent. By the time they reached the first floor both men were near exhaustion when two firemen, in Draeger, came towards them.

"You Clerkenwell?" asked Teddy.

"No, Euston," came the reply.

"Help us get him out," demanded Teddy.

With conditions somewhat improved in the street, ambulance crews were waiting as they saw the four firemen carrying the engineer towards the loading bay exit ramp. They swiftly cut away all his clothing and started to douse the man with water spray from a fire brigade hose-reel. An ambulance man substituted the bit of hose for an airway, not giving the discarded, lifesaving, hose a second glance. Bottled distilled water was applied to the man's eyes and he was lifted onto a stretcher and placed in the ambulance before being whisked away, with a police escort, to Guy's Hospital.

Les and Butch descended the staircase at a more leisurely pace after locating the valves and shutting them both down. The first closed with ease, the second with the aid of the injured engineer's wrench. In the street, cold store employees were still being treated by ambulance crews but there was less pandemonium. Even the naked Southwark fireman had been found some overalls to wear. Other ET crews in full protective clothing would finish the ventilation, and with the cold store's power switched back on their engineers would engage the building's fans to safely dissipate the remaining ammonia gas.

Returning to the station, it was cleaning and testing their BA sets and the Draeger suits for the Lambeth ET crew – well, most of them anyway. Ken was headed off to the mess to make them all a cuppa and to get out the special tin of biscuits, reserved for the tender's crew after working jobs. As Alfie left the station that evening the rubber suits were still suspended from broom handles, so as to help them dry completely, before being returned to their storage boxes. They looked like alien scarecrows hanging from the appliance room balcony as Alfie thought, "Well, that was an interesting afternoon."

The following day Alfie reported for his night duty at around 5.30 p.m. Out of habit he looked in at the watchroom to see what he was riding. He would have been surprised if it hadn't been the tender. He saw that Les had laid-in for watch and that Butch had taken public holiday leave. Freddy Floyd's name had been pencilled in to ride the ET, which was now down to five – its minimum number of riders.

After roll call Alfie was ordered up to the station office by the Sub Officer. As he went in Teddy was standing by the Station Officer, who was seated at his desk.

"That was quite some trick you pulled off yesterday, Alfie" said his guvnor. "The man is still critical although he's stable. The doctors think he has probably lost the sight in one eye. You saved his life yesterday, Alfie. Teddy has already given me a blow by blow account of your deeds. I am reporting your actions to Division as worthy of meritorious conduct."

As the Station Officer stood to shake Alfie's hand the station call bells started playing their tune and all three headed towards the appliance room.

"Great job yesterday," said Teddy as they waited in the appliance room to see what was going out. Lambeth's pump-escape, pump and turntable ladder were off.

"Time for another cup of tea," said Alfie as the tender's crew, including a none too happy looking Freddy, made their way back upstairs to the mess room.

That evening Lambeth's machines are in and out like a fiddler's elbow. All except the ET, that is. Then, just before midnight,

Lambeth's house lights illuminate the station as the call bells sound yet again. The blue-coloured call light tells the ET crew that it's their shout.

"It's a 'BA required' fire at a Bayswater Hotel," shouts the dutyman as he passes Teddy the call slip and the route card, not that Ken needed one.

The emergency tender picks up speed as it crosses over Lambeth Bridge heading north. Its crew are already rigged in their distinctive yellow bagged Proto sets. They sit silently as the appliance radio crackles into life. A priority message is sent from the Bayswater hotel making pumps eight. They listen intently, knowing it's going to be a long night.

(Fiction)

A Flicker of Flame

THE STATION OFFICER PICKED up his battered, but much thumbed, pocket Oxford Dictionary. He found the word he was seeking and studied the range of definitions. *"The zone of burning gases and fine suspended matter associated with rapid combustion: a hot, glowing, mass of burning gas or vapour: the condition of active, blazing, combustion: burst into flame: something resembling a flame in motion, brilliance, intensity, or shape: a violent or intense passion: a person that one has an intense passion for."* Such a simple five-letter word was 'flame', yet it influenced so much of what he did and who he was. He thought of the young man. A man who had died instantly even before the flames engulfed his body. A body which was only identified from his dental records. It would take the police a few days to locate the man's next of kin. Unbeknown to the Station Officer, he would discover her before they did.

The old lady was a creature of habit. Her early life had been one of service. She was born towards the end of the last century. Once a nanny's assistant in a grand country home she had, through her own hard work and study, become a children's nanny herself. Her first lover also turned out to be her last. When he took the 'King's shilling' they were engaged to be married but he never returned from the Great War; neither did his body. His faded, uniformed, image now stood in the silver plated photograph frame he had given her for her 21st birthday. The frame looked as old, worn out and tired as she did. It showed more tin than the silver plate that once covered it. Age had taken its toll on the picture frame and the old woman in equal measure. Her only living relative was her dead sister's son who, although he had remained in the Southwark area, she hadn't seen in years.

Situated in Waterloo, a part of Southwark, it was only a relatively short walk across the bridge to Covent Garden and the palatial homes where she had once worked. Not that she walked 'there anymore, living in Cornwall Gardens, a maze of forgotten back streets hemmed in by bleak Victorian tenement building. She might as well have been on a different planet. She thought she was. Most Londoners preferred to forget that it even existed. The local council seemed to have overlooked it completely. Prying eyes would watch those lost and hurrying through the dirty side streets from behind their equally dirty window panes and nicotine-stained net curtains. Given her surroundings, it was hardly surprising that she considered herself a prisoner in her own home.

Despite the name, no grass ever grew in this dark and depressing labyrinth. The narrow alleys of blackened brick tenements blocked out the sun for most of the day. All colour had leached away after decades of the multitude of chimneys spewing out their smoke and soot, occasionally filling the streets with its smog. In her two-room, fourth floor, dwelling in Charles Court, just around the corner from the Old Vic Theatre, the meagre fire burning in the grate drew moisture out of the room's damp and crumbling plaster.

For her there was no escape from the gloom except, possibly, at night. That was when she lit the candle that stood on the bedside cabinet. Its reflected light was much friendlier than the naked single light bulb hanging from a twisted flex on the ceiling. Through the hole in her wall, where once had hung a door, the candle's light cast shadows into her day room which served as her kitchen, diner and lounge. In fact it served her every daily purpose. Her bedroom had only enough room for her narrow single bed, the small bedside cabinet, and the clothes she kept in a battered leather trunk in one corner.

In cold weather warmth was a luxury. Her broken window panes were stuffed with anything that came to hand – old newspapers, rags, and sometimes bits of cardboard from the food boxes occasionally brought around by the nearby Southwark Cathedral's missionary. He found it hard to believe that such obscenities were allowed to persist in his city in this so-called age of enlightenment and equality. At least that is what Prime Minister Thatcher had recently called it!

Very few now called the old lady by her first name, Mary-Ann. In fact few even knew it. Even her kindly neighbour only ever called her Miss Fellows. She had a crippled hip and it confined her to her two rooms. Harry, the neighbour, helped her out by cadging food from local restaurants. But not tonight, so she had gone to bed hungry. She had been reading by candlelight. It was her habit. She loved the candlelight as much as she loved her books. She had read them all many times. She would read until her eyelids grew heavy with sleep. Tonight she put the book down too close to the candle, much too close. Her eyes were already closed as the book pushed the enamel candle holder to the very edge of the cabinet. There was more holder off the cabinet than on it.

Gravity took control and the lit candle fell to the floor. It remained alight and the heat of its flame ignited the newspaper behind the cabinet which ignited the bedclothes hanging down. This, in turn, set fire to the underside of her ancient mattress. All the while toxic smoke rose upwards towards the ceiling.

Some compounds found in the smoke from fires are highly toxic; others can cause irritation to the skin and mucous membranes. The most dangerous of these compounds is carbon monoxide. It is an odourless but lethal gas and is sometimes accompanied by the gases hydrogen cyanide and phosgene. Smoke inhalation can therefore quickly led to incapacity and loss of consciousness. Sulphurous oxides, hydrogen chloride and hydrogen fluoride in contact with moisture respectively form sulphuric, hydrochloric and hydrofluoric acid, which are corrosive to both lungs and materials. When sleeping neither the nose nor the brain senses smoke, but the body will wake up if the lungs become enveloped in smoke; the brain will be stimulated and the person will be awakened. The old lady was now coughing and gasping for her breath. Her eyes were desperately trying to focus in the dark, smoke-filled room. Suddenly it all got brighter, much brighter. In her last living moments she believed that someone had come into her rooms and turned on the electric light. Light radiated all around her as the smouldering mattress found the oxygen it needed and the whole bed exploded into flames.

Those reporting for their first night shift started to drift into the fire station just before 5 p.m. They would report for their night duty right up to the change of watch at 6 p.m. You could set your watch by Eric who always arrived at the station exactly six minutes prior to roll call. Morning or evening, Eric never failed. This particular afternoon, as they reported to the Edwardian station, the pump bay was missing its pump. However, it was not missing the array of various equipment it carried as it littered the appliance room floor. Hose, ladders, small gear, adaptors and extinguishers seemed to fill every available space. It never ceased to amaze the uninformed observer just how much kit a fire engine actually carried.

The pump had been taken out of service with a mechanical fault. One of the day watch had been sent to collect a spare fire engine and it looked very much that the first task of the night shift was to re-stow the reserve appliance when it arrived at the station.

"Funny how the bloody spare comes in after that lot go off duty," muttered Bunny to no one in particular.

There was not much love lost between the two watches and there hadn't been since the aftermath the first national fireman's strike some eighteen months earlier. Of the four watches, the day shift had a poor reputation across the other three watches. Unlike his watch their Station Officer had refused to strike. He had not let them forget it either. He was now an even greater 'jobsworth' than he was before that winter of '77/78. He relished reminding them that he was enjoying the considerable pay rises earned on the backs of their actions. The watch reacted in any way it could, with the result that standards had fallen and were still falling. However, since such problems were kept on the station; Divisional HQ was largely in the dark about what was happening. But matters were coming to a head.

As if on cue the spare fire engine returned to the station during the 6 p.m. roll call. In fact, those on parade could hear it coming down the street. It had blown the exhaust and sounded more like a tank than a fire engine. Still another would have to be found. It was eventually, arriving just before 8 p.m.: supper time! Supper would have to wait as they re-stowed and then tested the spare pump. It looked like it had been around the block a few times too, probably seen more service than their junior buck, the 'JB', who had only recently passed his four yearly qualified fireman's examination.

Although, as the older hands would remind him, it did not contain that much of a test these days not since the union had kicked over half of the former content into touch.

Their 'Guvnor' was a good man. He was rated triple F: fair, firm and friendly. He had mellowed over the years, the last ten of which he'd been stationed here as the watch Station Officer. When he first arrived he had inherited a troublesome watch. He set about sorting it out and had. Not averse then to holding the occasional conversation behind the back of the drill tower with those intent on making others' lives a misery, his little 'chats' had the desired effect. He had now built up a professional team of competent firemen that he was privately very proud of. He had not done it all on his own. Six years ago he won the junior officers' 'lottery', getting one of the best Sub Officers he had ever worked with. They made for an amusing looking pair when seeing them standing together. The Station Officer was short and squat and the Sub Officer tall and lanky.

In fact the guvnor was border line regulation height and had a somewhat portly figure, although no one other than his wife would remind him of his increased girth. His Sub Officer, on the other hand, was built like a beanpole. At six feet eight inches tall he was too tall to wear the gas-tight suits carried on the emergency tender that he had ridden in charge of at his last station. It proved to be a problem and the solution was to send in a shorter officer and transfer him out. He and the guvnor made for a formidable team, especially on the fire-ground: each watching the other's back, anticipating the other's moves and leading from the front. But station work routines were law and the guvnor did not alter from them. The Sub Officer was loyal to his boss's wishes. Meals were served at the allotted times and stand-easies lasted not a minute over the assigned fifteen minutes as laid down in Brigade Orders. However, with a fire-engine to be re-stow, tonight's supper was put on hold.

"I was really hoping to catch the new BBC comedy tonight, *Yes Minister*. It started at 8 p.m. Bloody missed it now," said Eric as he wound on the 240 feet of hose-reel tubing carried on either side of the pump. "They have electric motors that wind on these tubing's now, you know," he grumbled as he stood on the roof of the appliance, pulling the tubing hand over hand on the roof-mounted drum.

Finally at 8.45 p.m. the pump was put 'on the run' and the men ambled up to the mess room for their delayed supper. The lead story on the 9 p.m. BBC radio news bulletin that night was the British Steel announcement that more than 11,000 jobs would be axed from its plants in Wales by the end of the following month.

"That's strange," piped up Alan, the mess manager, who as well as being an excellent cook was also an even better wind-up merchant. "Funny how Margaret Thatcher announced last week that State benefits to strikers would be halved and now the steel workers losing their jobs get reduced benefit when trying to defend their industry."

He was looking directly at Eric, who made no secret about being a Tory. The watch was waiting for the bullets to start flying – even the guvnor had a wry smile of anticipation on his face – but it never happened. The station bells rang out. Their first shout of the night.

The fire in Charles Court, Cornwell Gardens had already taken a firm hold. Mary Ann was no longer recognisable. The strong flames had consumed the cardboard covering over the broken window panes and the strong breeze shot through the gaping hole fuelling the hungry fire. What few contents the old lady had were consumed as the temperatures rose and the flames spread. The rotting plaster simply fell from the walls and ceiling, exposing timber rafters and wall battens alike. Angry flames were seeking whatever new fuel lay in their path. They found few obstacles in a building where maintenance and repair had long since been forgotten by the uncaring landlords.

The teleprinter ordering slip read: 'Fire. Charles Court. Cornwall Gardens, Waterloo.' It ordered their pump-escape and pump, and as an 'A' risk category area the call attracted an additional fire engine. The Station Officer was surprised to see that Soho's pump-escape was the third engine; normally one from Lambeth or occasionally Westminster fire station would attend. The answer came as the two fire engines were no more than one hundred yards from the station and a senior officer, whom the Station Officer only knew by name, made 'pumps 12' at Hyde Park Corner, Westminster.

As Southwark's two fire engines sped their way along The Cut, towards Waterloo, the high buildings prevented any view of Cornwall Gardens. It was somewhere you had to be right on top of to find. However, the strong smell of burning, a working 'job', was unmistakable. But it could be the Hyde Park Corner blaze, thought the Station Officer. Plumes of smoke rising high into the night sky, cooling and falling back towards the ground, could spread their taint way beyond the area of the fire.

The engines turned right just before the Old Vic Theatre. You could easily have thought you were transported back to a London of yesteryear. Every vestige of a modern London seemingly disappeared. Buildings over one hundred years old dominated the narrow streets and narrower alleyways.

The buildings were typical of those built by the Peabody or the Guinness Trusts. These Trusts had originally built across central London over one hundred years before to provide improved accommodation for the poor. George Peabody, an American banker, diplomat and philanthropist, was the first seized with a desire to "ameliorate the condition of the poor and needy in this great metropolis". The Guinness Trust followed in his wake. The building with flames coming out of a fourth floor window may have looked similar to those belonging to the Trusts, but this and the surrounding buildings were now owned by much less scrupulous landlords. Maintenance of the five-storey terraced buildings, sub-divided into small, squalid flats, was not high on their agenda. They just wanted a maximum return on their investment.

A central entrance fed onto a common staircase which served the four flats on each floor, two at the front, two at the rear. A narrow corridor gave access to the individual flats, leading off an unprotected stone staircase. Just four feet of pavement separated those in the ground floor flats from the kerb. The party walls only extended into the pitched roof areas every two building widths, thus making a common roof space spread over the eight top floor flats.

Generally, the public has no idea of the hazards firemen encounter when they attempt a rescue. They risk their lives on every fire. As the first two fire engines arrived the crews saw the enormity of the task confronting them. Already several people, including children, were trapped on the upper floors, pleading for rescue. Fire and thick smoke was blasting from one particular top floor window. Smoke was also coming from others too and the roof was already alight. Seeing those waiting for rescue and assuming that were would be others, plus the extent of the fire, the Station Officer sent a 'priority' assistance message making pumps six, breathing apparatus required and requesting a turntable ladder. He already knew that an ambulance would be despatched to the incident, but his experience told him to request another so he did.

The pump-escape crew needed no instructions. They hit the ground running. Even before the driver had stopped moving the crew were pulling the escape ladder from the rear of the appliance and the bespoke carriage wheels hit the road with a resounding thud. As the driver moved his engine clear, the crew had already turned the wooden escape ladder 90 degrees and Eric was starting to extend the ladder to its full working height. The Sub Officer's choice of who to rescue first was made for him. Two windows away from the room gushing flames a hysterical woman was hugging her two children who were also crying with fear. There were others, but they looked in less imminent danger, if only marginally.

Parked cars made for an awkward pitch. The ladder stood at an obtuse angle to the window five stories up. The JB was already up on the main extension shouting to the mother to stay put and mind the ladder as the top landed heavily on the supporting brickwork just below the window sill. The Sub Officer followed him up the ladder. There was more screaming in the background: a man's voice bellowed something about his "trapped kids".

Many things happened at once. The guvnor was assessing the incident, keeping a weather eye on his crew's actions. He had already shot through the ground floor entrance to see what was happening at the back of the building. From the rear, an enclosed and restricted yard, he was relieved to see that no one else was shouting for help from the upper windows. Not yet, anyway. Alan, the pump's driver, had parked on the other side of the road, clear of the flats' frontage. The two riding the back of the pump had put their compressed air breathing apparatus sets on en route, facemasks hanging loosely about their necks. Hose was flying from the locker and Alan was legging it up the road. He had engaged the pump when he stopped and 'dropped' the water tank to provide water for a covering jet. He was running, with a standpipe, key and bar, towards the nearest hydrant some 150 feet away on the next corner. Aided by a firemen wearing his BA set they set about laying out the twin lengths of 2½ inch hose and connecting it to the pump inlets before Alan ran back to the hydrant to turn the water on. He had not even had time to rig in his fire gear.

On the fourth floor flames were being caught in the strong breeze and threatening the fireman at the head of the escape. A second fireman directed a jet into the burning room and was ready to protect his colleagues from the flames.

The JB had hauled himself up over the sill, which was 18 inches higher than the head of the escape ladder. He clambered through the open sash window head first. The room was full of smoke. Although not enough to stifle breathing it was enough for the woman to fear for her children's lives. The room was hot and getting hotter. With the Sub Officer just below the window sill, and balancing precariously on the ladder, the JB handed down the first child, a toddler, clearly suffering from shock. The Sub passed the child to a fireman immediately below him who descended the ladder with the screaming child. The Sub Officer was passed a second child, a boy of about nine or ten. He started his descent the ladder and heard the reassuring sound of two-tone horns blasting out and moving ever closer.

Soho's arrival coincided with the JB assisting the mother, who was in a highly agitated state, out of the top floor window. Soho had intercepted the informative message Alan had sent for his guvnor. The message gave Control brief details of the fire and the estimated number of people involved. Soho's adrenaline levels were high. Its crew did not require a script to do what needed doing. With three of their crew already rigged in BA sets, the Station Officer indicated the next priority rescue. Their escape was slipped with ease and pushed towards the building at speed. The driver of the Soho's pump-escape moved off up the road, directed to do so by the Station Officer, who was reserving the space he had occupied for the imminent arrival of the turntable ladder. Well, he was praying it was imminent.

The JB was on the head of the escape ladder. He had to constantly talk to the woman in an attempt to keep her calm. She was in danger of losing it completely despite her children being safely on the ground. Another fireman was making his way up the escape ladder to assist the JB who had managed to coax the woman to sit out on the window sill.

"Right, now turn around and find the top of the ladder with your feet," he said in a composed voice. "Then you can climb down the ladder and I will be right here behind you," he continued.

She found the first round, then the second whilst gripping the window sill for dear life.

"Right, now move your hands to the top of the ladder," he instructed.

She tried to do it all in one movement, making a sudden grab for the sides of the ladder with her hands. She failed. Her feet slipped off the rung and her body followed her feet through the gap. She was falling. Total panic consumed the woman. She thought she was going to die. In a reflex action the JB slipped his arm under the woman's right armpit and stopped her falling. However, in the process and with the weight of her downward motion, she dislocated her shoulder blade. Now her screams were 50 per cent fear and 50 per cent pain. The JB and his colleague retrieved the woman and turned her to face the JB. With her good arm clinging to his neck, and the colleague moving her feet one rung at time, the trio made a painfully slow descent to the ground.

Soho's crew, on the other hand, were moving at a different speed entirely. Who removed the loft hatch in the adjoining block, which gave access the common roof void, would never be discovered. Whoever it was, their actions allowed thick toxic smoke and heat to fill the top floor corridor and the stairwell serving the flats. In the furthest flat, where the man had been shouting about his trapped children, he was still shouting. Soho's leading fireman was the first up the ladder. As Soho had a straight pitch of their escape ladder it rested directly on the window sill. The leading fireman was followed by a fireman in BA and then another. The three entered the man's flat via the window. The room was full of acrid smoke. The leading fireman held the sobbing man by the window, where he took in gasps of fresh air. The two fireman had turned on their BA sets. Between the sobs the man said he was unable to reach his two children who were in the rear bedroom.

The smoke banked down to the floor. Visibility was only a couple of feet. The BA pair could hear the sound of coughing but found no obvious bedroom door. An internal door was concealing the children's bedroom door. But the coughing guided the pair towards the children's room. Once inside only one child was coughing; the other was not moving. Each man picked up a child and rushed back towards the open window. The leading fireman took the unmoving child and applied CPR, inflating the child's lungs before carrying it down the ladder. But already on the ladder was their father being assisted down. As one BA fireman exited the window the other passed the second, coughing, child. The escape ladder was full of people either being rescued or led to safety.

Soho's turntable ladder arrived before any of the 'make-up' pumps. Clerkenwell's emergency rescue tender had followed it over Waterloo Bridge. The turntable ladder driver read the Station Officer's intentions without a word being exchanged. He positioned the 100 foot ladder mid-point between the two pitched escape ladders. Soho's young 'acting' leading fireman took his place on the ladder, and hooked on, even before the TL jacks were down, its driver not stopping to rig in his fire-gear. The TL driver, a career-long Soho fireman in his early fifties, was a consummate operator of his beloved appliance. Sat at the rear console he elevated, trained and extended his ladder in one smooth, faultless motion, aiming for the remaining faces on the top floor. The Station Officer, still in charge, told him, "After the rescues, rig for a water tower," before returning to oversee the fire situation.

The two adjoining buildings had four flats across the top floor frontage. One flat was burning 'like a bastard,' the fire within having spread into the roof. At two of the other flats escape ladders were at work, rescues were in progress and increasing volumes of acrid smoke were drifting out into the street. The turntable ladder was extending the acting leading fireman towards the last of the flats, whose sole occupant was getting increasingly distraught waiting for rescue. Whilst this flat was less affected by smoke than some of the others, it was a moot point to the young woman living there, who thought she was going to vomit from the vile smoke she had breathed in. Finally she did, all down the front of the young leading fireman as he climbed into her flat. He had been followed up the turntable ladder by a member of the ET crew wearing a BA set.

In the flats to the rear, families had managed to make their way down to safety via the internal staircase. Alarmed by the smell of smoke, so had a family in the adjoining building, again using the internal staircase. However, the young asthmatic teenager in the rear corner flat had not been so fortunate. The smoke pushing down through the open ceiling hatch filled the narrow communal corridor. It had greeted him as he attempted to leave his flat, his parents having popped out for a drink at the pub prior to the fire starting. He had only taken a couple of gasps of acrid smoke before he suffered a convulsive fit. He collapsed, unconscious, to the floor.

It had been a relatively straightforward task to transfer the woman from the last of the flats onto the TL and into the arms of the ET fireman, who assisted her down to the ground. The young leading fireman spoke to the TL operator via the intercom.

"I am just going to have a quick look around."

With that he headed for the front door. The smoke was making his throat raw. He crawled across the floor. The front door was bolted shut. It was a close fitting door; it prevented even more smoke percolating in. Releasing the bolt and opening the door filled the flat with smoke.

"Bollocks," the leading fireman said, regretting his decision to have a look around.

He was just about to close the door again when he saw something, or rather someone, out in the corridor. The teenager appeared lifeless. Crawling on his belly the Soho man reached out and grabbed an arm and dragged the teenager back into the flat. He could feel no pulse as he gasped for breath. The smoke now hung almost down to the floor.

The sudden increase in the smoke billowing from the flat's window caused alarm for the experienced fireman operating the TL. "Get that bloody woman down here and quick," he shouted up to the ET fireman. Not that the ET man needed much encouragement: having seen the smoke himself, he was urging the woman to move faster. What his vocal encouragement failed to achieve was made up for as he half-tugged and half-dragged her down the bottom section of the ladder. Here he passed her over to the operator, who had jumped up from the console, to finish the job. Heading back up the TL at speed, he started up his compressed air BA set, not knowing what to expect when he reached the top.

What he had not expected to see, as he poked his head through the window, was the young acting leading fireman trying to breathe life into the teenager whilst keeping himself alive at the same time. The flat door had not closed and smoke filled the flat. What little breathable air there was hugged the floor. The young officer was sucking it into his lungs and then blowing it into the lungs of the teenager. He did not think he could continue it for much longer when a hand touched his head. With the ET fireman now in the room the pair managed to lift and place the unconscious youth up by the window opening. With the ET fireman back on the turntable ladder the teenager was placed over his shoulders. The boy's limp form added to the weight of the heavy BA set the ET man was wearing, but he could not wait for assistance. He had to get down the ladder and recommence the resuscitation. His arms and legs were throbbing – the pain caused by oxygen starvation due to his exertions – as he sped down the ladder. It was a coughing and spluttering acting leading fireman who unceremoniously exited the flat window and followed him down the ladder.

All these events happened over an extremely short period of time. The street resounded to the clamour of reinforcing appliances seemingly arriving all at once, their crews eager to get in on the action, much of which had been occurring in parallel to the ladder rescues taking place in the street. As one ambulance took a casualty away a second was arriving, its crew heading in the direction of the teenager being brought down the turntable ladder. Three police cars added to the mix, the last bringing the duty Inspector from the local 'nick'.

The two fireman who had arrived on Southwark's pump had been running themselves ragged. One had provided a covering jet, the other helping Alan set into the hydrant. Both had made herculean efforts to get water onto the fire. With residents escaping down the internal staircase the pair, with the aid of Alan, had pitched the extension ladder to the second floor staircase window. They had left Alan their BA tallies, before taking a 1¾ inch hose line into the building via the ladder and laying it out on the landing below the top floor. Contrary to proper BA procedures, whilst one pulled more hose up onto the landing the other legged it back down to the window, half-hollering and half-gesticulating for Alan to turn the water on. In those first few frantic minutes, with so much to do, there was not a spare pair of hands to be found. Every fireman was playing an active part. Those at the bottom of the ladders were just as vital as those at the top.

The pair in BA rapidly made it up onto the top floor before turning left and heading to the blazing flat. Despite the protection given by their breathing apparatus sets, the heat drove the pair down to the floor. They were crawling forward on their bellies having to endure the energy-draining heat before being able to direct their jet directly onto the fire. But the fire was coming to meet them. Having burnt through the upper section of the old lady's door, superheated gases and vapours had ignited. A flame front was moving along the ceiling and directly in front of the pair. Their water spray from their jet gave a cooling effect but it was marginal. They never felt any real benefit from it although it gave them the impetus to push on. The vaporising water spray, hopefully, would prevent a flashover, something that seriously worried the pair. Suddenly their hose line became lighter; it moved easier. Four members of Clerkenwell's ET crew had joined them. Together they reached the flat door and directed the jet into the blazing rooms.

All this time the fire in the roof void had been advancing. Thick black smoke was also punching out into the night from the adjoining building's upper floor. With rescues complete, additional crews made use of one of the escape ladders and brought a second hose line to bear on the ceiling hatch. Flames were visible through the smoke, seemingly determined to force the firemen back from whence they came, but they did not succeed. The men held their ground and pushed on with attacking the fire. Other firemen brought a short extension ladder up the inside staircase so the fire in the roof could be reached via the hatch opening. Finally, and with the TL converted to a water tower, the fire in the old lady's flat was finally subdued. The fire in the roof soon followed suit, with hose-reel jets replacing the bigger jets: the last thing the Station Officer wished to see now was excess water cascading down the internal staircase and flowing out into the street.

The Assistant Divisional Officer (ADO) arrived and took charge as the last rescue was being carried out. He and the Station Officer shared a strong mutual respect so he allowed the other to maintain his sound plan of attack. Order flowed from the initial frenzied activity. The punishing heat and smoke conditions abated. Despite their desire to get into the thick of it, two of the reinforcing crews were allocated salvage work, thus minimising unnecessary water damage on the lower floors.

Reports that the old lady was missing had been slow to surface. Once they did, there was nothing to be done except look for her remains. The process to consume a human body by fire, as in a cremation, usually takes 90 to 120 minutes in temperatures of around 1000°C; larger bodies can take longer. By all accounts the old woman was small and frail. Sixty minutes had elapsed since the time of first 999 call, so there would be something to find, however unpleasant it may be.

The asthmatic teenager was in a critical condition as he arrived, under police escort, at the hospital. Despite the endeavours of the medical teams he would not survive the effects of the carbon monoxide poisoning. Unlike the old lady he died without a single burn to his body. The same could not be said for the charred remains that would soon lay in the refrigerator of the local mortuary as it awaited the post mortem by the forensic pathologist. In due course the closing chapter of her life, and death, would be played out at the Coroner's Inquest, together with that of the unfortunate teenager.

As the ADO was sending his 'Fire surrounded' message the Station Officer was on his third ascent to the top of the building's staircase. He was checking on the progress of the damping down in the roof space and the final searches of the affected flats, but he was desperate for a fag. Reaching the top landing he reached into his fire-tunic pocket for his baccy tin. Things were much calmer now; the Brigade photographer was taking pictures, the police surgeon having certified the remains of the old woman dead. The Station Officer stood in the corridor and took stock as he removed one of his pre-made roll ups. It was his habit always to have a couple ready and waiting. All the lads had performed well, bloody well in fact. He would have expected nothing less and made a mental note to ring his opposite numbers at Soho and Clerkenwell to pass on his appreciation and formal thanks to their PE, TL and ET crews.

He held his lighter, an old petrol lighter that he had for years. With the cigarette between his lips his thumb pushed down on the lighter. There was a spark, then a flame. He looked momentarily at the flame. The product of fire that produces both light and heat, only today it had brought death and destruction. He watched as it flickered and danced in the darkened gloom. Suddenly the chest pains began. They hit him like a train crash. As he dropped his lighter his right hand grabbed his upper left arm and he let out a mournful groan. Time drifted out of sync. His last thought was: "This is no bloody heartburn!"

By the time the first fireman ran to his aid the pain had spread to his neck, his jaw and, for some reason he could not comprehend, just above his belly button. Short of breath, he was breaking out in cold sweats. It was the police surgeon who saved his life. She had ran back up the stairs as soon as she heard the commotion and the fireman shouting urgently for an ambulance crew. It was her decision to crush the aspirins and put them under the tongue of the ashen Station Officer. She was certain he had just suffered a major heart attack. Rushed to hospital under police escort he was again in the midst of controlled mayhem of people working desperately to save life. Only this time his was the life being saved.

The hours became days and days turned into weeks.

The first fully implantable pacemaker had been fitted in 1958 to a man who, at 43, had been suffering from a cardiac arrhythmia, something which had worsened as a result of a viral infection. The procedure was now commonplace. The Station Officer, also 43, had been seen by the hospital's top heart specialist, a pre-eminent cardiologist. He had learnt lots about the procedures he was now required to undergo and of the people who would carry them out, people like the 'electrophysiologist': a cardiologist who specialises in heart rhythm disorders. He also knew one other thing for definite. His days of riding a fire engine were over, probably his time with the Brigade were too.

The night duty immediately following the fire in Cornwall Gardens was a surreal one for the watch back at the station. Routines had to be performed, duties attended to. Despite the congratulations of others heading their way they all felt the same: empty inside. What news they got from the hospital was stilted and sparse. Their guvnor remained in a critical condition. The doctors were not hopeful at this stage. Their Divisional Commander attended the station to thank them for a job well done and to say the Brigade would do all it could to support the guvnor's family, which consisted of his wife only. There were no children. There was no real plan of action either, what followed just happened. Their guvnor was more than just their Station Officer, he was their companion too.

He had had his moments. He was a bit of a stickler for the rules, but he cared deeply about them and would go out on a limb to argue their case. His wife, who had a job in the City, had bought everyone on the watch a Christmas hamper during the firemen's strike in '77.

"It probably cost her a grand if it cost her a penny," Alan had said at the time.

It was payback time. The whole watch rallied round. Worrying about her husband's fate took its toll. She was not coping well and discovered she didn't have to. She found herself with a new-found family, her husband's watch. They in turn trusted each other's decisions and actions. No one wasted time discussing the next steps, they just got on with what needed to be done. Transporting the wife to and from hospital, jobs done around the house, caring for the guvnor's garden, servicing his car: all was taken care of. Each weekend his wife was invited to someone's home for dinner. Nothing was too much trouble.

The guvnor was never short of a visitor either. Alan was sternly lectured one night by the duty ward sister for trying to smuggle in the guvnor's baccy tin! It was a strange sort of bollocking, one that ended up with Alan inviting her out for dinner and she accepting.

In a corner of Eltham cemetery, three weeks after the fire, a double funeral took place. Police inquiries into the death of an unidentified man had led back to Mary-Ann Fellows. She was buried alongside her estranged nephew in paupers' graves. The only people who bothered to attend were Mrs Fellow's kindly neighbour, the Southwark Police Inspector (who had discovered their family connection), the four undertakers and the 'duty' vicar who conducted the burial service. Even as they moved away the council's mechanical digger was already filling in the graves.

It was five months after the old lady died that his watch and friends gathered for the guvnor's farewell bash. It was not so much a goodbye as an *au revoir*, since their Station Officer was now a Technical Officer (a non-operational Station Officer) in the Division's Fire Prevention Branch. Having given up smoking completely he had nevertheless requested an unexpected leaving gift, something to replace the one he had lost in all the confusion on that fateful night.

It was handed to him in its presentation box, one which he opened before smiling faces. He lifted it and pressed the igniter of the solid gold ingot, petrol-filled lighter. Tears filled his eyes as he watched the flame and recalled that last memorable 'shout'. He had thought his watch had made him proud then. But he knew, looking at his wife, and with tears filling her eyes, that they had made him so much prouder since. He hoped that they knew it. But just in case his short speech told them how he felt in typical fashion. He and his wife were not the only ones wiping away a tear by the time he finished his heartfelt, hilarious, farewell words.

(Fiction)

Rescues in NW2

MIKE HAD BEEN OPERATIONAL for exactly two years when he reported for the second night duty of that tour. At 20 years of age he was not considered a big bloke, nor was he overly athletic. He weighed in at 11 stone 2 pounds and had a 32 inch waist line. On parade, that November evening, he was detailed to ride the pump-escape and designated as the station's dutyman. This North London fire station, once in the former Middlesex Fire Brigade, still received its fire calls via telephone from the control room at Wembley. The Sub Officer rode in charge of the PE and Station Officer Vic rode the pump. With the normal appliance routines completed, and after a cup of tea, the guvnor left the Sub Officer to take the watch for evening drills. It was an uneventful evening. No fire calls– what firemen call 'shouts' – until *that* call.

It was a bitterly cold night. Snow had already started to fall by the late evening. No one went to bed at the designated time, although, like all older fire stations, firemen had put down their army-style fold-away beds after supper anywhere they could find a space. The station had no dormitory and there was a definite pecking order on who had the best bed spaces. As the watch's 'junior buck', the 20 year-old found himself at the bottom of the list. All had to sleep using the Brigade-issue blankets (horrible scratchy things) since the guvnor did not allow any personal sleeping bags on the station. It was one of his many foibles. Most of the watch slept in their overall trousers and a tee shirt. It ensured a quick response when the 'bells went down'. But being the operator of the control room – or, as London stations call it, 'watchroom' – his bed space was secure in the station control room that night. As the station control room operator it was his duty to answer any calls from the Wembley control room, write down the call details on a special form and actuate the dispatch lights which would inform the other firemen which fire engine(s) were going out.

At 2.24 a.m. his light sleep was shattered by the bells going down and the automatic house lights coming on all around the station. He leapt from his bed and was at the watchroom switchboard within a second. With pen in one hand and switchboard phone in the other, flicking switches, he listened intently to the control officer. He wrote down the address and the route card reference. The station's pump-escape and pump were ordered to a fire at 203 Northwood, NW2. Switching on the two coloured appliance dispatch lights, red and green, in the appliance room, he let the crews know that both machines were being ordered. He heard the wooden appliance bay doors crash open as the two drivers waited impatiently on their appliances, revving the engines up. Handing an ordering slip first to the Sub Officer, together with a route card, he repeated the process with Station Officer Vic before Mike climbed into the rear of the PE.

As the drivers drove out of the station the cold night air hit them. There was a thick covering of snow all around. The call was to the far side of their stations ground, almost into West Hampstead's patch. The drive took five to six minutes; because of the snow, the fire engine drivers were careful to maintain control of the machines. When they entered Northwood the PE was still in front, the pump a safe distance behind it. As the PE cleared a long and slow right-hand bend it was the Sub Officer and the driver who first witnessed the unfolding drama in the near distance.

Then, in his short career, the young fireman saw a sight most firemen speak of yet many hope they will never see. It was a dire fire situation. People were screaming for their lives. They were trapped in the burning, three-storey, terraced building. It was a combined shop and dwellings. Its occupants were desperate to be rescued. Coming from the opposite direction, with different weather conditions, the supporting station's fire engine had arrived at the incident seconds ahead of Willesden's own two machines. Their crew had dismounted and were running to slip their 50-foot wheeled escape ladder before extending it to the top floor window. A window where people were shrieking for help. Acrid, thick, angry, smoke was forcing its way from the windows of the property. Fierce flames were shooting into the street from the lower levels.

Before his PE had even stopped he had jumped to the ground. He knew his task was securing a supply of water so that an immediate attack on the fire could commence in concert with the attempts to save these people's lives. Grabbing the hydrant equipment from its locker he ran to the nearest water hydrant which was just slightly to the left and in front of the property on fire.

The building involved was a café, its accommodation above. It was some 25 feet wide and went back about 70 feet deep. As he ran to connect a standpipe to the hydrant, some ten feet from it, the ground floor suddenly exploded into a ball of fire. It seemed the entire building was engulfed in searing flames. The fire in the ground floor café had flashed over. What had been a serious incident escalated in those few seconds to a desperately dangerous one. Flames, like a plumber's blowtorch, roared across the pavement. The resultant fireball rose up over the roof of the house. The flames were so fierce that they burned the side of the other fire engine that had, in all the urgency, been parked too close to the front of the building. The heat was so severe that it first scorched and was now setting alight the wooden wheeled escape ladder which had been pitched to the upper floors. The pump operator of the supporting fire engine had a miraculous escape; he barely avoided being severely burnt, as the resultant flash-over almost consumed him while he operated the side-mounted pump controls.

The force of the explosion knocked our young fireman over. He dropped the hydrant equipment and was forced to back away because of the severity of the heat. He shielded his face with raised arms. When he looked up to where people had been a moment ago there was nothing to be seen except a wall of flame. Why he did what he did next he still has no idea. He had never witnessed anything like it before. He was given no instruction: gut instinct drove him to do what he did.

He ran back towards his own station's pump. Skidding on the snow, he stopped at the pump's rear cab and, jumping up into the cab. he grabbed a Proto oxygen breathing apparatus set. The pump's driver, a senior fireman, seeing the young fireman's obvious intentions, screamed at him,

"No Mike!"

The older fireman had never shouted so intently. The young fireman was not listening. Dispensing with all the starting-up and booking-in procedures required for the breathing apparatus, he threw the set over his shoulders, stuffed the mouthpiece into his mouth and turned on the set's main valve. In his haste he chose not to secure the set to his body or fit the mouthpiece to his head harness. Now, as he ran towards the burning escape ladder, he put the BA goggles over his eyes and placed the nose clip on his nose. With a long push of the by-pass valve, which inflated the set's breathing bag, he drew in through the mouthpiece the first breaths of pure oxygen.

Another fireman had already got a jet to work, using the one-hundred gallon water tank supply. The young fireman barked out his instructions, instructions that were muffled by his mouthpiece. He shouted for the man on the jet to extinguish the flames on the escape ladder and to try and hold back the fire. He climbed the escape ladder at speed. The fireman on the jet looked on in disbelief but complied with the shouted command as the fireman on the ladder rapidly rose higher.

He felt the effects of the blistering heat as he ascended the burning ladder. He also felt the spray of cold water on his neck and hands as the fireman below sprayed him and tried his best to keep the flames at bay. Nearing the top of the ladder the flames enveloped his whole body but the fireman below relieved the situation: by directing his jet, he managed to keep the flames away from his mess-mate climbing the ladder.

He had reached the top floor window sill. It was where he had last seen those pleading so desperately for help. The heat rising from below was intense. In fact, he thought he might not be able to endure it. But he was determined to get into that room. So, taking a leg lock on the ladder, he first used his axe and attempted to cut away the window frame and enter the room. He failed. Within the first couple of blows of his axe he knew he was not making any impression on the wooden frame. He had no choice but to get into the room using the restricted window opening. The head of the escape ladder had been extended into the narrow open window. The top of the ladder was taking up most of the available space closest to the window sill.

This was the very space where, only moments before, those inside the room had been shouting frantically for rescue. He managed to twist his body around on the top of the ladder and, somehow, entered through the window opening feet first. As he forced himself through the gap his fire helmet was knocked off his head and fell into the street below. He wriggled and forced himself through the restricted opening, his feet feeling for the floor. He felt the unconscious figures right under the window. He had no option but to stand on them in order to get into the room.

He realised, as he entered the room, that his time in there would be very limited. The temperature was intense. He was starting to cook. But then, why would he not? The room was like a ruddy oven! The floors below him were ablaze. Already, at the back of his mind, doubt was creeping in. How could anyone possibly survive in such conditions without breathing apparatus? The temperature was like nothing the young fireman had ever experienced. It sapped his strength. His fears were starting to grow: a fear that said if he did not leave the room right now he might never get out at all – alive, that is. Suddenly he felt very alone. It was his overwhelming sense of duty that made him stay.

He bent down to the two figures at his feet. He found a limb and started to lift. The first body felt very heavy as he attempted to lift it towards window sill. The seconds were turning into minutes. Each time he seemed to get the unconscious casualty up onto the sill, the body slipped back down to the floor. He could not keep it in the right position as the exposed skin had become greasy from the heat and smoke. He changed his grip in order to lift it higher, but the dead weight proved too much. Once again it fell to the floor. He grasped the ladder in a last determined attempt to give himself more purchase when he felt another fireman's hand grab his own.

He took the offered hand and directed it towards the casualty he was trying to lift. Now as he lifted, the other fireman knew what he was trying to do and pulled from the outside. The fireman at the top of the ladder was joined by others. None were wearing breathing apparatus and, being crammed at the head of the escape ladder, they took terrible punishment from the heat and smoke pouring out from the windows below. However, between them they were able to get the first unconscious person out through the window and onto the shoulders of one of the firemen, who started to descend the ladder. Others on the ladder were assisting, preventing the fireman performing the rescue from falling. The difficult process of getting the first casualty down the ladder prevented others, wearing breathing apparatus, from getting up and joining in the search and rescues.

With the first unfortunate soul hurriedly cleared from the base of the ladder a fireman, wearing BA, raced up the ladder to try and enter the room. However, inside the room the second casualty was already being lifted and passed out through the window opening. The top of the ladder was like a log-jam. Those wanting to get in had no alternative but to accept the next casualty and start another difficult descent. Below, meanwhile, a breathing apparatus crew from his own station were getting increasingly anxious. They were desperate to get into the room to help their young colleague, knowing what he was doing required an entire crew. However, they were unable to help him because of the casualties being brought out of the window and down the escape ladder.

The firemen working on the escape ladder were shielded by covering jets of water. Whilst this prevented the actual flames from getting to them, they still had to contend with the severe heat and smoke which continued to envelope them in powerful waves.

Back inside the top floor room small pockets of fire had broken out. Mike could see the glow of the flames through the smoke. He sensed that this was the only room in the building not to have flashed over. He realised that the fire was still raging beneath him. He could hear the flames consuming anything that burned. He had visions of the floor giving way beneath his feet, pitching him into the inferno below. It was then he found a third unconscious soul, a child. Those in the room craving rescue had been breathing in the hot gases mixed with the smoke. It clearly must have burnt their throats as their laboured breathing and the guttural sounds made for a sickening noise. Carefully lifting the child, he carried he body back to the window where he placed it on the shoulders of a waiting fireman.

He thought he could not take much more of this punishment. It was time for him to get out. He had already rescued three people and was feeling exhausted. His decision to leave the room changed when he thought he could hear more strangulated breathing sounds coming from within the room. He knew he could not leave now, so continued to search. On hands and knees he crawled through the debris covering the floor. He felt the worrying rising temperature coming off the floor. The smoke was now so thick that he could not see a hand in front of his face.

On the far side of the room he found two more unconscious people. Both were large individuals and he was running on empty. He did not have the strength to move them unaided. Crawling back to the window he removed his mouthpiece and shouted down, "Two more are still in here." Although he could see nothing below but the smoke he heard the huge gasp and cry of awe from below. It came from the large crowd who had gathered to watch. They had cheered each time a rescue was performed by the firemen.

Returning to the bodies he thought, "I really do need some bloody help in here." Then, as he started to drag one of the unconscious bodies towards the window his strength finally failed him. The body was too large. The intense heat and the previous effort sapped his remaining reserves. He turned when he heard a sound coming from the window. He crawled back to it and saw the outline of a crewmate wearing breathing apparatus. The other fireman was struggling to get through the window opening. As he helped his colleague through, he removed his mouthpiece to tell him of the discovery of two more casualties before taking him to where they lay. The arrival of a colleague gave him renewed strength. Between them they dragged and lifted the nearest person back towards the window where a fireman was already waiting to receive the body onto his shoulders.

Although the crowd could see the rescues they could not appreciate that this public display of professionalism was no mean feat of strength or skill by the firemen, whether in the room or on the escape ladder. To them, standing in the safety of the street, it all looked very exciting. But to lift a dead weight, pass it through a restricted space, then onto the shoulders of a fireman, who was struggling to stay balanced on the 50-foot ladder whilst manoeuvring an unconscious person onto their shoulders: this tested these men to their limit. The firemen below their colleague as he carried the casualty assisted as much as they could, but all were taking huge punishment from the smoke and heat from a fire still burning beneath them.

With the fourth rescue taking place on the ladder the pair inside returned to the fifth person. However, when they returned to the window there was no fireman waiting to receive the casualty. They were recovering people faster than they could be carried down the ladder. There was no alternative: they had to carry the person down themselves. So, exhausted, he climbed out of the window and stood at the top of the ladder. His colleague lifted the casualty and assisted in getting it across his shoulders.

It was only with great difficulty that the two achieved the task. With the ladder still occupied by the fireman carrying down the fourth person, no one could ascend the ladder to assist in helping him carry the fifth person down.

As Mike started to carry this heavy burden down the ladder, every step down tested his resolve. He started to feel light-headed. Then he felt the reassuring hands of a fireman beneath as he guided his feet onto each rung of the ladder. He had only descended 10 feet or so when his exhaustion made its presence known. He knew he was going to fall off the ladder, together with the body he was carrying. His strength had given out, there was nothing left in reserve. He was totally spent.

Spitting out the BA set's mouthpiece he shouted to the fireman below to grab the casualty. He hoped he might fall from the ladder without taking anyone with him. But the fireman below was having none of it. He shot up the ladder and, with huge force, used his arms to envelope him and the body onto the ladder. The slight respite from the weight he carried allowed him to recover slightly. The pair shared the body's weight and after some very difficult manoeuvring the pair continued to carry the limp form to the bottom of the ladder where it was swiftly removed by others.

After the briefest of respites he re-joined other BA firemen searching the top floor. It was the home station's Leading Fireman who told him that he had been ordered by the Officer in Charge of the fire to leave the room and return to ground floor level outside. In the desperate search for still more bodies he ignored this order, believing there were still some areas of the room not searched. All three now began a last frantic search of the remainder of the room. It was during this search he realised he was becoming a danger to himself and the others. He could no longer think properly and had not an ounce of strength left. He was very close to passing out.

As he started his descent the firemen already on the ladder had to descend to allow him off. It was as he was stepping off the ladder he collapsed. Willing hands caught him and carried him across the spaghetti of hose to a clear area of pavement where he was laid down to recover as an ambulance crew checked him over and administered oxygen. As the breathing apparatus set was being taken off of him Station Officer Vic came over to him to ask how he was. This wise and accomplished Station Officer said:

"For you, young man, this job is over."

Placed on a stretcher he was carried to the waiting ambulance. He passed numerous fire engines and other ambulances at the scene. So much help had arrived that he was not aware of. Concerned firemen looked his way and gave him a smile and the thumbs-up sign. No further people were found in that room.

In the ambulance an attendant started to remove shards of glass from the young fireman's hands, which were bleeding freely from the cuts from glass that had shattered in the initial explosion. His hands were also blistered from the heat. Alongside him, on the other side of the ambulance, was a man lying on another stretcher. His face was burnt and his hair badly singed. The man sat up and asked;

"Are you the fireman who entered the fire first?"

He replied that he was. The man, clearly in some pain, asked to shake the fireman's hand and with a strange calmness muttered softly:

"I think you are very brave."

The man had managed to rescue himself by jumping out of a first floor window, 15 feet above the ground floor. Another man had rescued himself by climbing down a drainpipe. It later transpired that the young fireman had been in the top floor room for 27 minutes, mostly on his own, searching for and rescuing five people.

He was taken to hospital suffering from heat and smoke exhaustion to be checked over by the duty Accident and Emergency doctor. However, scant attention was paid to the young 'exhausted' fireman in the busy A&E Department that fraught morning, as the medical staff fought desperately to save the lives of some of the people who had just been rescued. Two hours later he was released; collected by a senior officer, he was delivered back to his station.

As he sheepishly entered the mess room he was greeted by big smiles from all the watch. He informed Station Officer Vic that he had been discharged and was fit to continue his duties. Not a man to be overcome with emotion, the guvnor told the returnee he should get back onto the machine he had been detailed to ride at roll call – and with that, he was back in the 'box'. Nothing more was said of the incident. They all just sat and drank tea, looking at each other, smiling through their blackened faces. They were filthy, smelt of fire debris, smoke and grime. Their work overalls were soaking and soiled. Zilch was said as to what had just happened only a few hours before. It was beyond anything any of them had ever experienced before. Nobody knew where to begin or what to say. After washing, and a change of clothes, they drifted slowly back to their beds where most just lay on top of their blankets, unable to sleep.

Returning to his bed in the station control room, his mind was a whirl of thoughts and emotions. He could not sleep either. Each time he closed his eyes a vivid memory of the fire flashed across his mind and he was forced to open them again. (In fact these flashbacks went on for many weeks afterwards before he was able to return to a good sleep pattern, free of harrowing images.) In the next hour Willesden's station bells summoned both machines to another incident. During the search of the premises, where a fire was reported, the security guard complained that the crews stank of fire and smoke. One of the firemen replied:

"We had a bit of a fire earlier mate."

The others just looked at him and smiled. It was something of an understatement. That was the last call of their shift. They all left the station that morning for their two rota leave days.

Parade on their next first day duty was normal. At 9 a.m. the firemen were detailed as to their riding positions for that day. After the appliances and equipment were checked, and other normal procedures carried out, the young fireman was ordered to report to the station office. As he knocked and entered the office he was immediately ordered to stand to attention. He stood in front of an unexpected array of officers, both his own and the off-going watch officers. His guvnor set about giving him the biggest bollocking of his short career. He was told, in no uncertain terms, that he had broken nearly every rule in BA procedures and had endangered himself in the process. With a ferocity that was making some of the others standing there quake, the Station Officer continued that if he ever caught him doing anything like that again he would be charged under the Fire Service's discipline code and would likely be sacked. By the time the Station Officer had finished this verbal assault the 20 year-old fireman was visibly wilting under this quite unexpected onslaught.

The Station Officer then stood up from his chair and moved swiftly from behind his desk. His stern face suddenly broke into the widest of smiles as he came towards the pale-faced young fireman. He offered his hand, then, changing his mind, he moved closer and enveloped him in a huge friendly hug. He looked at his 'junior buck' and said:

"In all my considerable years your actions were the single most heroic act he had ever seen. I am very proud to have you as a crew member on my watch."

He ended by saying he was going submitting a report and was going to recommend him, and others, for bravery awards. The other officers then came over to him. Each shook his hand as they warmly congratulated him. As he left the station office he was in a daze. Privately, he wondered why there was such a fuss about what he done. He felt sure plenty of others would have done the same.

The word was also now out on the 'wire'. Word that this watch had had a 'fair' old job and did 'some' rescues. Those on Willesden's other watches bitterly regretted missing the sort of job that was only seen very rarely in the fire brigade. On 'shouts', firemen he had never met before would ask to shake his hand and say that they had heard of what he had done. He was very humbled to be treated in this way, especially by those he knew were far more experienced firemen (and officers) than himself.

It was later in that tour the watch held its own debrief on that fire. It was the guvnor's way that after a proper 'job' they would sit down and learn from each other. They listened to each man to get an understanding of the whole job. It was only then that the young fireman discovered that simultaneously to his rescues the Sub Officer had led a crew into the front door of the building, only to find an inferno raging. With a jet of water he had led the crew, none of whom was wearing breathing apparatus. They fought their way up a collapsing staircase whilst attempting to extinguish the fire as they went. Moving into the first floor accommodation, at the rear of the building and after a search, they had rescued two more people whilst taking a huge amount of physical punishment in the process.

It transpired that nine people were in the building at the start of the fire. They were in various letting rooms on the first and mezzanine floors and in the family accommodation on the second floor. In addition to the two people who had rescued themselves, one of whom had spoken to the young fireman in the ambulance, seven people were rescued by the brigade. Three of them died later in hospital, two from the top floor and one from the first floor.

Epilogue

Years later, and after his promotion to Leading Fireman and now on another fire station, our hero was informed that the police wished to interview him again about the Northwood fire. During the interview, where he had to make a formal police statement, the incident in the ambulance seemed of special importance to the police. He asked the detective Inspector about its significance. He was informed that the man who accompanied him in that ambulance had set fire to the café in Northwood and many other places over the subsequent years. He was responsible for the deaths of eight people in total. Finally caught, he confessed to his many arson attacks. The man was due to appear at the Old Bailey. He was subsequently found unfit to plead and was sentenced to be detained at Her Majesty's pleasure in Broadmoor Hospital, a prison for the criminally insane.

Fireman Michael Wallman and Fireman Brian Hudson (Willesden), Fireman Alan Fosbrook (West Hampstead) and Fireman Alan Cox (Hendon) were each awarded a Chief Officer's Commendation for their actions when five people were rescued from a fire at Cricklewood Lane, North West London in November 1969. Three of the five people survived. Fireman Michael Wallman was subsequently awarded the British Empire Medal (BEM) for Gallantry.

(Fact)

Old Fire Stations Never Die...

GREAT MARLBOROUGH STREET FIRE station was built in 1887. It was a Metropolitan Fire Brigade station, one of an increasing number being built by the Metropolitan Board of Works, the forerunner of the London County Council (LCC) which came into being two years later. Like most fire stations then, and those that followed, it was a freehold site. It was built at a cost of £13,000, which puts the cost in today's prices at slightly more than £1.5 million.

The fire station was both the workplace and the home for the firemen and their families. They were on call twenty-four hours a day and the station strength consisted of one Station Officer, fifteen firemen, two coachmen (who drove the engines) and two pairs of horses. Station No 72 was in the Soho district of the West End; its horsed fire engine, horsed escape cart, manual escape ladder and manual hose cart covered this part of the Victorian capital. It was one of 102 fire stations (including the three river stations) protecting the then London area from fire and disaster. For some reason station No 72's complement of firemen was higher than the norm, which averaged around 10 or 11.

During the latter part the 19th century the population of this part of Soho continued to increase steadily. The area was one of the most densely populated parts of London and also one of the poorest. The unsanitary conditions in which many inhabitants lived encouraged Victorian philanthropists to turn their attentions to Soho. This is reflected in the establishment of six hospitals in the area between 1850 and 1875 to deal with local health problems as well as various charity houses providing temporary shelters for homeless men and women. So whilst the working conditions of the firemen was onerous, the living conditions for their families, at the fire station, were considered better than many working within the locality.

By the turn of the century, and now under the control of the London County Council, the firemen of the London Fire Brigade (which changed its name in 1904) were bound hand and foot to their fire station. If any dared to try and improve their conditions of service they might as well resign as their position would be made untenable. Attempts to form a Union, and get it to argue for better conditions, were frowned upon by the LCC. London's firemen's grievances were left unsatisfied right up to the declaration of World War One. It stayed that way until 1918, when finally there was a concession of one days leave in ten, and a wage increase of five shillings a week, worth £15 today.

Self-propelled fire engines had been gradually replacing horse-drawn steam engines since their introduction in 1902. The last horse-drawn appliance was withdrawn from Kensington fire station in 1921.

The days of the Great Marlborough fire station were numbered. It would be one of some 20 London fire stations closed from 1920 until 1922, when its doors were closed for the last time. Both its firemen and the motorised fire engines transferred to other locations. The development of faster and improved fire engine designs had meant many fire stations, in close proximity to each other, were no longer deemed necessary. It was the largest cull of London fire stations in the Brigade's long history.

The station had been well built. It remained pleasing to the eye. It was sold and found new uses and new owners. However, it never lost the look of a former fire station. It survived both the ravages of the Blitz and subsequent rocket attacks on London during World War Two.

Then in the late evening of 11 April 1970, a violent explosion rocked the building. Its effects ripped through the basement and ground floor of what had become a dress manufacturer. Once again London firemen filled the Great Marlborough Street address, this time to combat the fire which, as they raced through London streets, was spreading rapidly through the building. As Soho's crews turned into the road, flames were issuing from all five floors of this former Victorian fire station. Help was summoned from the surrounding stations. As the fire grew in intensity further reinforcements came from the adjacent divisions. Twenty-five pumps and specialist fire engines would gather at the scene as the old station was swiftly consumed.

The history of the building was not lost on the crews amassing in the narrow streets of Soho, although they had little time to reflect on the fact. Adrenalin-charged firemen toiled as heavy, water-filled hoses were pulled and carried, whilst weighty ladders were pitched. Firemen climbed, and then negotiated parapets of the adjoining buildings to fight the flames, some to endure the radiated heat from the inferno which scorched their hands and faces. The building could not be saved, but neither would its contagious flames be allowed to contaminate the adjoining buildings.

The hot and smoky atmosphere filled the street. Inside the building, flames weakened all they touched. Floors and internal walls started to falter then collapse, throwing clouds of bright sparks skyward. The gable wall, first unsteady, became dangerously unsafe. Fifty-foot wheeled escape ladders were hurriedly withdrawn as the firemen's muscles and sinews strained to move both themselves and their heavy equipment out of harm's way.

There was an unspoken mutual respect and confidence in the actions of others at the scene: a synergy which was displayed in the combined efforts directed to subduing and then defeating the fire. Men moved ever nearer as the deluge of water dampened the flames. However, not all escaped unscathed. A Station Officer, moving across a smoke covered flat roof, stumbled and fell through a roof light onto the floor below. He shattered his knee but was seen to fall. He was swiftly brought to safety, but in great pain, by firemen who rushed into danger to rescue their fallen colleague.

As night turned into day exhausted firemen, and their officers, wet, tired and cold, sought succour in a cup of tea supplied from the Brigade's canteen van. Soon they would return to their stations. The charred shell, with only steam rising from its ashes, gave little clue to its past life. There was no obituary for the old fire station. That day's papers gave no more than a passing comment to the dramatic events in Soho that night. An occurrence where, once again, London's firemen prevented the spread of a far more devastating fire into the surrounding West End streets. As for the old fire station itself, it ended its days in a most appropriate way, its honour guard the very people it once had served.

(Fact)

Yesteryear's Fires:
Soho's Denmark Place

UNTIL THE RECENT TRAGIC North London Grenfell Tower fire in 2017 the worst post war UK fatal fire occurred in a club and drinking bar in London's Soho in the summer of 1980. It killed 37 and injured another 30. Outside of terrorist attacks it remains the worst mass murder on mainland Britain, since the fire resulted from an arson attack. The majority of those who perished were believed to have been Spanish and Latin American customers and staff of the club and bar.

Located at 18 Denmark Place were two unlicensed, but popular, bars. Both were located on the building's top two floors. Named 'The Spanish Rooms', they were a late night bar, frequented by locals, and a salsa club popular with Latin American immigrants. Admission to either bar was restricted to members who obtained entry by shouting up from the street below in order to obtain a key. Access was through the locked front door and up a fire escape enclosed with plywood. Being unlicensed the bars were obscured from the outside world by boarded up windows. The door in Denmark Street that led to the fire escape was bolted shut. The Metropolitan Police were planning to shut the place down on Monday 18 August 1980. A farewell party was being thrown over that fatal August weekend.

On the night of Saturday 16 August, John 'Gypsy' Thompson, aged 42, had entered 'The Spanish Rooms' and started drinking there. Thompson, a petty drug dealer, was known to the police. Believing that he had been overcharged for the drink, he began an argument and then a fight with the bartender. Thompson was ejected from the building and the entry door was locked behind him. Thompson had found a two-gallon container outside the club before hailing a taxi; he then travelled to a 24-hour petrol station in Camden. There he filled the container with petrol before returning to 18 Denmark Place. In the darkened alley of Denmark Place he poured the petrol through the letterbox of No 18's front door, followed by a piece of lit paper.

The petrol erupted with explosive force, the burning petrol swiftly igniting the staircase owing to its timber construction. Flames and superheated gases rose upwards with great energy and force. The resultant fireball found those on the upper floor. The searing heat peeled skin whilst clothes caught fire. People could not easily escape their fate due to the boarded up windows, the locked fire escape and the lack of any fire safety precautions owing to the bars' unlicensed status. The club, being unlicensed, was off the London Fire Brigade's inspection radar.

The fire moved quickly up and through the building, destroying the main entrance and the exit from the bars. Some patrons tried to escape via the back door but found it locked. Others smashed windows and jumped out onto the street below. On Denmark Street there was a music shop that backed onto the clubs and some patrons were found here trapped behind the security shutters, fearful the fire would follow them. Some were luckier than others.

Soho's firefighters, in their Shaftesbury Avenue station, were still up having recently returned from another call on a typically busy Soho night shift. They were chatting in the mess-room. In fact they were listening rather than chatting: listening to their guvnor, Station Officer Turk Manning, who was reminiscing about the 'good old days'. At 3.33 a.m. the station bells sent the Green Watch crews on their way once again, However, the address given was 'Denmark Court, off Charing Cross Road' and Turk Manning knew that there was no Denmark Court on Soho's ground. He contacted the Wembley Control room immediately by radio message and told them so. Whilst the crews waited for the control room staff to check the address someone came running up to Soho fire station to report a fire in Denmark Place. Manning instructed his crews to attend Denmark Place.

When Soho's crews arrived, Turk Manning looked down

Denmark Place. He saw what he thought, at first, was a rubbish fire some way down the narrow alley. As he went to investigate a man came out of the night, a man who Turk Manning thought might have been in a fight by the way he looked and staggered. The man, clearly distressed, said,

"There are people in there– lots of them."

As Station Officer Manning reached the building he saw smoke escaping from around the shuttered windows, then flames appeared from the first floor before showing from the second floor windows too. The fire was spreading and very fast. Instructing that a hydrant be set in and jet got to work, Station Officer Manning sent a priority message making 'pumps four – persons reported'.

Soho's crews had struggled to break into the locked door as shards of hot sparks and glowing embers showered down on them. They watched as people ran off into the night despite some clearly being injured. But from inside the building, other than the sound of burning, nobody was heard calling for help or giving shouts of despair.

As entry was finally made from Denmark Place the firefighters saw the fire consuming all before it. The staircase was fully engulfed in flame. Turk Manning had sent a fireman to check the other side of the building. When the fireman arrived he had found six people trapped behind security grills of an adjacent shop. Once entry was effected, the people inside were rescued, all suffering various degrees of serious cuts or burns. It was through that shop that the first effective attack on the fire was made. Turk Manning had also instructed Soho's turntable ladder be pitched to see what rescues it might be able to perform and to assess the true extent of the fire from its high vantage point.

With Assistant Division Officer Tom Kennedy en route from Paddington, the 'A' Divisional headquarters, the Wembley mobilising controls' Officer of the Watch rung the Divisional Commander, Roy Baldwin, at his Paddington quarters to inform him of the incident. Baldwin was not required to attend an incident of this size but responded instinctively. Baldwin was later to comment, "Manning would not normally make-up unless he had a good job and his 'fours' were normally worthy of a six!"

At 3.41 a.m. eight minutes after the time of call, Station Officer

Manning made pumps six. Baldwin would take command of the fire two minutes after he arrived at the scene. Details on the ground were scant about who and how many people might still be in the building? Baldwin found the street filled with 'foreign-looking' people, all seemingly in great distress. None would give answers to the firefighters' requests for information about who else might be inside the burning building. It was a policeman who informed Baldwin that the building was used as illegal club and that as many as 150 people may have been inside it.

It was Soho's Sub Officer, Ron Morris QGM, who led his crew to the main staircase and made a successful attack on the fire, although it was not out by any means. Now Baldwin and Manning could make a preliminary survey of the devastating effects of the fire. Baldwin's message back to the Wembley control room gave the initial body count as eight. But what was evident to the experienced fire officers looking at the severity and pattern of burning was that this was no accidental fire. The smell of an accelerant, most likely petrol, was still present at the base of the staircase. The fire was deliberate and Baldwin sent a request for the Brigade photographer to attend the scene and the police to commence their investigations.

The main fire was put out in just under two hours. Crews had used three jets and breathing apparatus. Now as the damping down started the death toll rose to thirteen as five more charred bodies were found on the second floor. The total number in the clubs prior to the arson attack was never actually determined but 50 people were recorded as escaping the blaze and 30 of those were treated in hospital for a variety of injuries and some with serious burns.

It soon became difficult for the crews to give Baldwin a definitive number of fatalities. The speed of the fire was so rapid that many of the bar patrons died where they were sitting or standing. So firefighters found bodies slumped exactly where they had been when the fireball hit them, some apparently still clutching glasses. Bodies were piled one on top of another or filling tiny spaces after they had crawled in attempting to escape the horror of the flames. Others had tried to escape by clawing at the walls and windows. Some did break through into the guitar shop behind the club on Denmark Street and used electric guitars to smash through its front window. It took forensic experts two months to identify all the victims and who came from eight different countries.

Now the daunting task of body recovery began. It was a harrowing assignment for those concerned. Baldwin was later to comment to the Press that he had nothing but praise for the firefighters performing their unenviable job. "It was above and beyond the call of duty and I am proud and privileged to serve with such men."

As Soho's Green Watch left the scene at 9 a.m. they were replaced by other stations' crews including Soho's Red Watch. They continued the task of removing the charred bodies, many unrecognisable, from the scarred building. Lowering the bodies to the ground proved problematic too. Despite the firefighters' desire to handle the bodies with dignity, some body parts fell to the ground whilst another broke in two, hitting the ground with a sickening thud.

'Gypsy' Thompson was arrested nine days later while drinking at a club a short distance from the crime scene. He was tried at the Old Bailey in May 1981 and charged with just one murder, that of Archibald Campbell, 63. (It was apparently simpler that way.) His trial clashed with that of the Yorkshire Ripper, drawing most reporters to the next-door court. Thompson's life sentence earned a few column inches. When he died of lung cancer on the anniversary of the fire, in 2008, handcuffed to a hospital bed, nobody noticed.

Footnotes

The initial call was A24 (Soho) pump-escape, pump & turntable ladder and A23 (Euston) pump. Euston's pump-escape went on a minute later with multiple calls. A22 (Manchester Square) pump-escape and pump came on at make pumps six. Euston's pair entered via the music shop with Station Officer Weston in charge. Euston made their way up the rear fire escape and met Soho's crew on the first floor landing. It was then decided that Euston would take the first floor and Soho would take the second floor. By the time Euston's pump-escape was relieved by Homerton's pump, the body count was 27.

More striking than the actual fire was the speed at which it was forgotten. There were headlines the next day, once the bodies had been counted. "If it was arson, it could be the worst mass murder in British history," *The Sunday Times* reported on its front page. (This was before Harold Shipman got caught.) *The Observer* quoted a fireman: "I have seen worse fire damage, but I've never seen dead bodies packed together like that before." Then the coverage fizzled out.

Look today and online searches reveal only a few mentions. Two or three little-known books devote a passage or two to the mass murders, although Martin Lloyd-Elliott's *City Ablaze* (1992) gives a comprehensive account. Many of the victims' families still know very little about the fire. Seven years later, when 31 people died in the King's Cross Underground fire (again on Soho's ground and at which Station Officer Colin Townsley GM, from Soho, was one of the victims) inquiries, services, documentaries and memorials followed. Princess Diana even unveiled a plaque. Yet at Denmark Place there was never any memorial service. There is no plaque! The only commemorative plaque in the area is devoted to the inventor of the diving helmet. Moreover, there was never a public inquiry. The clubs were illegal; there seemed to be few lessons to learn, no institution to blame. This also means there is no official account. The Metropolitan Police's archive contains only basic facts, which it only releases in response to a Freedom of Information request. Finally: No 18 Denmark Place was gutted for demolition in 2016. It, like the dreadful fire, to be forgotten.

(Fact)

The IRA's Bombing Campaign, 1971–1993

THE VIOLENCE, DEATH AND suffering of the sectarian 'Troubles' were not just confined to Northern Ireland. In the 1970s the 'Provisional' Irish Republican Army (IRA) initiated a campaign of terrorist violence in England, bombing a number of military and civilian targets. London became a particular target of choice. From the Irish terrorist perspective the mainland campaign had several objectives. Among them was shifting some of the paramilitary violence of the Troubles offshore. It also reduced the dangers to Irish civilians and the IRA's own supporters, plus it exported some of the suffering felt in Northern Ireland to English cities, most notably London.

Like most politically-based terrorism, the UK mainland campaign was also designed to make the British people feel unsafe, create a climate of fear and generate public and media pressure on the British government. Therefore, for this reason, the 'Provisional' IRA, or Provos, often targeted high profile events or locations, including the Houses of Parliament, Ten Downing Street, Oxford Street, Harrods department store and military ceremonies in Hyde Park and Regent's Park (where both troopers and horses from the Blues and Royals Regiment were killed and maimed).

The Irish terrorists also assassinated prominent British figures, including Lord Louis Mountbatten and the Conservative politicians Airey Neave and Ian Gow. In November 1975 IRA gunmen shot dead Ross McWhirter, a co-founder of the *Guinness Book of World Records,* outside his Middlesex home.

From 1969 until 1997 the 'Provisional' Irish Republican Army conducted its paramilitary campaign primarily in Northern Ireland and England. Its aim was to end British rule in Northern Ireland and to create a united Ireland. The Provo's mainland campaign claimed the lives of 175 people, injuring more than 10,000 men, women and children, and caused property damage exceeding one billion pounds.

The 'Provisional' IRA had emerged from a split in the Irish Republican Army in 1969, partly as a result of that organisation's perceived failure to defend Catholic neighbourhoods from attack in the 1969 Northern Ireland riots. They gained credibility from their efforts to physically defend such areas in 1970 and 1971. From 1971–72 the terrorists went on the offensive and conducted a relatively high intensity campaign against the British and Northern Ireland security forces and the infrastructure of the state.

The Provisionals did declare a brief ceasefire in 1972. A more protracted one followed in 1975 when there was an internal IRA debate over the feasibility of future operations. However, the armed group reorganised itself in the late 1970s into a smaller, cell-based structure, which was designed to be harder to penetrate. They now tried to carry out a smaller scale, but more sustained, campaign with the eventual aim of weakening the British government's resolve to remain in Ireland. In the 1990s they also began a campaign of bombing economic targets in London and other English cities.

On August 31, 1994, the full IRA Council called a unilateral ceasefire with the aim of having their associated political party, Sinn Féin, admitted into the Northern Ireland peace process. This process included the Provisional's too. The organisation ended its ceasefire in February 1996 but declared another in July 1997. The IRA Council accepted the terms of the Good Friday Agreement in 1998 as a negotiated end to the Northern Ireland conflict. In 2005 the organisation declared a formal end to its campaign and had its weaponry decommissioned under international supervision.

The prolonged, and concerted efforts, by the Provisionals to bomb their way towards a political settlement revolving around the Irish 'Troubles' had deadly effect. Their actions brought the London emergency services into the capital's front line because of their continuing and indiscriminate bombing. It brought about heightened tension within the capital city and beyond. Accordingly, London's then security precautions were increased and these would become a part of everyday life for years. In fact they have remained in place; just the nature of the terrorist has changed. (The terrorist attacks in the 2000s brought about a series of devastating suicide bomb attacks in London carried out by Islamic radicals.) Heightened security is now an everyday reality. Recent, random and fatal attacks in London and elsewhere indicate that it will continue into the foreseeable future.

Back then, as in the present day, the pressure fell on the security services, in particular the Metropolitan Police and its Special Branch, to combat and prevent the terrorists' aims. As today, when attacks took place it was the police who led the investigations in their determination to bring the perpetrators to justice. During the years of the IRA's bombing campaign the Brigade, the ambulance service and London's medical services could do little to prevent the bombing. However, when an attack took place they were right in the thick of it. Whilst fearful of the possibility of secondary devices they nevertheless frequently put themselves in harm's way, to save life and to deal with the consequences of such cowardly attacks.

There are so many tales to tell of those worrying times. This just happens to be my own story and the bombing of the **Palace of Westminster**.

On 17 June 1974, 17 days after my arrival at Southwark Fire Station as the new Sub Officer on the White Watch, the IRA made an audacious terrorist attack on the very seat of British government. Just before 9 a.m. a powerful 20-pound explosive device shattered the normal tranquillity of Westminster Hall, in the Palace of Westminster. It brought additional chaos to the morning rush hour in Central London. The *Daily Telegraph* described the attack as "one of the deadliest bombings of the IRA's mainland campaign."

Despite the reverberating sound of the explosion throughout Parliament and the vicinity of Parliament Square, there was no indication of the unfolding drama for us until Southwark's station bells summoned us to the scene some ten minutes later. It was Westminster, Soho and Lambeth's appliances, eight fire engines in total, which made up the initial attendance at this historic and national heritage site. Alongside Buckingham Palace, it was one of the Brigade's most high-profile special risks. Both Westminster and Lambeth fire station crews heard the thunderous explosion. They knew it sounded close and were impatiently waiting to find out just where they would be ordered to. Adrenaline started pumping through the veins of these crews as they thought of the carnage that the terrorists' wanton actions had unleashed on the capital this time.

The ringing of station call bells, and the teleprinter ordering, brought them the answer. Westminster Hall had been the terrorists' target and these crews were to deal with the consequences. The dominant sound now pervading Westminster's streets was the cacophony of emergency vehicle two-tone horns: a sound that filled the air with the characteristic warning as the fire engines and other emergency vehicles raced to the scene. Fire engines, ambulances and police cars all converging on a common destination – one of the world's most famous and iconic landmarks. Smoke was already rising into the morning sky as Westminster's appliances headed down Victoria Street, Lambeth's crossed over Lambeth Brigade and Soho's crews sped down Whitehall.

The scale of the explosion, and the first signs of the resultant fire, left the officer in charge of Westminster Fire Station in no doubt that without immediate reinforcements he would not be able to contain the blaze. Even before his arrival he made, "Pumps twelve, breathing apparatus required". Pulling into the Palace of Westminster courtyard he was confronted by a serious fire that had taken hold in the northeast wing of Westminster Hall. Smoke was billowing from the Gothic windows and the massive roof timbers were already alight. The Great Hall was filled with the dust of centuries along with thick smoke drifting in from the side annexe to the hall where the device had been planted. Among the organised chaos of the early stages of evacuation, the task of assessing the situation and liaising with other emergency services, the officer in charge's plan of attack started to unfold.

As Westminster and Lambeth's crews started to pitch wheeled escape ladders to the upper floors, Soho crews donned breathing apparatus sets, water supplies were secured and jets of water were got ready to bring into play. Liaison with the police, responsible for the security of the Palace of Westminster, tried to establish whether people were still inside the Great Hall and, if so, who and where?

Southwark's pump-escape and pump formed part of that 'make-up' attendance. We joined the second wave of attack. Our fire engines raced through the Elephant and Castle and on towards Westminster. We were eager to get into the fray. Traffic had been brought to a standstill around both County Hall and Waterloo station as the police closed Westminster Bridge to all traffic. Our two appliances weaved their way through the thickening traffic, congestion that was getting worse by the minute. But driving on clear stretches of the opposite side of the road, the drivers closed in on the incident, the sound of our ringing fire engine bells marking our progress.

Just 14 minutes after the initial call we passed through the outer police cordon, located on the southern side of Westminster Brigade. The bridge was closed to all but emergency vehicles. It was completely empty save our two engines. We had a clear uninter-rupted view of Big Ben and the Palace of Westminster, but not of the dramatic scenes being played out behind them. We could only see the huge column of smoke rising skyward from behind the House of Commons. Reaching Parliament Square we saw the concerted attack already underway by those first to arrive. Escape and exten-sion ladders had been pitched to upper windows. Firemen were pulling heavy hose lines into position and crews in breathing appa-ratus had entered the smoke-logged Great Hall's northern corner.

A turntable ladder had been positioned ready to direct its monitor onto the roof of the Great Hall. Thick brown smoke was giving way to flames, which were breaking through the ancient slated roof and windows shattered by the explosion. Westminster's Station Officer was still in charge. He stood in front of the Great Hall's historic wooden main entrance doors directing operations and dealing with the multitude of tasks that befalls a fire officer in this type of situa-tion. He had the fire being fought from the inside, searches under-way together with jets directed into the burning building by firemen from vantage points on the external ladders.

I reported and was told to make an entry, in breathing appa-ratus, to find and attack the fire internally using the corner turret staircase with our pump-escape crew backing us up. We were to search the rooms off the stone spiral staircase, a staircase that was believed to led to the roof void where fire was seen taking a firm hold. Wearing our one-hour Proto oxygen sets, three of us started to climb as our PE crew fed in the hose line as far as they could without the protection of breathing apparatus. The first few feet were easy. It was relatively smoke-free and progress was swift, especially as the PE crew was lightening the hose-line. At first floor level we met the heat barrier and proceeded more cautiously, our exposed ears starting to tingle under the effects of the heat and hot gases. The smoke got thicker. Off the staircase we found small storerooms and offices. Each was checked as we passed, a simple chalk mark left on the door to indicate it had been searched. The height between floors was unusual, the ceilings reaching up some 15 feet from the floor. By the second floor, some 45 feet up spiral staircase, conditions became uncomfortable. The heat was reflected off the walls and, even more worryingly, off the stone stairs.

Stone staircases involved in fire, and where cooling water is suddenly applied, can result in severe spalling of the stonework. In certain circumstances this led to serious structural weakening and in extreme cases, collapse. This was only something we had read about in the Manuals of Firemanship and a little knowledge is a dangerous thing! It was my first experience at encountering such conditions. We were, to say the least, a tad concerned! The fact that some stonework was already spalling off the walls did little to boost our confidence, but we maintained our progress upwards anyway.

On the third floor level we started ventilating. Both the heat and the smoke levels eased, but the exertion of pulling, and manoeuvring, the water-filled hose-line up the winding staircase had taken its toll. The oxygen levels in our BA sets were getting worrying low. Even if we made it to the top, with the hose line, we would not have sufficient oxygen supply to do anything with it. So, leaving the hose on the staircase, we quickly made our way to the top to see if access into the roof void was possible. It was not and neither had fire broken through. The heat and smoke we experienced was being forced through ventilation ducts connected to the Great Hall's roof. Now with one of the crew's oxygen supply very low we retraced our steps back down the staircase, leaving the hose line in situ, and accompanied by the sound of its low cylinder pressure-warning whistle actuating continuously. With only minutes to spare we exited the Hall. After collecting our tallies from the BA control point we reported our findings, something which added little to the overall scheme of things.

However, the fire was now contained. Crews were working hard to minimise further damage from the fire which involved the ancient roof. Free of our BA sets we were the first crew to climb up onto the roof of the Great Hall. The early frantic activity had now given way to a much steadier pace. Crews were isolating, and investigating, hot spots before cutting away and tackling the pockets of fire.

With an escape ladder pitched to the northern upper wall my pump's crew climbed over the high parapet before we used hook ladders (as improvised roof ladders) that enabled us to work on the pitched slated roof. The slates were enormous. Each was about two feet wide, three feet long weighing about 75 pounds each. With smoke percolating between the slates we saw the orange glow of smouldering timbers near the ridge of the roof. Ordered to use care in removing the slates, which were over 100 years old, we manhandled them, one by one, safely to the ground.

Openings were made into the roof exposing the smouldering timbers. Steady progress was made in extinguishing the fires in the accumulated debris between the battens and timber roof trusses. After four hours at the scene, and with our task unfinished, we were relieved. Other crews took over and we made our way back to Southwark. On Southwark's teleprinter was the "stop" message from Westminster Hall; 12 jets and two turntable ladder monitors had been required to extinguish the blaze and a total of 40 BA sets were used.

On 13 February 1975 a telephone call from Brigade Headquarters asked if I had led my crews at the Westminster Hall fire. I said, "Yes," and was told to get my pump over to Brigade Headquarters at lunchtime. When I inquired why I was told:

"You and your crew are to be presented to the Queen."

"OK," I said, thinking it was a typical fire brigade wind-up.

I rang the Divisional HQ to ask what they knew about the afternoon's excursion to Lambeth. They said it was the real McCoy, it was a Royal duty.

That February afternoon the Queen was touring the headquarters of the Metropolitan Police, the London Ambulance Service and the Brigade to pay a personal tribute to the emergency services involved in dealing with the aftermath of the recent spate of IRA bombings. We were one of eight London Fire Brigade crews, together with some senior officers, who were to represent all those who had attended terrorist incidents. Whilst we felt honoured to be selected we were conscious that we had not, so far, had to deal with the horror and human misery that some of the Brigade's crews had confronted. They witnessed the dreadfulness of mass, or individual, slaughter and the possibility of being drawn into a terrorist trap, thus falling victim to a secondary explosive device. I had not seen such awful injuries, harm which one human being inflicts on another. I was horrified that innocent individuals were targeted for someone's political gain. I knew I was lucky. I wanted it to stay that way.

Like four bright new pins we arrived at Lambeth, the Brigade Headquarters. We were given a briefing in the Officers' Club (a hallowed haven at Brigade Headquarters where mere mortals like ourselves were normally denied access). The Deputy Chief Officer gave the briefing so we knew this was all high-profile stuff. He told us that we would stand informally in our individual crews. The Chief Officer would introduce the Queen and she would spend a short time with each crew before moving onto the next. He said, actually he insisted:

"You will address the Queen as 'Your Majesty' when she first speaks to you. After that you will call her 'Mam'. That's 'Mam' as in spam. You do not speak to her unless she speaks to you. Clear?"

The eight crews, from London's central divisions, who had first had personal dealings with the bombings waited for the Royal guest. Paddington, Knightsbridge, Chelsea and Westminster crews from the A Division; Clerkenwell and Barbican from the C Division; whilst Lambeth and we represented the B Division. Exactly at the allotted time the Queen's car arrived. She was welcomed by the Chief Officer, Joe Milner. As Lambeth fire station's crews, dressed in their fire gear, formed a Royal honour guard the Chief escorted the Queen towards the reception area and to those waiting.

Her Majesty looked vibrant, and chirpy, as she entered the Officers' Club smiling and cheerful. It was not a sombre occasion at all. Whilst we were naturally somewhat nervous, the Queen moved from group to group, putting us at ease with well-informed questions. Dressed in a shapely coat, with mink fur collar and fur-lined cuffs, a smart hat and carrying her trademark handbag, she moved effortlessly between the various crews with the Chief acting as host. He introduced each station represented and then remained in the background whilst those present savoured their moment of having this special audience with the Queen.

No doubt her question format was probably the same for all three visits she made that day, meeting London's emergency service crews. Nevertheless she possessed a remarkable gift and demonstrated a presence of being genuinely interested in what stories each group had to tell and enjoying the humour that makes dealing with such incidents possible. She left each crew with a warm and friendly smile before moving on to repeat the process all over again. With no formal speeches forty-five minutes later the Chief escorted Her Majesty back to the Royal car and she was gone.

Timeline of the London terrorist bombings

31 October 1971: A bomb, claimed to be placed by the Provisional IRA, exploded in the roof of the men's toilets at the Top of the Tower restaurant. The restaurant was closed to the public for security reasons in 1980, the year in which Butlin's (the operator of the restaurant) lease expired. Public access to the building ceased in 1981. The restaurant never reopened.

8 March 1973: The Provisional IRA conducted its first operation in England, planting four car bombs in London. Two of the car bombs were defused: a fertilizer bomb in a car outside the Post Office in Broadway and another at the BBC's armed forces radio studio in Dean Stanley Street. However, the other two exploded, one near the Old Bailey and the other at the Ministry of Agriculture off Whitehall. Ten members of the IRA unit, including Gerry Kelly and Marian Price, were arrested at Heathrow Airport trying to leave the country. As a result of the explosions one person was killed and almost 200 people were injured. Gerard Kelly, who later became a member of Sinn Féin's *Ard Chomhairle* (National Executive) and a

Member of the Northern Ireland Assembly, was then aged 19. He and eight others, including Hugh Feeney and sisters Marian and Dolours Price, were found guilty of various charges relating to the bombings on November 14, 1973. Kelly was convicted of causing explosions and conspiracy to cause explosions, and received two life sentences plus 20 years.

23 August 1973: A bomb was found in an abandoned bag in Baker Street station ticket hall. The bomb was defused. A week later another bomb was found by a member of staff at the same station and was also defused.

24 December 1973: The Provisional IRA left two packages which exploded almost simultaneously in the late evening on Christmas Eve. One was in the doorway of the North Star public house, at the junction of College Crescent and Finchley Road, Swiss Cottage; this exploded, injuring six people. The other exploded on the upstairs veranda of the nearby Swiss Cottage Tavern where an unspecified number of people were injured.

26 December 1973: A bomb was detonated in a telephone kiosk in the booking hall at Sloane Square station. Nobody was injured.

5 January 1974: Two bombs exploded within three minutes of each other: the first at Madame Tussauds, the second during the Boat Show at Earls Court Exhibition Centre. Police confirmed a telephone warning had been given shortly before both explosions, allowing evacuations at both sites. There were no fatalities or injuries reported. It was later confirmed the devices had been planted by the IRA.

17 June 1974: A bomb exploded at the Houses of Parliament in London, causing extensive damage and injuring 11 people.

17 July 1974: An explosion in the Tower of London left one person dead and 41 injured. This was the second bomb in London on that day: at 4.30 a.m. there was an explosion at government buildings in Balham, South London. Nobody was injured in the morning blast but there was substantial damage to surrounding buildings.

1 October 1974: Bombs containing coach bolts were thrown at both

the Victory Club in Seymour Street, near Marble Arch, and the Army and Navy Club in St James's Square, SW1, where 70 members of the Royal West Africa Frontier Force are having their annual reunion.

22 October 1974: A five-pound bomb was thrown at Brooks Club, 400 metres from the Army and Navy Club. Len Murray, General Secretary of the TUC, was inside the restaurant. Former Prime Minister Edward Heath, who was dining nearby, attended to see the damage. Three wine waiters were hurt.

7 November 1974: King's Arms, Woolwich, a bomb was thrown through the pub window. A barman and a soldier died in the explosion; another soldier had a leg blown off. Twenty-eight other people were injured.

25 November 1974: Small bombs, using pocket watches as timers, were planted in three pillar boxes: one in the Caledonian Road in north London, one at Piccadilly Circus and one at Victoria station.

30 November 1974: Two bombs are thrown into the Talbot Arms in Little Chester Street, Belgravia,

17 December 1974: After an unidentified woman phoned a warning into the *Mirror* newspaper, a bomb subsequently exploded in New Compton Street in Soho. Then a second detonated at the Museum telephone exchange in Chenies Street WC1, killing 35-year-old telephonist George Arthur. A third terrorist bomb went off at the Draycott Avenue telephone exchange in Chelsea.

19 December 1974: A car with 160 sticks of gelignite inside it was left outside Selfridge's in Oxford Street. Following a warning to the *Sun* newspaper the area was evacuated as Christmas shoppers huddled in the basement rooms of nearby pubs. There was a massive explosion and a great deal of damage but no deaths or injuries. The explosion was estimated to have caused £1.5 million worth of damage.

1974: A bomb was defused in Harrods department store in Knightsbridge, London.

February 1975: The Queen visited the London Fire Brigade

Headquarters and was met by the Chief Officer Joe Milner who introduced Her Majesty to representative crews that had attended various recent IRA London bombings.

28 August 1975: Seven people were injured when a bomb exploded in Oxford Street, London and outside the south-east corner of Selfridge's store. A telephone warning was issued to the *Sun* newspaper five minutes before the explosion.

5 September 1975: Two people were killed and 63 injured when an IRA bomb exploded in the lobby of the Hilton Hotel in the West End.

22 October 1975: On the same day as the 'Guildford Four' were wrongly convicted of a pub-bombing, a man telephoned the Holland Park home of the Conservative MP Hugh Fraser and his wife, author Antonia Fraser. He asked what time the MP left in the morning. A bomb had been fitted to one of the Frasers' cars outside their house at Campden Hill Square, London W8. A noted cancer researcher, Professor Gordon Hamilton-Fairley, was walking past the car when the bomb exploded prematurely, killing Prof Hamilton-Fairley immediately.

3 November 1975: Several people were injured by a car bomb in Connaught Square, London W2.

6–12 December 1975: Four IRA members held two people hostage in the Balcombe Street Siege.

13 February 1976: A bomb weighing 30 pounds (14 kg) was found in a small case at Oxford Circus underground station and defused.

15 March 1976: An IRA bomb exploded on a Metropolitan Line train at West Ham station, on the Hammersmith & City section of the line. The bomber, Vincent Donnelly, took the wrong train and attempted to return to his destination. However, the bomb detonated prior to reaching the City of London. Donnelly shot Peter Chalk, a Post Office engineer, and shot and killed the train's driver Julius Stephen, who had attempted to catch the perpetrator. Donnelly then shot himself, but survived. He was apprehended by police.

16 March 1976: An empty train was severely damaged by a bomb at Wood Green station. The train was due to pick up fans from an Arsenal football match, but the bomb detonated prior to arriving at the station. It injured a passenger standing on the platform. Three men were sentenced to 20 years imprisonment for this attack.

27 March 1976: A bomb exploded in a litter bin at the top of an escalator in a crowded Earl's Court exhibition hall. 20,000 people were attending the *Daily Mail* Ideal Home Exhibition at the time. Seventy were injured, with four people losing limbs.

30 March 1979: Shadow Northern Ireland Secretary Airey Neave was murdered as he left the House of Commons car park by a car bomb planted by the Irish National Liberation Army, another IRA splinter group.

January 1981: A bomb was left at the RAF barracks in Uxbridge. The device was discovered and the 35 RAF musicians and 15 airmen living there were evacuated before it exploded.

10 October 1981: A bomb blast on Ebury Bridge Road, next to Chelsea Barracks, killed two people and injured 39.

26 October 1981: A bomb planted in a Wimpy Bar on Oxford Street kills Kenneth Howorth, a Metropolitan Police explosives officer who is attempting to defuse the device.

20 July 1982: Hyde Park. The first attack occurred at 10:40 a.m. A nail bomb exploded in the boot of a blue Morris Marina parked on South Carriage Drive in the park. The bomb, comprised of 25 lbs of gelignite and 30 lbs of nails, exploded as soldiers of the Household Cavalry, Queen Elizabeth II's official bodyguard regiment, were passing. They were taking part in their daily Changing of the Guard procession from their barracks in Knightsbridge to Horse Guards Parade. Three soldiers of the Blues & Royals were killed outright, and another, their standard bearer, died from his wounds three days later. The other soldiers in the procession were badly wounded, and a number of civilians were injured. Seven of the regiment's horses were also killed or had to be euthanised because of their injuries. Explosives experts later discover that the Hyde Park bomb was triggered remotely by an IRA member inside the park. The soldiers that died were Lt Anthony Daly, and Troopers Simon Tipper, Vernon Young, and Raymond Bright.

The second attack happened at about 12:55 p.m. A bomb exploded underneath a bandstand in Regent's Park. Thirteen Military bandsmen of the Royal Green Jackets were on the band-stand performing music from the musical *Oliver* to a crowd of 120 people. It was the first in a series of advertised lunchtime concerts. Six of the bandsmen were killed outright and the rest were wounded; a seventh died of his wounds on 1 August. At least eight civilians were also injured. The bomb had been hidden under the stand some time before and triggered by a timer. Unlike the Hyde Park bomb, it contained no nails and seemed to be designed to cause minimal harm to bystanders. The seven who died were Bandsmen Graham Barker, Robert Livingstone, John McKnight, John Heritage, George Mesure, Keith Powell and Laurence Smith.

10 December 1983: A bomb exploded at the Royal Artillery Barracks in Woolwich. The explosion injured five people and caused minor damage to the building. The bomb exploded in a guard room, leaving a crater 15 feet deep. A Christmas party was underway in the Sergeants' Mess, around 300 yards away, when the bomb exploded. The Scottish National Liberation Army claimed responsibility for the bombing, stating that "More will follow". However, Scotland Yard believed that the IRA were behind the attack. The IRA admitted responsibility for the attack.

17 December 1983: Harrods was bombed. Six people were killed (including three police officers) and 90 wounded during Christmas shopping at the West London department store.

16 May 1990: Wembley. IRA detonated a bomb underneath a minibus, killing Sergeant Charles Chapman (The Queen's Regiment) and injuring another soldier. No one has ever been convicted of Sergeant Chapman's murder.

20 July 1990: A large bomb was detonated at the London Stock Exchange, causing massive structural damage.

7 February 1991: A mortar attack took place on 10 Downing Street whilst the Prime Minister, John Major, was in residence.

18 February 1991: A bomb exploded in Paddington Station, damaging the building's roof but caused no casualties. Three hours later a second bomb exploded at Victoria Station. One man was killed and 38 people were injured.

29 August 1991: Three incendiary devices were found under a train at Hammersmith tube station.

23 December 1991: Two IRA bombs exploded, one on a train at Harrow-on-the-Hill station, causing no injuries, and a smaller one on a train at Neasden depot.

10 January 1992: A small device exploded in Whitehall Place, SW1. No reported casualties.

28 February 1992: A bomb exploded at London Bridge main line station, injuring 29 people.

10 April 1992: The Baltic Exchange bombing. A large bomb exploded outside 30 St Mary Axe in the City of London. The bomb was contained in a large white truck and consisted of a fertiliser device wrapped with a detonation cord made from Semtex. It killed three people: Paul Butt, aged 29, Baltic Exchange employee Thomas Casey, aged 49, and 15-year old Danielle Carter. Several people were critically or severely injured. The bomb also caused damage to surrounding buildings (many of which were further damaged by a second bomb the following year). The bomb caused £800 million worth of damage – £200 million more than the total damage costs resulting from all 10,000 previous explosions that had occurred relating to the Troubles in Northern Ireland. A new skyscraper was built on the site of the previous historic building.

11 April 1992: A large bomb exploded underneath the A406 flyover at Staples Corner, causing serious damage to roads and nearby buildings including a B&Q DIY store. It caused the closure of the junction. The blast was so powerful it could be felt many miles away.

12 October 1992: A device exploded in the gentlemen's toilet of the Sussex Arms public house in Covent Garden, killing one person and injuring four others.

16 November 1992: A bomb was planted at Canary Wharf in the

Docklands. The device was spotted by security guards and was deactivated safely.

17 December 1992: A bomb, hidden in a litter bin in a third-floor men's lavatory, of John Lewis department store, Oxford Street, was detonated just after 11 a.m. Fifteen minutes later a second bomb exploded at the rear of the store whilst shoppers and staff were being evacuated. Four people were injured.

23 January 1993: A bomb exploded in a litter bin, outside Harrods, injuring four people.

27 February 1993: A bomb left in litter bin exploded outside a McDonald's restaurant in Camden Town. It injures several people.

24 April 1993: Bishopsgate bombing. A huge truck bomb exploded at Bishopsgate. It killed journalist Ed Henty, injured over 40 people, and caused approximately £1 billion worth of damage, including the near destruction of St Ethelburga's Bishopsgate church, and serious damage to Liverpool Street station. Police had received a coded warning, but were still evacuating the area at the time of the explosion. The insurance payments required were so large that Lloyd's of London almost went bankrupt under the strain, and there was a crisis in the London insurance market. The area had already suffered damage from the Baltic Exchange bombing the year before.

October 1993: Over an eight-day period, a series of IRA bombs are left in various London locations. On 1 October, four bombs were left in the Finchley Road. Three exploded, causing damage to buildings and several injuries caused by falling and flying glass. On 4 October, pairs of bombs were left in Highgate (one failed to explode), in Hornsey, and Archway, causing significant damage but no injuries. On 8 October, bombs exploded at Staples Corner and West Hampstead, again causing damage but no injuries.

9, 11 and 13 March 1994: Heathrow Airport. A series of mortar attacks were launched at the international airport by the IRA who fired 12 mortar rounds. The resulting security operation partially paralysed the capital's main air routes.

9 February 1996: Docklands bombing. The IRA bombed the South

Quay area of London. The truck bomb ripped through London's Canary Wharf office development, killing two people and wounding 39 others, and causing around £150 million in damage.

15 February 1996: A five-pound (2.3 kg) bomb placed in a telephone box was disarmed by Police on the Charing Cross Road.

18 February 1996: A bomb detonated prematurely on a bus travelling along Aldwych in central London, killing Edward O'Brien, the IRA terrorist transporting the device, and injuring eight others.

23 April 1997: Britain's transport industry claimed losses of at least £30 million after a series of IRA bomb alerts in southern England brought traffic to a standstill. In the London area, the Heathrow airport and the M25 motorway were closed.

(Fact)

Spectacles, Testicles,
Wristwatch and Wallet

HISTORY IS DEFINED BY periods in time. In English history, for example, there are the Tudor, the Elizabethan and Victorian ages. During the 150 years of the London Fire Brigade's history it was the same. Looking back, during the 1950s, '60s and '70s, London's firemen were defined as 'Proto' men. A common denominator in their fireman's armoury was the Proto breathing apparatus set. It was developed from the earliest versions to the Mark IV set, but for most of us who carried a BA head-harness in our cork helmet or inside our Melton fire tunic pocket, it was the Mark V Siebe Gorman oxygen BA set. Improvements to the set came with the heaviest of price tags: the lives of other firemen. Ours was the Proto age.

Life in a Proto BA set was a work in progress. Lessons learnt saw better procedures and modifications to the set. Yet for those that wore them little in the way of our fire kit had changed at all. From the late 1930s and for the next forty years, other than the slight changes to fire helmet design – which remained black and made of cork – we looked the same. In fact we were practically identical. The same can't be said for the subsequent forty years which saw a revolution in uniform design and resulted in the better equipped London firefighters of today.

I loved wearing a Proto BA set. Less than a year after leaving training school, starting on Lambeth's Red Watch and having passed my probation, I was off on my BA course. My fireman's apprenticeship had just moved up a notch. It was a big notch too.

We all took a similar journey. On the course we learnt the art of the BA shuffle: the testing of a floor with your front foot whilst keeping your body weight on the back foot as we moved in thick smoke in BA. The 'spectacles, testicles, wristwatch and wallet' describes the movement of your arm when trying to avoid obstacles which might impede your progress as you took the next shuffling foot forward at a fire. We memorised the flow of oxygen through the BA set. We used the 'Rat-run', which had bugger all to do with rats but was a smoke- and heat-filled underground obstacle course used in BA training. We discovered that your ears act as an excellent thermometers. They let you know just how bloody hot it was crawling down into a basement fire in a Proto set. A set that gave you both life-sustaining oxygen as well as a large dose of confidence.

Once I was a qualified BA wearer the next stage of my internship started. Old hands would keep a weather eye on us new BA boys. However, some of their old (bad) habits were also passed down as we also took out the mouthpiece to confer, contrary to proper procedures! Occasionally the set was worn with little consideration for BA discipline. Thrown over a fireman's shoulders, the mouthpiece was put in unconnected to a head-harness as a snatch rescue was performed and where the sucking in of acrid smoke had dire consequences for the rescued and the rescuer alike. Other times the procedures were followed to the letter. Times when as you entered a smoke-filled warehouse or basement, even with the protection of the Proto set, you were forced down to the floor by the intensity of the searing heat.

My own BA apprenticeship lasted four years before wearing the coveted London 'yellow' breathing bag and riding Lambeth's emergency tender (ET). I soaked up the experience like a sponge. The experience and know-how I acquired from the senior ET hands lasted throughout the rest of my career. Once again, as the junior buck, I was being taught new aspects of my chosen craft. It was a daunting prospect riding alongside such revered and well-regarded firemen, hopeful that some of their skills and expertise would rub off along the way.

When it came, Chief Officer Joe Milner's introduction of ever more BA protection on fire engines was welcome. Whilst the arrival of the compressed air sets increased firemen's protection from toxic and noxious gases and smoke I greatly bemoaned the demise, and loss, of the 'old' Proto set. The duration of the Mark V set, the safety net it afforded the wearer with its longer 'entrapped procedure' melded perfectively with my philosophy of 'one hand for the job and one for me'. But such was progress in the 1970s. That said, I remain proud and honoured to be included the era of the Proto firemen. That despite the odd difficult BA job, which made my sphincter do an excellent impression of half-crowns and threepenny bits, the set never let me down. So thank you Seibe-Gorman, good job.

I doubt there is one former 'fireman' or firefighter who does not recall, as if it were yesterday, their first fatal fire. Many remember their first slip and pitch of the escape ladder in anger. I know I do. The same goes for your first real BA fire. Did I make any real difference to the efforts of others on the day? I doubt it. But did this fire make much of a difference to me? Well, all the difference in the world. Until then I had called myself a fireman; after this fire I actually believed I might become one.

I had arrived at Lambeth's Red Watch in January of 1967. I was aged 18. I passed my Proto BA course thirteen months later. I was qualified to ride BA in February 1968.

Unattached, and kicking my heels between night shifts, I had found myself a regular part-time job for the Victoria Wine Company delivering wine to the rich and famous around Victoria, Pimlico and Chelsea between night duties and on my first leave day. On this particular April day, and parked along Millbank for a lunchtime sandwich, I watched three of Lambeth's fire engines, the pump-escape, pump and turntable ladder, turn right out of the station and head east alongside the river on a shout. The appliances passed Lambeth Bridge and disappeared down Lambeth Palace Road in the direction of Waterloo station. Looking eastwards, along the Thames, I saw the tell-tale signs of a 'job'. A column of thick smoke was rising skyward in the distance. As I finished my sandwich the column grew thicker and reached ever higher.

Frustrated at not knowing what was happening, or where, I returned to my wine deliveries. By the mid-afternoon the distinctive taint of smoke, which only comes from a serious fire, filled the air. I thought Lambeth must have a 'job' on its hands. Rushing to finish my deliveries I left the shop and walked quickly from Victoria to the fire station, eager to learn more. I arrived around 4.30 p.m. and saw a stand-by pump in the station. So whatever had happened was still going on.

Quickly changing into my overalls I went down to the watchroom to read the teleprinter messages from the fire-ground. Multiple calls had been received at 1.02 p.m. to the Eldorado ice cream factory in Stamford Street, SE1. It was later established that most of the factory employees were in the first floor canteen when the fire was discovered. An employee, walking from the canteen across the main storage area towards the staircase, saw fire among a stack of corrugated cardboard cartons. Once the employee had raised the alarm, the canteen was quickly evacuated and a few of the staff attempted to tackle the fire with fire extinguishers. However, the speed and intensity at which the fire was developing trapped two of the men in the canteen. The dense smoke filled the first floor and prevented them from reaching the staircase and their escape route to safety. They ran to the windows, their only possible way out!

The fire in Stamford Street was on Southwark's (B23) ground. Their pump-escape and pump, plus Lambeth's machines and supported by Cannon Street, made up the augmented attendance. Smoke was pouring from the windows along the whole of the first floor and a man was shouting for help as Southwark arrived. It was Southwark's guvnor who sent a priority message, "Make pumps four persons reported."

Southwark's crews attempted to rescue the man via a 30-foot extension ladder and they discovered the window opening too small for the man to climb through. As the smoke in the building appeared to be impenetrable, the crew set to work with hand tools to cut their way, via the metalled window frames, to release the man. Lambeth's turntable ladder crew saw another man shouting for urgent help at a first floor window. In quickly, and decisively, siting the ladder and rescuing the man, the TL driver and the officer in charge were later formally congratulated for their swift actions. It was not the first time a 100-foot turntable ladder had been used to rescue a person from the first floor, but it was unusual.

Southwark's 'guvnor' was Station Officer Arthur Money. He assessed the building as being "One, two and seven floors about 150 fifty feet by 120 feet." The whole of the first floor was smoke-logged and with rescues being carried out on the front and side of the building he made "pumps eight – BA required." This highly experienced, and long-standing, Station Officer gave instructions for BA crews to enter the first and second floors as it seemed likely that other employees might well be trapped in the building. A few minutes later the first senior officer arrived from the Divisional headquarters at Clapham. He ordered three more pumps with BA. (It is what they did back then.) With the arrival of more pumps, ladders were pitched to the windows on the Stamford Street frontage and additional BA crews entered the building, taking with them charged, heavy hose lines. They experienced great difficulty in penetrating the fire area. The build-up of heat was considerable due to the combustible nature of the storage, the size of the area involved, its low ceiling height and general lack of direct ventilation. Even those firemen working on the external iron fire-escape were subjected to extremely punishing conditions. The smoke was hot, dense, black and extremely difficult to work in. It was obvious that this was going to be a prolonged, and difficult, BA job: one which necessitated relays of Proto BA crews gradually forcing their jets, a foot at a time, into the building until the seat of the fire was located.

As the duty Assistant Chief Officer took charge, more BA pumps were requested. By 2.30 p.m. the "BA incident box" was requested, together with one hundred extra oxygen cylinders. The BA Instructors from Southwark Training School rushed to the scene to assist with the servicing of the many Proto sets.

Over the next few hours relays of BA men slowly, and painfully, worked their way further into the building. Even hugging the floor, men's ears blistered under the severe effects of the heat they had to endure. Many, as they exited, were told to recharge their sets and return to the fray. Additional 'immediate relief' appliances were summoned to relieve exhausted crews, although none of the fire engines already there left the smoke-filled street in Southwark. The arrival of these additional BA pumps enabled crews who had been at work more time to recharge their sets and catch a breath.

Lambeth's pump-escape and pump returned to the station, with exhausted crews, prior to the 6.00 p.m. change of watch. Brigade Control ordered our pump to exchange crews and return to the scene. With the BA sets serviced I was one of three Red Watch men riding the pump and we carried on where others had left off. It was their herculean efforts which had moved the hose lines forward. Hose lines we now followed and used. We were committed twice. I experienced the extremes of heat and the draining conditions that others had endured all afternoon. It was a bloody lot different from Croydon's BA Chamber or the Divisional BA drills at Southwark's 'rat-run'. It was totally different from sticking a BA set on for 10 or 15 minutes at a typical house or maisonette fire!

When the 'stop' message was sent by Deputy Chief Officer Frank Mummery late that evening, fifty pumping appliances, four emergency tenders, two turntable ladders, plus Lambeth's canteen van attended the fire before the first proper relief crews were finally ordered.

We worked into the night before we too were eventually relieved. We returned the following morning on the 6.00 a.m. reliefs. We were back the second night duty too. Now just damping down, we saw the full intensity of the fire. Large swathes of concrete had spalled off beams, exposing the steel reinforcements. Huge sections of the lower surface of the floor had spalled completely; hundreds of thousands of lolly sticks were also destroyed, the major fuel of this extraordinary blaze and my first proper 'Proto' BA job.

Going down London's sewers in a Proto BA set was something completely different. It was not everyone's cup of tea either. It was rather like using hook ladders: a love or hate thing. This time, instead of up you're going down. Still at Lambeth fire station I had four years' operational experience under my belt and put in for an emergency tender (ET) course. It was something I never wanted to rush into as I felt it was necessary to get some decent BA jobs before making such a move. Historically ET crews were held in high esteem. They were expected to deliver the goods at difficult BA fires, or at special operations requiring BA, in addition to their wider rescue role. This 'gaining experience' view was not shared by all at Lambeth. On Lambeth's other watches young firemen (I was only 22) put in for an ET course as soon as they had passed out in Proto BA. They argued that they would gain the experience by riding the

ET. This was not a view held by the Red Watch's ET men, the very firemen I would ride alongside.

The role of the Brigade's ET crews were occasionally extremely demanding and sometimes dangerous. In the late 1960s the ET crews were seen by many senior officers as "Leete's commandos", named after the then Chief Officer Leslie Leete. In the 1950s the Brigade only had two ETs: one at Lambeth, the other at Clerkenwell. These crews would combat their individual fears of hot confined humid spaces, or face the risk of a sudden unexpected explosion of flammable gases or liquids, whilst working as an elite crew. They greatly supported, and contributed to, the efforts of fire-ground crews. Their synergy resulted in getting difficult tasks done and leading by example. Occasionally their skills made the difference between life and death, for example in the rescue of a trapped BA fireman. These situations required every ounce of the ET crews' combined expertise. It was not the place for a mere novice, in my view. It was the widely-held view of those that rode Lambeth's ET on Red Watch too. So it was with their blessing that I applied for the next available course. The course came almost immediately, supported by my guvnor's endorsement, but not before our monthly salary slips changed from pounds, shillings and pence (£. s. d) to pounds and pence on Monday 15 February 1971 as we all went decimal.

I attended Southwark Training School for my three-week course. Southwark was the centre of the Brigade's ET training. It serviced the seven ET stations' qualification needs. As well as incorporating intensive BA training, the course covered the rigorous and demanding roles expected of its crews, including visits to specialist installations and premises. One of these was London's sewer system. Later, taking crews on a sewer visit became a bit of a party piece when I was stationed at Southwark, West Norward and Brixton.

Taken to Southwark's Cornwall Road, close to the South Bank, we were greeted by the 'Ganger' of one of the then GLC's sewer crews. It was where we were introduced to this strange subterranean world. The sweaty brickwork of the egg-shaped tunnel closed in on us no sooner than we had squeezed through the manhole cover opening in the middle of the road. We had descended a vertical metal ladder that took us 30 feet below London's streets. Our first visit was without breathing apparatus. The warm and humid smell of detergent contrasted with the cold water flowing around our feet. This familiarisation of this strange claustrophobic place let us see where sewer men spent their working day. With each step the dull turgid screen of mist parted to allow us through. The shafts of light from our torches picked out the glistening highlights of geometrical lines of brickwork, creating its own *son-et-lumière* with each step we made. Distorted shadows transformed us into phantoms wandering in a Victorian aquatic underground maze.

We were wading along the tunnel in single file. Cold greyish water flowed eastwards at knee height and pushed against the backs of our waders, urging us on. We could not walk upright. The tunnels were only five feet high. Cramped, we moved forward at a stoop, shadows mirroring our movements on the damp brickwork. After a while the Ganger, at the head of the file, turned round.

"Keep in your place," he said, "and if you get lost, then don't start doing anything clever like trying to find us. Just stay where you are, we'll find you."

The Ganger was the head of a team of five 'flushers' who spent their working hours cleaning the bowels of London. He had on heavy waders that came up to his waist. Beneath them he wore thick thigh-length woollen socks like leg warmers. Above the waders and the leg warmers he was garbed in a blue overall jacket kept in place by a belt, and the all-important safety harness. Although the tunnel we were trudging through was generally oval-shaped, the sewer bed was flat and covered by a layer of sediment that felt like a mix of sand and grit. Our fireboots sank into it with every step.

"That's what we call muck down here," the Ganger said. "It's full of little pockets of gas, waiting to overpower the unsuspecting sewer worker. That's why if you ever get called to get us out of one of these tunnels only ever come down in your breathing apparatus, otherwise we will all be in the shit, literally."

From that simple inconspicuous manhole cover we had entered just one of the many lifelines of the metropolis, twisting and turning beneath the roadways: 1500 miles of Neo-gothic sewers. Some were much smaller than the ones we were in that day. Others were almost like caverns; storm relief sewers that directed away 1,000,000 gallons of rain water, thus protecting the capital from flood damage during torrential rainfall.

For our second visit we wore breathing apparatus. There was a different manhole, down near the Elephant and Castle, and after a 40 foot descent we entered a tunnel no taller than four foot. Our backs started to ache within the first 50 feet. The bottom of our breathing bags were dragging through the sewer water. As we negotiated this subterranean waterway we were conscious that a rain cloud bursting some miles away might fill these tunnels with torrents of water, thus sweeping away the unwary worker. The only protection against this possibility was the 'Top-man'. Armed with his two-way radio he provided regular weather forecast updates, something that for those working below can mean the difference between life and death.

We practised the rescue techniques necessary to lift, carry and raise an injured sewer worker. Later, in the comfort of the class-room, we supplemented our practical experience by learning of the health and biological hazards such rescues can expose the rescuer to. These include Weil's disease (spread by rats' urine, the virus of which can get into the body through cuts and scratches and end up in the brain) and in most cases would lead to an unpleasant death. Hepatitis is more common, but is not the only organic peril since other bacteria will cause a range of potentially life-threatening conditions. It is therefore vital that the washing and decontamina-tion procedures are rigorously followed once crews return to street level. Just as potentially lethal are the reactions of different chem-icals mixing in the sewer system. This can produced a cocktail of toxic gases, hence the importance of the sewer safety lamp which has been designed to warn of its presence.

The ET course was very 'hands on'. We lifted, pulled, cut, spread with the full range of rescue equipment carried on the ETs. We visited various lift installations and learned how to recognise the differences between electrical, mechanical and hydraulic systems, how to shut them down and hand-wind the lifts, how to open or remove lift doors and release the 'dead' brakes so that we could move a lift either up or down.

Our explorations covered the London Underground system too. We learned the lifting points on varied Underground rolling stock and how to isolate the power supply to the tracks. We went beneath escalators; we entered cold store refrigeration plants (where the hairs in our nostrils froze within seconds). We performed drills wearing the full protective clothing then only carried on the ETs: gas-tight suits which would be the firemen's only protection when dealing with serious leakages of toxic gases and refrigerants such as ammonia.

At the end of the course, its participants – Sub Officers, Leading Firemen and firemen – were examined by Training School senior officers. Every aspect of the demanding course was covered; attendance alone was no guarantee to gain a pass. The camaraderie, which was established between us all, helped ensure the expected high standards were fully met. Finally, armed with our new skills and knowledge, we returned to our respective stations to put it all into practice.

I did actually attend two sewer incidents whilst riding Lambeth's ET, one in Brixton Road and the other in North London. Brixton Road was a sewer collapse and the crews at Brixton (B30), under the command of their Irish Station Officer Declan Butler, did an exceptional job of extracting the injured sewer workers. We just helped. North London was a way to go from Lambeth and by the time we arrived it was done and dusted. Full marks went to the local station crews.

Whilst the local South London sewer gangs were always willing to give us a visit, there were some on my various White Watches who did not share my enthusiasm for seeing what lay right under their feet!

(Fact)

The Ghost in the Smoke

by Kevin McDermott

MICK STOOD ON THE side of a south London street trying to find a taxi. In the gathering gloom of that damp May evening he foolishly waved and shouted "Taxi" at anything that resembled a cab. It was at a time like this that he wished he had learnt to give one of those piercing whistles that always seemed to work for the hero in the movies. Suddenly he saw the familiar shape of a London taxi cab approaching and he breathed a sigh of relief when he saw that its yellow 'For Hire' sign was lit. He was standing on the edge of the roadway frantically waving when the cab swung in towards the kerb and caused him to jump back sharply.

"Yes mate?" said the driver, bending towards the open window.

"Euston railway station, please," said Mick, and listened as the driver gave a sharp intake of breath, the kind of sharp intake of breath that Londoners always seem to give when they feel they are about to do you a favour. "Have you got a problem with that?" Mick queried.

"No mate," replied the cabby, "but I've just come from that area and the bleedin' traffic is murder. If you are rushing for a train you could be in trouble."

"That's alright," said Mick. "As it happens I am going for a train but I've still got a few hours to spare so there's no rush."

He placed his one piece of luggage beside the driver and climbed into the rear of the cab. He watched as the driver entered the fee for the solitary suitcase along with a few other incidentals on the meter of the taxi. "Christ!" he thought to himself, "there's nearly two quid on the meter already and we haven't turned a wheel yet." It certainly would have been a lot cheaper to take the underground to Euston, but with his aching head he couldn't possibly put up with the rush hour crowds and the inevitable crush on the Tube. Besides, he had just spent three hectic days in London, and felt like leaving it in style. As he sprawled back in to the relative comfort of the taxi's broad rear seat, he knew he had made the right decision.

Mick was a retired London fireman now living in Ireland. It was his attendance at the annual fire brigade reunion that had brought him back to London for the first time in ten years. As the taxi crawled its way slowly in the bumper to bumper traffic, his befuddled mind relived the events of the previous night's reunion and he thought about some of the old mates that he had met for the first time in ten years. The reunion followed the usual pattern: small groups of men standing around, pints in hand, laughing, joking, and reminiscing about the various old smoke-eaters from times past. Many of London's more spectacular fires were fought all over again, and they drank a toast to the men who had gone to that great fire station in the sky. When eventually the reunion started breaking up, was Mick just a little misty-eyed as old friends shook his hand and left him with a final requiem?

"Great to see you again you old sod, keep in touch and look after yourself now."

He spent what remained of the night sleeping off the effects of the few pints in a friend's flat near the Elephant & Castle. Now he was eager to get away from a London that seemed to be awash with people, traffic, and petrol fumes.

The sudden braking of the taxi shattered his train of thought. Peering through the now rain-spattered window, he realised that he was in fact travelling through an area of the city where he had spent nearly twenty years of his fire-fighting career. He was bending forward and looking up at the floodlit dome of Wren's masterpiece when the cabby spoke for the first time since the journey began.

"That's St Paul's Cathedral," he said. "It's well worth a visit if you ever get the chance." He then went on to give Mick a verbal tour of the famous church. Mick pretended he was interested. He didn't have the heart to tell the cabby that not only had he been inside the cathedral on numerous occasions, but he had also humped lengths of hose up that spiral staircase. On one occasion he had even sent a jet of water over the cross during the annual exercise that the fire brigade held there.

As the cab moved slowly along the now drizzle-soaked and brightly lit streets his mind went back over the years to the 1960s. As a young fireman he had ridden a fire engine through those very same streets. Along with a tightly-knit crew he had shared the excitement, the sometime amusing but mostly tragic incidents that had occurred in some of the buildings he was now passing. Even now in his mind he could still picture the fire engine weaving its way through the traffic, and still hear the unmistakable sound of the now defunct engines' fire bells echoing around the walls of the high buildings.

As the taxi turned a corner and stopped at a red traffic light Mick's eyes were drawn towards a brightly lit office block standing on the corner. A slight chill went through his body as he realised where he was. "Well, I'll be damned," he said to himself, "so they finally pulled it down." He was referring to an old block of flats that had stood on that corner since the days of Queen Victoria, and where he had once experienced a very eerie and unexplained phenomenon. An incident that he had never managed to come to terms with. In the preceding years it had haunted him to such an extent that every time he passed those drab looking dwellings, the question always crossed his mind. Was it a ghost or just a figment of his imagination?

It had all started after he had reported for night duty one November evening. The first call out came just as the crew was sitting down to supper and was to a chimney fire in Prince Albert Dwellings on the corner of Albert Street. On arrival at the block of flats they could see the thick sooty smoke pouring from one of its many chimney pots and their first task was to find out which flat contained the offending fireplace. The crews split up and, starting at the top of the building, they gradually checked each flat in turn until only the basement flat remained. Mick banged on the door of the basement flat and shouted: "Fire brigade here, we want to check your fireplace".

After some delay the door was opened by a middle-aged, red-haired woman. Straight away Mick could see the raging fire in her grate. She had piled the fire high with newspapers and the flames were roaring up the chimney. They had found the source of the chimney fire.

When eventually the chimney fire and the fire in the woman's grate had been extinguished, the crew was amazed to see that the flat was stacked to the ceiling with bundles of old books and newsprint. In fact it looked more like a waste paper warehouse than a private dwelling. They crew listened as their Officer-in-Charge lectured the woman on matters of safety and pointed out the dangers of storing so much flammable material in a private flat. She didn't take too kindly at being lectured by the Station Officer and as the crew was leaving her flat she looked daggers at Mick. In fact it was a look that made him feel slightly uncomfortable. He laughed when one of his mates said, "Bloody hell Mick, I don't think she liked you, maybe she has a thing about Paddies."

During the course of the evening the crew dealt with a few minor incidents and had just settled down for the night when the call bells rang throughout the station. The time was 1.15 a.m. and once again the station became alive and noisy. The opening and closing of the pole house door added greatly to the noise as the men slid down the pole to where the two fire engines stood ready for action. Struggling into his fire tunic and boots Mick climbed aboard one of the fire engines just as the address from the teleprinter was handed to the driver. "Prince Albert Dwellings," he shouted. "Hold tight… doors". The big red doors swung open and the two fire engines drove forward into a traffic free street and once again headed for Prince Albert Dwellings.

"There's smoke coming from that window," said the policeman pointing at the basement flat.

"Christ!" swore Mick. "It's the same bloody flat we were in earlier, but it's more than a chimney fire this time."

The fire crew tried to descend the stairs to the flat but were beaten back by the heat coming from below. The officer in charge ordered Mick and his mate to rig in their breathing apparatus sets and to make the descent protected by a curtain of water spray. Turning the setting on the hose nozzle to the appropriate position and sheltering behind the resulting water spray, both men inched their way slowly down through the searing heat which by now was starting to crack

146

the glazed tiles on the stairway. When eventually they arrived at the door of the burning flat they saw that its exterior was starting to char and blister. This was a sure sign of a massive build-up of heat inside, so Mick and his colleague prepared themselves for the inevitable flashover which would occur when they broke the door down.

A couple of good kicks from a size ten fire boot was all that was needed and the already weakened door gave way with a bang as the fresh supply of oxygen turned the interior of the flat into a fire ball. Suddenly the hose went limp. As the jet of water became a useless trickle, both men realised that the hose had burst somewhere behind them. His colleague indicated that he was going back to sort out the problem and Mick found himself alone and helpless, staring into the inferno.

He watched in awe as the fire raged through the flat, consuming everything in its path. He was gripped with fear as he watched the many stacks of newspapers turn black and then burst into flames. As he stood there in a sort of trance he realised that things seemed to have gone very quiet, and he could even hear the clicking of the valves inside his breathing apparatus. He was also aware that although the exposed parts of the skin on his face had started to burn, a cold shiver was running through his body. Suddenly he gasped and caught his breath as he saw the figure of a red-haired woman coming slowly towards him through the flames. He was still trying to scream when the hose stiffened and the nozzle in his hand kicked violently as a jet of water hit the apparition and it disappeared in a cloud of steam and smoke. Now all hell broke loose as more firemen arrived with extra hose and they slowly fought their way into the flat. By the time they had the fire under control the ceilings had collapsed and the flat was completely destroyed. Although Mick half expected to find a woman's body where he had last seen her, they found only rubble. As the cold light of dawn filtered through the burnt out flat the badly charred body of a middle-aged woman was found under the debris of what was once a back bedroom. The report of a subsequent post mortem stated that she had died of smoke inhalation sometime between the hours of ten and eleven the previous night.

"Here we are, Guv," said the cabby. "Euston station. That will be six pounds exactly."

Mick awoke from his doze in the back seat and realised that they had arrived at his destination. "Sorry," he said, "I must have dozed off, I was miles away."

The cab driver handed him his suitcase and laughed as he said, "You must have had a bad dream back there, because the way you screamed I thought you saw a bleedin' ghost."

Mick handed over his fare and threw in a couple of pounds as a tip. "Thank you very much," he said to the cabby, "and sorry if I gave you a scare. You were right... I *did* see a ghost, but I think it's being laid to rest now, thanks to a new office block."

The cabby watched dumbfounded as Mick walked away toward the station entrance. "What a weird geezer," he thought to himself, as he swung his cab around and joined yet another queue of London's traffic.

(Fiction)

PHOTOGRAPHIC SECTION

AM INDEBTED TO THE copyright owners for their kind permission to reproduce the images in this section. In particular, a special mention is owed to the London Fire Brigade: without their existence, this book would not have been possible.

- London Fire Brigade (LFB)

- Massey Shaw Education Trust

- Alan Dearing

- Owen Rowlands

- Nigel Saunders

- Darren Shirley and Kevin Wright

- Harry Simmons

- Michael Wallman

- Paul Wood

SIR EYRE M. SHAW, K.C.B.

The legacy of Eyre Massey Shaw. See "Eyre Massey Shaw", page 15.
(Massey Shaw Education Trust)

The Massey Shaw, Dunkirk, 1940. See "A Fire-Float Went to War", page 22.
(Massey Shaw Education Trust.)

See "The Case of the Peculiar Out-Duty...", page 27. *(Owen Rowlands)*

The Bishopgate Fire, 1964. See page 47.
(LFB)

Left: Divisional Officer Sydney Gompertz Gamble, Second Officer, London Fire Brigade
See "The London Fire Chief Who Never Was", page 57. *(LFB)*
Right: OXO Building. See "The OXO building incident, SE1", page 63. *(LFB)*

Left to right: Brian Hudson, Michael Wallman BEM, Keith Wright.
See "Rescues in NW2", page 93. *(Michael Wallman)*

155

Great Marlborough Street station. See "Old Fire Stations Never Die…", page 106. *(LFB)*

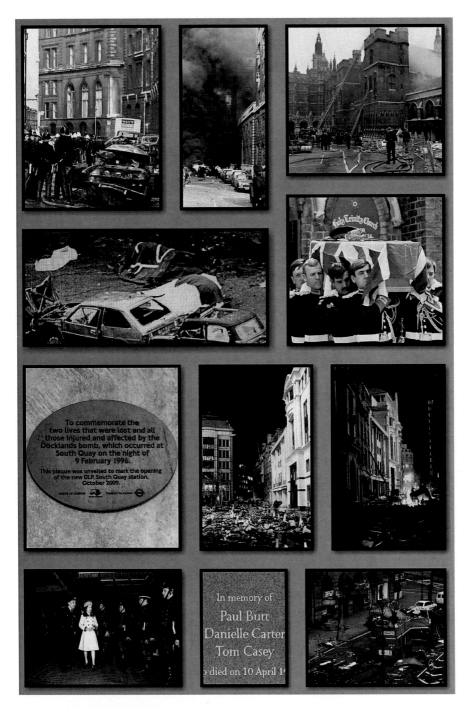

See "The IRA's Bombing Campaign, 1971–1993", page 116.
(LFB, Alan Dearing, Author's collection; collage by Paul Wood)

Wooden ladders – iron men.
See "Spectacles, Testicles, Wristwatch and Wallet", page 133. *(LFB)*

The Queen visits Lambeth, meeting Joseph Milner. See "A Firemen's Chief Officer:
'Joe' Milner", page 167. *(LFB)*

New Cross. See "Anatomy of a Fire", page 183. *(Nigel Saunders)*

Harry Simmons, Senior Control Officer, London Fire Board
See "In Control", page 216. *(Harry Simmons)*

Scenes from the Kings Cross Fire, 1987.
See "Yesteryear's Fires: King's Cross Underground Station", page 252. *(LFB)*

See "Firefighter Jack Waterman", page 260. *(Paul Wood)*

See "First Night Duty", page 275. *(LFB)*

See "Poles Apart", page 298. *(Author's collection)*

The author at 18. See "Old Dinosaurs... We Are Who We Are...", page 326.
(Author's collection)

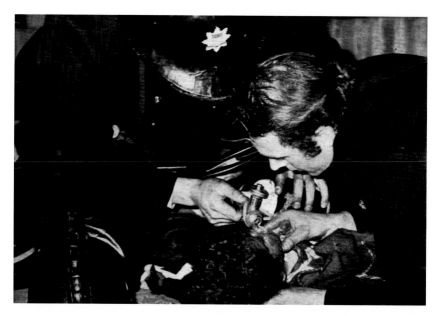

Rescue on the Old Kent Road. See "Old Dinosaurs… We Are Who We Are…", page 326.
(Owen Rowlands)

Today's London Fire Brigade: ever ready, ever willing; always there to respond
(Nigel Saunders)

The Grenfell Tower Fire, 2017. See "The Grenfell Tower fire", page 330.
(Paul Wood)

(Overleaf credit: Darren Shirley and Kevin Wright)

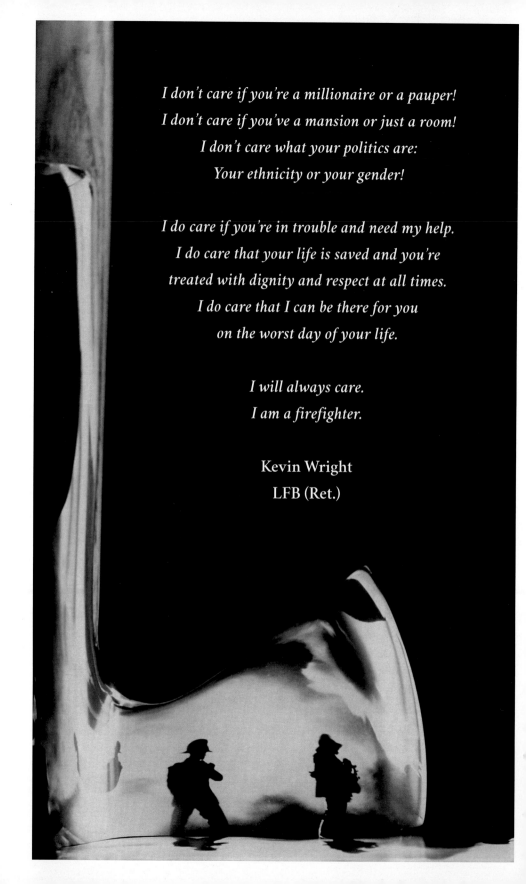

I don't care if you're a millionaire or a pauper!
I don't care if you've a mansion or just a room!
I don't care what your politics are:
Your ethnicity or your gender!

I do care if you're in trouble and need my help.
I do care that your life is saved and you're
treated with dignity and respect at all times.
I do care that I can be there for you
on the worst day of your life.

I will always care.
I am a firefighter.

Kevin Wright
LFB (Ret.)

A Firemen's Chief Officer: 'Joe' Milner

Joseph 'Joe' Milner CBE, OStJ, QFSM, 1922–2007; London's Chief Fire Officer. 1970–1976

WHAT MADE THIS SUCH a special time for an aspiring young fireman, serving at Lambeth fire station, remains a matter of conjecture. Maybe it was the exciting LFB life viewed through the eyes of a twenty-one year old? A young fireman that was being shown the ropes, and his craft, by the combined experience and wisdom of ordinary people who chose the life of a London fireman. Maybe being at a busy station helped, but it was also a time of big change. A new 'Chief' had brought with him new ways, new ideas. He also brought a fresh new style, one that ordinary fireman seemed to understand and could readily relate to where it really mattered, out on the fire-ground. However, it was also a time of considerable wider industrial unrest, even fraught at times. But it never seemed to be personal. There never seemed to be a lynch mob baying for the new Chief's blood.

It was only after his premature, and unexpected, departure from the Brigade, which many considered under a cloud, that I can say I got to know this man a little better – albeit briefly in the early 1980s and on a more regular basis in the late 1990s.

Joe was not a Londoner. His service with the LFB was only as its Chief Officer, yet despite the manner of his departure he only ever referred to his tenure in office with warmth and genuine affection.

He always remained loyal to its 'firefighters' and had worked hard, even in retirement, to support them via the then named Fire Services National Benevolent Fund (Firefighters Charity).

I remain convinced that Joe was a man of his time. A man gifted with a common touch. A man I remain proud to have served under. A man who should have been referred to as *Sir Joe...* had justice prevailed. If there is a league table of LFB Chief Officers he is up there with the very best. I do not feel the LFB will ever see his like again, but who knows given how the new Fire Commissioner, Dany Cotton, is doing? So a reminder of the man – Joe Milner.

Joe was born in Manchester in October 1922. He was the son of a Manchester labourer and his affinity to the working man (and woman) remained with him throughout his career and beyond it. Leaving school at 14 he worked for a short time with a firm of gas engine manufacturers before joining the Manchester Corporation's Transport Department. (As what was never recorded.)

With the imminent outbreak of war Joe joined the army in 1938 at 16 years of age. He served in the Royal Corps of Signals until his 18th year when he transferred to the Kings (Liverpool) Regiment in 1940. From 1942 until 1946 he fought in India and Burma. In 1944 Private Milner was a member of Orde Wingate's Long Range Penetration Force (The Chindits) and was flown into Burma by Waco gliders. His were the Broadway Landings, one of three selected sites to fight and harry the Japanese. Milner arrived at Broadway in March; 600 further sorties followed bringing in more men, by which time about 9,000 Chindits (supported by over 1,000 animals) were present in Burma. Between June and July the Chindits sustained heavy casualties and were slowly pulled out of Burma. The last Chindit left Burma on 27 August 1944. Milner's tour of duty was meant to last only 90 days but it was five months before the survivors, debilitated by malnutrition and disease, were finally pulled back into India. (No other units throughout World War II were kept in the field, deprived of any relief or recuperation, and are comparable to what the Chindits had endured.)

In 1945 Joe Milner once again returned to Burma. This time he was a member of the War Graves Unit and his, and his companions', task was to recover and properly bury the bodies of fallen comrades. He was working there for seven months.

Having been de-mobbed in 1946, Joe Milner applied to the Northumberland Region where he did his Nation Fire Service (NFS) recruit fireman training. Milner won the Under Secretary of State's prize for the best recruit. He was a fireman in the last months of the NFS.

With the return of fire brigades to local authority control in 1948 Joe Milner, who had risen in rank, first became part of the Middlesbrough fire brigade and then transferred to the North Riding of Yorkshire Brigade before finally transferring into the Manchester Fire Brigade in 1950. It was the same year that he passed his Graduates exam in the Institution of Fire Engineers (IFE).

At 29 Milner was selected in 1951 to become a Station Officer in the Hong Kong Fire Brigade, as it was called then. The following year·he passed his Membership exams of the IFE. Asked later why he has chosen Hong Kong to apply for he said: "I felt the call of the East. But more important I had a hunch that both Hong Kong and its fire service were due for radical transformation. I want to be in on the ground floor of a development like that."

He was proved to be right and the credit went to him for bringing about many of those radical, and successful, changes. He saw the service grow from just 500 firemen to 3000. It became the second largest fire-fighting force in the Commonwealth and one of the world's most efficient. During his first four years Joe Milner was in charge of the Kowloon District before running the Inspection Branch (later renamed the Fire Prevention Branch). Between 1955 and 1961 he was appointed a Divisional Officer, then District Officer before becoming the Deputy Director of Fire Services. He was awarded the Queen's Fire Service Medal in 1962.

Appointed Director in 1965 Joe Milner was a major force in bringing about change and modernisation to the Hong Kong Fire and Ambulance Service. Not least in his list of significant achievements were the introduction of the Brigade's 'Search and Rescue' Division, which accounted for 10 per cent of the Hong Kong force. He also introduced new smaller-sized fire stations rather than the few big ones, plus an attendance criterion of six minutes.

Confronted with such an impressive CV and a proven track record, the Fire Brigade's Committee of the Greater London Council selected Joe Milner to replace Leslie Leete, the retiring LFB Chief Officer. He took over the London Fire Brigade in June 1970 at the age of 47. A sea change had come to the Brigade. Many would soon discover their new Chief to be a forthright man who did not mince his words. He was in stark contrast to the outgoing Chief who had given the impression of being particular uncomfortable in the company of the lower ranks.

Joe, as he was to be affectionately called, was not tall and was slightly built. He had the appearance of a marathon runner although he was in fact an avid walker. Those on night duty in Lambeth's watchroom would regularly see him leaving the Headquarters' lobby at around 5 a.m. for his daily six-mile constitutional with his favourite pipe in his mouth. He would return some 90 minutes later, occasionally popping into the fire station watchroom to chat with the dutyman. (A practice that would have been a complete anathema to the previous post holder.)

For those around the Brigade then reading the new Chief's profile, produced for the in-house magazine, *London Fireman,* and listing Joe Milner's war record, it was akin to something taken from of the *Boy's Own Annual.* Soon many would meet the man in person as he travelled around the 11 Divisions, and was seen frequently on the fire-ground looking, learning, and gathering intelligence. Plus, one of Joe Milner's greatest strengths: listening to the views of his London firemen and their officers.

One of his first actions did not set the world alight but nevertheless set the tone of his tenure. He added the word RESCUE to the Brigade's fleet of Emergency Tenders. His aim was to remind the public of what the LFB did and the variety of services it performs. Things did not go all his way. His desire to have a complete name change to 'London Fire and Rescue Service' never saw the light of day.

In that first year his in-tray contained many issues requiring his urgent attention. But some things were beyond his control. The early 1970s had maintained the momentum of the late '60s with its growing political and industrial unrest, which was making its presence felt across everyday life. The widespread national dock strikes sounded the death knell of London's docks and gave rise to dire economic effects. The then Labour government lashed out in response at its traditional stronghold of support, the Unions. Inflation had risen sharply by the end of the previous decade as the reduced buying power of London firemen's meagre monthly wage more than demonstrated. Joe's arrival coincided with an increasingly powerful trade union movement sweeping the nation. (It also saw the removal of Labour's Harold Wilson and the arrival of the Tory Edward Heath as Britain's Prime Minister.) This increased power and the demands by the Unions for better working conditions were felt across the fire service too.

It was following another major dock strike the country faced a further local authority dustmen's strike. Once again London's communities were up to their knees in tons of uncollected refuse. The results of this action were not lost on London's inner city population or on its many fire stations crews who were having to cope with the health and fire hazards caused by the consequences of the continuing battle for better pay and conditions demanded by the dustmen's unions. Their employers resisted these demands, supported by the Government's unseen controlling hand. Rubbish rapidly accumulated all over again in the capital's designated dumping areas. Night after night fire engine crews travelled around the Central London fire stations' grounds dealing with these proliferation of fires or standing-by whilst the home station's crews were dousing putrefying rubbish fires, piled ten feet high in some cases. Leicester Square became a notorious 'emergency' rubbish dump and the stench, after just a few days, became almost overpowering. South of the river much less salubrious locations were used to pile the uncollected garbage. But regardless of where it was stacked, clambering over this mixture of rotting and smelly household and commercial waste was equally unpleasant. Joe Milner would, together with other senior officers, take to the streets to see at first-hand the conditions that their firefighters were having to endure.

For organisational leaders, and Joe Milner was one, the '70s were an extreme decade as regards its industrial relations record. The extreme left dominated many Unions, including the Fire Brigades Union (FBU). Progress and proposed changes in the London Fire Brigade's working practices were challenged and obstructed. The

Union's opposition was not necessarily supported by the whole of the London FBU membership but went ahead by a show of divisional representatives' hands. Union activists (better described as 'militant') would often carry the day.

The first, in a series, of FBU 'emergency only disputes' hit the Brigade during the middle of the Milner era. London firemen answered just 999 calls and at some of the more militant stations appliances were taken 'off the run' (out of service) for the most trivial of reasons. Maintaining adequate fire cover became a major issue at times for Chief Milner. This new type of fire brigade 'industrial' action grew incrementally throughout his time in office. Finally, but after Milner's sudden departure in 1976, the first national strike involving firemen started in November 1977. It lasted for sixty-nine long days.

After just a year in office, in August 1971, Joe Milner became one of only two Chief Officers in modern times to command a 50-pump fire in the greater London area. CFO Milner actually commanded his, whereas his predecessor merely attended one. Joe's fire was one of the fiercest and most difficult fires that the post-war London Fire Brigade had to face. It lasted nearly 30 hours and involving all three watches. The scene of the blaze was at Wilson's Wharf, Battle Bridge Lane just off Tooley Street in Bermondsey. It was ironic that this should be the same location that cost the life of London's first Chief fire officer, Superintendent James Braidwood, when in 1861 he was buried under a collapsed wall at a warehouse blaze that took several days to bring under control. (Braidwood's brigade was called the 'London Fire Engine Establishment'.)

Wilson's Wharf had been built on the site of that first devastating fire, part of the Hays Wharf Company's great rebuilding scheme, and had opened in 1868. Starting life as a coffee and cocoa wharf, it later became the company's first wine and spirit bottling department. Just over a century later it lay unoccupied, having previously undergone conversion to a refrigerated warehouse and cold store. The six-storey warehouse had an irregular shape and sat tightly wedged between other wharfs. On the riverside was a wide vehicular jetty where, previously, goods and products had been delivered to its 150 foot wide riverside access. It was also 150 feet from this side of the building to the far side, which faced Tooley Street. Various raised open and covered iron bridges connected it to the surrounding wharves.

A small fire had started during the removal of plant. Unable to stem the rapidly developing fire with an extinguisher, contractors beat a hasty retreat from the building leaving their oxyacetylene cutting equipment in situ. It was sparks from their hot cutting that had ignited combustible tape on the pipe-work insulation. It had spread to the building's insulation material itself, four-inch thick and very flammable expanded rubber. Even as the contractors were running out of Wilson's Wharf and local fire crews drew closer, the hot and smoky atmosphere was being trapped inside this disused cold store. Its windows and loopholes had been bricked up, making the building a veritable fortress and thus turning large parts of the complex into a vast brick oven. The fire was superheating the interior.

In the space of 45 minutes 'pumps' went from 15, to 20, and then 30. Command of the fire changed hands so quickly that no single plan of action could be properly implemented until Chief Officer Milner took command at 4.16 p.m. He faced daunting problems, taxing even his considerable know-how of commanding major incidents from his time in Hong Kong. He had all his Headquarters' principal officers at his disposal, including Deputy Chief Harold Chisnell. It would take their combined experience and expertise to direct operations at this incident: one which was now extremely serious due to the complex layout of the building, the thickness of the walls and lack of access points. The heat build-up, deep inside the structure, was likened to a potter's kiln operating at maximum temperature.

Despite the tenacity and doggedness of the firemen, the tremendous heat and smoke posed major problems for the fire-fighting crews in establishing a bridgehead to counter the blaze. Contractors working alongside firemen tried to break open some of the bricked up windows at the third floor level with power tools, but little or no progress was made. Meanwhile BA crews, who had made exploratory forays into the building, were slowly being forced back. The conditions were so severe that it blistered exposed skin. Concern about the fire brought complaints of smoke drifts from as far away as Bethnal Green and there were reports of smoke drifting into some Underground stations in the City of London.

With a conflagration of this magnitude Joe Milner considered that only two courses were open to him. One was to concentrate on subduing the fire in the main warehouse and arresting its development to the adjacent blocks. This would require him committing crews to extremely hazardous and punishing conditions. Furthermore it would require a total commitment in the order of some 80 pumps! The result would denude large areas of London of any fire cover for a protracted period. (During the course of this fire the Brigade dealt with emergency '999' calls to other incidents in the capital.)

His second option was to abandon the efforts to subdue the fire in the main warehouse and to concentrate on surrounding the fire and confining the spread to the area bounded by Battle Bridge Lane, English Ground and the river. The success of Milner's strategy depended on allowing the fire to break through the roof of the central warehouse and reduce the lateral transmission of heat and smoke by ventilation. The danger Milner faced was that once the fire broke through the roof there would be a serious threat to surrounding property and adjacent area from radiated heat and flying firebrands.

Following discussion with his command officers, Joe Milner decided to adopt the second option. At 5.12 p.m., he ordered that pumps be increased to 50. His operation proved successful and by 1.30 a.m. the next day the fire had been reduced to the fourth and fifth floors and entry had been effected by BA crews. Although heavy smoke was still being encountered, steady progress was made throughout the day and it was possible for the Chief to send the "Stop" message at 8.30 p.m. on the second day of the fire. The fire-fighting operations involved the use of 23 jets, eight radial branches, and one high expansion foam unit and in excess of 200 one-hour Proto BA sets using an estimated 315 oxygen cylinders.

The damage to the complex consisted of three-quarters of all floors severely damaged by fire, the remainder severely damaged by fire, heat, smoke and water, and one half of the roof severely damaged by fire, heat and smoke.

Joe Milner's brigade was very busy operationally throughout

his tenure. In fact, during Joe Milner's six-year reign the Brigade dealt with more 20 to 35 pump fires than the previous decade or the one that followed. But the Chief had new operational worries to consider. Its operational workload was further added to that year by the 'Troubles'. The Irish Republican Army (IRA) bombing campaign came to London in October 1971. The Post Office Tower (now called the BT Tower) was an IRA terrorist target. The bombing, although not resulting in any fatalities, did cause the closure of the building to the general public for many years. Joe Milner, like so many others, watched these events unfold on national and local news. However, the threat of becoming caught up in this new breed of incident was not only promoting discussion and speculation amongst station personnel, it was also increasing the concerns of wives, partners and firemen's families. It seemed the IRA could make an attack on any high-profile London landmark and the Chief was very aware, when on duty, his crews were concerned about their family members, many of whom worked in the capital and who could become an innocent victim of this hate campaign. Such things were beyond his control and his firefighters had a job to do, but his concern for the wider Fire Brigade family was ever-present whenever he met with his crews. (The IRA brought about 29 separate bombings to the capital whilst Joe Milner was the Chief in the early 1970s.)

By the end of that year Joe Milner had prepared plans for a radical shake-up of the way his Brigade was managed. His proposal were submitted to the GLC's Fire Brigade Committee and were accepted without modification. At its heart was a new Operations Branch headed by Assistant Chief Officer (ACO) Don Burrell. They were supported by the Technical, Planning and Development Branch headed by ACO Trevor Watkins DFC, plus a Mobile Group, whose role was to check the way policies and procedures were being implemented, led by ACO Ernie Allday. Additionally, the Fire Prevention Branch retained its existing role and there was revamped Training and Recruitment Branch.

On the evening of 30 October 1971 Chief Joe Milner gave a ground-breaking address to the Brixton Rotary Club at Kings George's House, in SW4. He nailed his colours firmly to the mast by publicly acknowledging the value and esteem with which he held his officers and the men and women of the LFB. Such was the importance of his moving and heartfelt talk that his complete address was later published in a special supplement to the *London Fireman* magazine.

He was not the only one to make comment on the workings and people of the London Fire Brigade. In a highly unusual break with normal protocols, the Fire Service Inspectorate, who were notoriously tight-lipped about what they observed in their Brigade inspections, commented most warmly on the enthusiasm of all ranks. They confirmed Joe Milner's own belief that the moral and the *esprit de corps* within the Brigade were high.

London, under Joe's stewardship, led the British fire service with its work in implementing a hazchem (hazardous chemicals) code which was considered to be ground-breaking work: much credit deservedly went to the late Charlie Clisby, then a Deputy Assistant Chief Officer. The system was adopted across the emergency services during 1972. In the same year Milner directed that the Brigade launch a TV advertising campaign warning of the dangers of portable paraffin heaters. These had been directly responsible for multiple fatalities and serious house fires. It was the first time a UK Fire Brigade had used TV advertising in this way.

The introduction of the 'Three-Day Week' presented special problems for Joe Milner and his principal management team. It was one of several measures introduced across the United Kingdom by the then Conservative government to conserve electricity, the generation of which was severely restricted owing to strike and other action by coal miners and the aftermath of an oil crisis. This resulted in widespread blackouts over the winter of 1973 to 1974. The phased blackouts left fire stations (and everyone else for that matter, except essential services such as hospitals) without power for three to four hours at a time. Mobilising was severely affected and orderings had to be given over the radio network. Fire stations had no stand-by electrical generators and the resultant use of emergency lighting in homes (i.e. candles) led to a number of serious fires.

The bombing of the Old Bailey law courts, at the heart of the British justice System, in March 1973 marked a dramatic shift in the tactics of the IRA in their attempts to bomb their way to achieve their political ends. The IRA exploded two car bombs in the heart of London and injured over 200 innocents. Sadly, one man died, not through the direct impact of the bombing but from a fatal heart attack. The bombers had callously chosen a day when thousands of commuters were forced to drive into central London because strikes had hit the capital's public transport services.

It was St Bart's Hospital that bore the brunt of the 160 or so patients that were either taken there or who made their own way to the hospital's emergency treatment department. The hospital had no warning of the bombing or of the impending arrival of so many patients. Accordingly, its procedures for implementing a major accident plan could not be used. Most of the walking wounded required treatment for cuts and abrasions, but 19 individuals were admitted and nine required surgery. There was much behind-the-scenes, top-level discussions on the role and safety of fire crews given the escalation in tactics of the Irish terrorists. Milner's view remained firm that where public safety was concerned his crews would remain committed to all lifesaving duties and in all circumstances. His view was widely supported by the Brigade's rank and file.

It was in the early months of 1974 that Joe Milner charged the Brigade to embark on its most intensive recruiting drive since the creation of the Auxiliary Fire Service in 1938. You could not look anywhere without seeing advertising space taken up in the national and local press, even on commercial television and radio, encouraging men to join the London Fire Brigade. Recruitment posters were even pasted on to the sides of fire engines!

Operational staff shortages were bad and getting worse. Appliances were being taken 'off the run' at an increasing rate because there were not enough firemen to crew them. Normal manning was quickly reduced to minimum levels and any spare firemen were constantly being ordered out to other stations to make up shortfalls. The FBU contested that some firemen were spending more time riding engines at the surrounding stations than at their own. More firemen were needed for the introduction of the forty-eight hour week, a reduction of eight hours from the existing fifty-six hour week. But Joe found himself operating in a very competitive market place. The Post Office, London Transport and the Metropolitan Police were all wanting extra staff and just as urgently.

However, the brigade of the early '70s remained an almost totally white-dominated operational workforce. The desire to see a reflection of the multiracial society that London was rapidly becoming sadly did not feature in its recruitment campaign. But many non-white applicants did apply.

By 1974 Joe Milner was really getting into his stride. It was the year that his promise of more breathing apparatus for his firemen was delivered. Compressed air (CA) breathing apparatus sets were introduced onto all pump-escapes; Proto sets on pumps were reduced to two per appliance with two additional CA sets carried. It was the same year which he introduced the Chemical Incident Unit into the operational fleet. This would attend the increasing number of chemical incidents and be mobilised to all radiation incidents. Joe Milner's time as chief would also see the introduction of yellow fire helmets and then yellow leggings.

The only operational fatality on Joe Milner's watch occurred at the end of 1974. Tragically, Fireman Hamish Harry Pettit lost his life at the Worsley Hotel fire which also claimed the lives of six occupants. It was in the early hours of Friday 13 December 1974 that two separate fires were deliberately started in the Worsley Hotel. The Worsley Hotel comprised a series of interconnecting houses and were four and five storeys tall. The hotel was located at 3–19 Clifton Gardens in Maida Vale, W9. The Worsley was used by the hotel industry to house both hotel and catering employees, many of whom came from aboard, and were either working or training in Central London hotels.

As further London crews arrived, along with increasing numbers of senior officers to direct operations, most of the occupants were accounted for as the immediate rescues were completed. The operations moved from rescue to fighting the fire. Crews took heavy hoses through the doors from the street and off ladders pitched to upper windows. One of these firefighting crews, three firemen led by a Station Officer, entered a second floor room to search out the seat of the fire. Whilst the crew were in the room, several of the floors above them, now weakened by the extra load of the partially collapsed roof and the weight of a large water tank, came crashing down on them. The devastation appeared concentrated on that one room. It was not initially known just how seriously the injuries to those trapped in the collapse might be. The release of their trapped colleagues became an immediate priority to the firefighters outside.

It proved to be a most difficult and protracted rescue operation. One by one, three of the trapped men were released: two firemen with serious burns and a Station Officer with a serious back injury. Tragically, when the body of the fourth fireman was found he was declared dead at the scene. It was the body of a 26 year-old probationer fireman, Hamish Harry Pettit, who had attended the fire with Paddington's (A21) Red Watch.

Chief Milner was no shrinking violet when it came to turning out from his Greenwich quarters to an incident. In addition to the 30 pumping appliances, three turntable ladders, three emergency tenders and other specialist vehicles that had attended this incident, Joe Milner saw at first hand the efforts directed to saving life and the building. The "Stop" message was despatched at 8.02 a.m. that morning, but damping down went on for some days. The fire proved to be the largest fire in Central London that year.

The Worsley Hotel fire was also the first major incident dealt with by the Wembley control room after the computerized mobilising system had been commissioned earlier that week. This was another of Milner's improvements to the Brigade mobilising practices. He had closed the Lambeth Control room the same year.

For a man not shy to recognise the bravery and commitment of his fire crews, this incident nevertheless resulted in one of the largest number of fire brigade bravery commendations from a single incident with four of the firemen subsequently receiving national gallantry awards from the Her Majesty the Queen. The highest bravery award in the London Fire Brigade is that of a Chief Officer's Commendation. Joe Milner 'COMMENDED': Fireman Hamish Harry Pettit (Posthumously), Temporary Sub Officer Roger Stewart and Fireman David Blair (West Hampstead), Sub Officer Ronald Morris and Leading Fireman Peter Lidbitter (Westminster), Station Officer Neil Wallington and Fireman Raymond Chilton (Paddington), Temporary Leading Fireman Eric Hall (Soho), Temporary Divisional Officer John Simmons (Brigade HQ) and Assistant Divisional Officer Tom Rowley (A Division HQ).

He also issued 'Letters of Congratulation' to: Assistant Chief Officer Trevor Watkins DFC KPFSM (Brigade HQ), Assistant Divisional Officer Gerald Clarkson (Brigade HQ), Assistant Divisional Officer Roy Baldwin (A Division HQ), Station Officer Keith

Hicks, Temporary Sub Officer Ian Macey, Firemen Donald Clay, Edward Temple and Peter McCarlie (Soho), Fireman David Webber (Paddington), Fireman David Harris(Action) Acting Leading Fireman Alan Trotman (Belsize) and Fireman Daniel O'Dwyer (Manchester Square).

In 1975 Joe Milner's own name appeared in the Queens New Year Honours list. He was made a Commander of the Most Excellent Order of the British Empire (CBE).

The following month he actually met the Queen but not at Buckingham Palace. Her Majesty came to see him at the Lambeth headquarters in February. After meeting GLC dignitaries, including former London fireman 'Paddy' Henry who was now the Chairman of the Fire Brigade's Committee, Joe Milner escorted the Queen into the Officers' Club where she met representative crews and officers who had attended recent IRA bomb incidents. Typical of the man he stepped back after introducing each of the eight crews to the Queen so as to allow those being presented to talk to the Queen.

The last day of February 1975 was a Friday. Joe Milner was in his Lambeth office as the 8.38 a.m. service from Drayton Park on the London Underground Northern line (Highbury Branch) left one minute late. It was formed of two three-car units of 1938 LTE rolling stock. On arrival at Moorgate station the train failed to slow, passing through the station platform area at 30–40 mph before entering the 66 feet (20 metre) long overrun tunnel with a red stop-lamp, a sand drag and a hydraulic buffer stop. The sand drag only slowed the train slightly before the train collided heavily with the buffers and impacted with the tunnel terminal wall.

The crash was declared a 'Major Accident' by both the Brigade and the London Ambulance Service. It was the LFB's most difficult special service incident in over a decade and London's worst-ever Tube train disaster. The crash left the station in total darkness, throwing up a huge volumes of soot and dust. Joe Milner both commanded the incident and maintained a regular presence throughout the initial rescues and then the recovery phase.

The five-day rescue operation involved 1324 firemen, 240 police officers, 80 ambulancemen, 16 doctors and numerous voluntary workers and helpers. The last body to be brought out of the tunnel was that of the driver, Leslie Newson, a 56 year-old husband and father of two children. It was London's Chief Officer who famously quoted "MY THOUSAND SELFLESS HEROES", in dedication to the literal thousand firefighters who spent five days rescuing survivors.

In the early summer of 1976 Joe Milner 'upped sticks' and resigned from the London Fire Brigade. There was no warning of his imminent departure, but he was always his own man. It is to those who were part of the upper echelons at the time to say if he walked of his own volition or was pushed. What is known is that that Joe's first wife Bella had died early that year and he remarried in the later part of 1976. So maybe he choose love over career, a career where he was seen as Caesar and where too many 'Brutuses' were running loose on Lambeth's principal floor.

In the September 1976 issue of the *London Fireman* the acting Chief Officer, Don Burrell, gave no mention to the departed Joe Milner, his achievements, his commitment to London's firemen or even a 'wish you well in your retirement'. The lack of comment was churlish, to say the least! If there ever was a 'leaving do' for Joseph Milner, the powers that be never thought to report the event in any future addition of the in-house magazine...

Postscript

In retirement Joe became an ambassador for the then-named Fire Services National Benevolent Fund (later the Fire Fighter's Charity). He happily took the invitation to return to London to attend a presentation following a sponsored Paris to London marathon row in the summer of 1981 to accept a substantial cheque on behalf of the charity. He never uttered an ungracious word about his departure from the Brigade, unlike some in principal rank who had kicked up a stink because Joe had been invited to the reception.

He travelled around in retirement but finally settled in Norfolk. Joe was a regular attendee to the then Retired Senior Officers Mess Club, under the watchful eye of its President Brian 'Bill' Butler. Despite his considerable travel distance Joe loved those evenings and the opportunity to swing the lamp and tell a tale or two. I was in regular contact with Joe then and never once did he comment on the manner of his departure, or of those that probably orchestrated it. He was a remarkable human being.

Joe wrote a novel, based on his own wartime experiences, that was published in 1995. *To Blazes with Glory* was a Chindit's tale; it was no doubt his tale too.

Joe died at his home in Caston, Norfolk, on 13 January 2007. His funeral service was held on 29 January at Holy Cross Church in Caston. The London Assembly merely noted "the recent death of former London Fire Brigade Chief Fire Officer, Joseph Milner CBE QFSM". There was no comment by any elected member of London's Fire Authority or a Brigade officer on how much the man had achieved and had done for the reputation of the London Fire Brigade.

(Fact)

Anatomy of a Fire

IT WAS SUNDAY EVENING. The night watch had already started their shift. Around London's fire stations most were enjoying the warm spring evening. With the change of watch routines completed and cups of tea drunk, firemen were engaged in their various 'stand-down' activities. Some already had greasy, blackened hands as the freedom of working the Sunday night shift meant private cars, or motorbikes, could be worked on – provided the guvnor said it was okay. At a couple of stations full blown engine overhauls were well underway. At other stations the sound of hands striking a volley ball, or excited shouts or groans, filtered out from the confines of the station yards into quiet surrounding streets.

At a sprinkling of fire stations the evening's operational activity had already started. The first of that night's 999 calls had sent fire engine crews on their way: some attending nothing more than a rubbish bin on fire, others to someone shut in a lift. On the outskirts of Croydon a much more serious fire had broken out. The volley ball games at Norbury, Tooting and Mitcham fire stations had come to an abrupt end, the station call bells summoning crews to their respective fire engines. In North-West London the M4 eastbound traffic had been brought to a complete stand-still. A major accident would keep the emergency services busy for the next four hours as the living were rescued and the dead extricated.

Before the night shift ended over 40 fire engines, including special appliances, would be mobilised to an area south of the Thames. For one particular man that night there would never be another sunrise.

At 28 years of age Private Ernie Cheeseman had been at Dunkirk and survived the ordeal. Later, transferred into the Eighth Army, he fought in North Africa and was at Tobruk in 1941 where again he survived unscathed. He was with the Eighth Army in the Italian Campaign that had begun with the allied invasion of Sicily. He got through that battle too. During the fighting on the Italian Front the Eighth Army had, from 3 September 1943 until 2 May 1945 suffered 123,254 casualties. Ernie had not been one of them.

It was ironic, then, that having escaped injury so often during warfare, Ernie would finally succumb upon his return to the UK. As he was travelling in a crowded troop ship, some poorly secured crates had broken free. Ernie had acted with his typical lightning speed and pushed his mate clear of the falling wooden boxes. He was not so fortunate: the heavy containers crushed both his legs. It was thought that his injuries were so severe that one of his legs might have to be amputated. He spent months in the military hospital, followed by months in the Army's convalescent home, which were more barracks than 'home'. Here Ernie learned to walk again. It was also from where he was discharged from the Army. He was awarded a paltry injury pension together with his three campaign medals, one of which bore the bronze oak leaf for his 'mentioned in dispatches' which he earned at Tobruk.

The intervening years had not been kind to Ernie. His injuries frequently came back to haunt him. It made regular, full-time, employment problematic. However, he remained a proud man and took whatever work he could find. He was not one to go 'cap in hand' to the welfare state. He was now in his longest spell of unbroken work in years – in his fifteenth month as the night security officer at an industrial estate on the border of Deptford and Lewisham in South-East London. It was only a short bus ride from his New Cross home. His rented three rooms, and shared bathroom, was in a terraced house adjacent to the Victorian-built fire station. When unable to work, through ill-health or simply unemployed, he frequently whiled away the odd afternoon watching the firemen at drills in the station's yard.

His was a regular face peering through the iron railings of the station gates in Waller Road. Over time he became known to all three of the New Cross watches, the Red Watch in particular. They often had to remind Ernie that they were not called 'firemen' anymore but 'firefighters'. But to Ernie, seeing women in the fire brigade was a strange state of affairs. Some of the other firefighters thought so too. But the Red Watch had one of them. She had recently been sent to the station. When watching the station drills Ernie couldn't pick her out when they were running about with their ladders or hoses: she was just another firefighter in a uniform. However, at the end of her day shifts, as she walked passed his ground floor flat window, he had decided that she was a very pretty young thing indeed.

While the Red Watch night shift got on with whatever tasks they had to do, Ernie had caught his bus for work and was now preparing for the first of his regular nightly rounds. He liked his job. It was not overly demanding and he was well regarded by the site's managers: their smart elderly uniformed security man with the limp.

The industrial estate, which Ernie was slowly patrolling, was not vast. In fact, it had just three separate buildings. Two were recently erected, both two-storey prefabricated structures. One housed the company's management offices and Ernie's meagre bit of office space. It was the main brick built building that dominated the site. It housed a document and data store although it had not started life as such. Originally built as a gin distillery, in the days when gin was the drink of choice for London's less well to do, it was subsequently converted into a cold store after the owners of the Gin Company went bankrupt. It had lain unoccupied for most of the 1970s before being bought up by the current owners. With relatively little conversion, it now held data records and was used for archive storage.

The building contractors had worked overtime that Sunday, their tools and equipment now secured away in a caged area on the ground floor of the main building. Temporary electrical wiring hung suspended on most of the floors from either ceilings or secured to the walls by plastic ties. It was part of the building's extensive re-wiring programme, which included the installation of a new fire detection system. Looking at the mass of wires everywhere, Ernie wondered how the electricians knew what went where. DIY was never his thing.

Because of the electrical works he was required to do an extra round: the first after reporting for work at 8 p.m, the last two hours before he finished at 8 a.m., and before he checked in the daytime staff who started arriving at 7 a.m. The additional round was scheduled for 1 a.m. He could walk round the whole site in little under the hour. A more agile person could have done it in 40 minutes but the flights of stairs made his injured leg ache. He could have chosen to use the goods lift. It served all the floors in the main building but it had broken down in Ernie's first month on the job. He had spent the whole night trapped in the lift before being released by the day shift the following morning. He had sworn after that:

"I'll never use that bloody thing again."

He hadn't and he had no intention of doing so now. After completing his first inspection Ernie returned to his comfortable, if small, security office, switched on the kettle, picked up his library book and started to read.

Up on the fourth floor, in a secured document store, coils from an extension lead were heating up. In their haste to get away early one of the contractors forgot to switch off the power supply to an arc lamp. This is what the coiled extension lead was feeding. The extension lead drum was acting as a resistor. Fumes were starting to rise as the lead's plastic insulation softened and started to melt.

When used as a Cold Store the main building was subject of a fire certificate under the Factories Act (1961). However, the change of use had the effect of making only the general office on the ground floor subject of the Fire Precautions Act (1971). Because of the few employees who worked full-time in the building, the legislation only required an 'adequate' means of escape and the provision of fire-fighting equipment. These were the ten-litre water extinguishers placed on each floor level, something Ernie checked every six months. The owners had recently decided to install a fire detection system at the same time as the building's extensive re-wiring. The installation had little to do with any pro-active fire safety culture. It was a good marketing ploy and would reduce their hefty annual fire insurance premium.

At about 12.47 a.m. flame finally erupted from the overheated coils of electrical cable. It made contact with an adjacent pile of cardboard document boxes, boxes which contained reams of paper records. Before the circuit breaker tripped the flames were already 25 centimetres high. Now, radiated heat reached the racks of document containers. Some were made of plastic, others plywood and the remainder cardboard. All were flammable and several caught fire. As the smoke rose so did the temperature. Loose paper, a few metres away, spontaneously ignited. A flame front moved rapidly across the floor. It steadily consumed the available oxygen in the secure, enclosed, storeroom.

The construction of the storerooms reflected the building's former use as a cold store. Its insulated ceiling and walls were still covered with timber panelling. Floors were concrete and the flat concrete roof had an asphalt covering. Only the open floor spaces had had its former thick insulation removed. The buildings contents were typical of any data and file store.

The interior storage areas were sub-divided by mesh grills that went from the floor to the ceiling. These areas provided storage space for less sensitive or non-confidential data. More valuable archives, and commercially sensitive documents, were in the secured storerooms. Normal access to all floors, in addition to the goods lift, was via an internal concrete staircase. An external metal fire escape, located on the opposite side of the building, connected to the fire exits and provided access to the lift motor room on the roof.

Other than the few windows on the internal staircase there were no other window openings. The old distillery windows had all been bricked up decades ago and had remained so ever since. Air movement in the building was by forced ventilation and fans. Any windows or doors that may have been left open Ernie had closed during his first round.

UK firefighters sometimes mix up the terms 'backdraft' and 'flashover'. London's firefighters are no different when it comes to detailed knowledge of these uncontrolled fire reactions. Whilst both are dangerous violent events they are different. 'Backdrafts' do not often happen at fires. Only a few firefighters will ever see it; even fewer will actually experience one. A 'flashover', which is a sudden full room/space involvement in flame, happens far more often. Firefighters might see one at their next fire call.

Whilst a 'backdraft' is an explosion, a flashover is not. There are shock waves during a backdraft that have the force to break the confining structure around the explosion. Windows and doors may break, superheated smoke and flame may blast out a doorway or part of a building may even collapse. A 'flashover' is a rapid fire development. It stops short of an explosion's speed of chemical reaction. Oxygen-fuelled air sets off the 'backdraft' explosion. Should a firefighter crew enter a confined smoke-filled fire area and bring fresh air with them, a 'backdraft' explosion might occur. The trigger of a 'flashover' is heat, not air. The science of a 'flashover' is that heat, which is re-radiated back into a burning space from the ceiling and walls, raises the flammable gases and furnishings in the room to the auto-ignition temperature and triggers a flashover.

One of the main differences between a 'backdraft' and 'flashover' is the point in the fire in which they occur. There four stages to a fire: ignition, growth, fully developed, and decay. The first begins when heat, oxygen and a fuel source combine, resulting in fire. This is a small fire which often (and hopefully) goes out before any of the subsequent stages. Finding a fire in this stage provides the best chance of extinguishing it or escaping from it.

The second stage is growth. This is where the building and/or the contents and oxygen are used as fuel for the fire. There are many things which affects this fire growth, such as where the fire started, what combustibles are involved and ceiling heights. Although this is normally the shortest of the four stages, it's when a 'flashover' can occur, potentially injuring or causing fatalities to firefighters.

It is when the growth stage has reached its maximum, and all combustible materials have been ignited, that a fire is considered to be fully developed. This is the hottest phase of a fire and the most dangerous stage for anybody trapped within.

Finally, there is decay. This is usually the longest stage of a fire. There is a significant decrease in oxygen reaching the fire due to the actions of firefighters, lack of fuel, or both putting an end to the fire. Common dangers here are the existence of non-flaming combustibles. This can potentially start a new fire if not fully extinguished. There is also the danger of a backdraft as oxygen is reintroduced to a volatile confined space. A 'backdraft' explosion occurs when there is smoke in a confined fire space and which generates flammable carbon monoxide gas which is explosive (in the proper mixtures with air or oxygen). This gas is also deadly at concentrations far below the levels at which it is explosive. A 'flashover', on the other hand, only occurs in the growth (second) stage of a fire.

This firefighting science was totally alien to Ernie as he started his second round of the night. He had never heard of a backdraft or a flashover. His preferred reading always took him to the fiction shelves in the New Cross lending library. It was at the subsequent inquest, where evidence presented, confirmed that Ernie had checked both the outer buildings prior to entering the main building. He had 'punched-in' at the ground floor security point at 1.12 a.m. when starting his sweeps of the various floors. He took his time. He was in no hurry.

As he reached the top of the stairs and access to the fourth floor he got a whiff of smoke. There was nothing he could see but it was a large space, a mixture of storerooms and caged racking. Turning on the light switches did not have the desired effect. Only a few random ceiling lights came on. "Bloody electricians," thought Ernie, as he turned his torch on. Its bright beam cut through the darkened floor space and the whiff of smoke became a definite smell. As he negotiated the maze of mesh cages, and on the far side of the floor, he saw smoke in the torch's beam. Ernie went to check the storerooms. Starting at the furthest point he was working his way back towards the staircase.

When he reached the third storeroom he saw smoke seeping under the hinged metal double doors. Normally each secure storeroom had a soft metal, unique, seal passing through the eye-holes of the door bolt. The doors could not open without breaking a date stamped seal. Checking the integrity of each door seal was high on Ernie's must-do list during his nightly rounds. However, the contactors' requirement for easy access had seen self-locking plastic ties used at the end of their working day. However, whenever a secured storeroom was opened it triggered a warning light and sounded a buzzer on the security indicator board in the site's main office.

Despite his outstanding war record Ernie did not consider himself a brave man. In fact he erred on the cautious side these days. So before opening the doors he had returned to the floor's fire point, grabbed a water extinguisher and smashed the glass covering the fire alarm call point with his torch. The evacuation bell filled the building with its warning clamour, even if there was no one to evacuate. However, Ernie knew the alarm automatically transferred to the alarm company's control centre somewhere in north London.

As he returned to the storeroom, smoke continued to creep beneath the doors. He cut the plastic tie with his pocket-knife and released one of the two thick door bolts. He wished he could have bent down low to the floor. He had seen the firemen do that at their drills at the fire station but Ernie's knee would not give. So, with his fire extinguisher at the ready, he nervously prepared to open one of the two storeroom's solid doors. On the other side of the door the fire had consumed almost all the available oxygen. It laid dormant, waiting. Left undisturbed, it may well have just have smouldered prior to going out completely.

The last sensation Ernie ever felt was the inrush of air on the back of his neck. Air surged in towards the smouldering mass that filled the enclosed space. It is highly unlikely that Ernie's brain had time to register the violent force of the explosion. The energy released by the 'backdraft' threw Ernie like a rag doll. It smashed him into a supporting pillar some three metres away. As his unconscious body slumped to the floor his bare skin was already horribly scorched. Flames from the storeroom rushed out, seeking new fuel.

The actual speed with which the fire progressed from within the storeroom is uncertain. The fact that the fire extended from its point of origin into the fourth floor is undeniable.

The lady at the fire alarm control centre in Tottenham was required to follow certain protocols. At premises without any on-site security arrangements all alarm calls were directed straight to the fire brigade. Where a security presence was in place the fire alarm control room rang the premises first to verify it was a genuine alarm. She pushed the speed dial which connected her to Ernie's security office. She gave it a couple of minutes before finally putting the call through to the fire brigade

Back in the day, when the building had been a cold store, the Fire Brigade's 'special' attendance had been entered on the mobilising card index system. According to the card, the address given to the Brigade indicated that it was still a cold store. The card system detailed what fire engines to send in response to 999 calls. The control officers followed their normal mobilising procedures, unaware of the building's change of use. When the card was first made out Lambeth had been the only control room for the whole of the London County Council (LCC) fire brigade area. When a 999 call was received the control officer would refer to the relevant index card. Each card, which covered every known street/road in the LCC area, listed the home station, the nearest six stations, plus the nearest special appliances, such as a turntable ladder or a foam tender. But Lambeth's fire control room had long since closed, its functions transferred to the three remaining Greater London Council (GLC) fire control rooms. There was one at Croydon, Stratford and Wembley. Croydon covered all of Greater London south of the Thames.

Although the card index system was meant to be kept up to date, there were literally thousands of card index cards and some slipped through the net. So whilst each card now reflected GLC fire stations, the attendance listed on the card related to the building's former use. All cold stores required a 'special' attendance. So as the control officer read off the attendance printed on the card she looked at the incident disposition board that dominated the control room. It told her which fire engines were available.

The special attendance required two pump-ladders, two pumps, plus an emergency tender on all fire calls. The address showed it to be on Lewisham fire station's ground. In normal circumstances the engines from Lewisham and Deptford fire stations would have been sent, but Deptford's pump was already attending another call. Lewisham's ET had been sent on relief to the major fire in Croydon. So it was Deptford's pump-ladder, with a temporary Leading Firefighter in charge, Lewisham's pump-ladder and pump, with a Sub Officer in charge and New Cross's pump with its Station Officer in charge who were ordered. The nearest emergency tender was East Ham, so Croydon Control had to request Stratford Control to order the emergency tender.

Station Officer Simon Reece was third-generation London Fire Brigade. He joined when his dad was still serving. They had even attended fires together although from different stations. But the pair had never seen eye to eye. Simon's grandfather had remained a London fireman; his dad had made it to Leading Fireman, with Simon running his own watch. Simon was now the senior Station Officer in the Division having held his current rank for ten years. He was well respected and much liked, not only by his own Red watch but his by peers and superiors alike. The words that rank and file used to sum him up were firm, fair and extremely competent. Of average height and average build, he was anything but average when it came to running his watch or on the fire-ground. He had been the

Divisional Commander's natural choice for taking the first female firefighter at New Cross.

Lauren Simpson was New Cross's female firefighter. She had just completed her first six months' probation. She was riding the pump as it pulled out of the station and turned left into the New Cross one-way system in Queens Road before turning right into Kender Street and towards Lewisham.

Lewisham's two fire engines just beat Deptford's pump-ladder to the site's gated entrance. All three booked in attendance via Lewisham's pump. As Simon Reece turned into the roadway Lewisham's Sub Officer had already given instructions for the padlocked chain securing the gates to be cut off after his shouts to "Open up" had gone unheeded. As the gates where pushed back Reece had an uneasy feeling. He knew Ernie worked here. The old chap would never have been far from the entrance unless there was something wrong. On the other hand, Reece and the other crews could see no obvious cause for concern. There was no evidence of a fire from the street, yet the fire alarm indicated something very different.

Ernie was not at his post, which was odd! Reece knew there had to be a reason. The four fire engines drove into the site. Lights from the security office attracted their attention and the fire alarm ringing in the distance heightened their concerns.

Reece was not a man who took situations at face value. The alarm was ringing for a reason. Maybe Ernie had had a fall and it was his way of summoning help? The fact that no smoke or flames were showing did not mean there was no fire. So Reece instructed the crews to set into the nearest street hydrant and to charge the dry rising main in the main building, the only building covered by the fire alarm. He instructed Lewisham's Sub Officer to investigate the main building with his PL crew and Deptford's crew. Reece, meanwhile, walked into the security office. He noted Ernie's empty tea cup and an open book on the old man's chair. As he muted the fire alarm he saw that the call point had been actuated on the fourth floor. Hearing another buzzer sounding he walked into the adjoining office and found the security panel. It indicated a storeroom had been opened on the same floor. Maybe it's a robbery, mused Reece. Did old Ernie go to investigate and was attacked?

Reece informed the Sub Officer, via his hand-held radio, what he had discovered and instructed him to start his searches on the top floor. He added that he would have a look around the main building's perimeter. Reece took George, his senior hand, and young Simpson with him. George was very much old school. He was not keen on the new ways of the LFB, especially women coming into the job. He was looking forward to the middle of next year when his 26½ years' service were up. He knew it was time to cash in on his damaged knee. Something he had cleverly disguised and knew he could use to retire early with an injury pension.

Reece was at the rear of the building when the Sub Officer informed him that light smoke had been encountered on the staircase at third floor level. He told Reece that they had made a quick recce of that floor and found nothing, including Ernie!

"So whatever is happening Guv, it must be on the next floor."

Reece sent an informative message to Croydon Control saying smoke had been found and that crews were investigating.

Lewisham's Sub Officer was an experienced officer. He had over 15 years serving in London's 'busy' A Division before transferring out into the 'sticks,' as he liked to call Lewisham. The transfer had cut down his travelling time from his Folkestone home. He made sure those with him were properly equipped before entering the building, even though the two crews didn't need any reminding of what to take when investigating a suspected building fire. Except for himself and one other, all the remainder wore their compressed air breathing apparatus sets (BA). Some carried hose, others lines, branches and some breaking-in gear.

Whilst on the third floor the Sub Officer, and the others, had a quick look around. They were keen to learn the possible layout of the floor above. But there was no knowing if the various floors mirrored each other! But after 20 paces into the floor space what they discovered told them that if the floor above was anything like this one then finding the fire, and fighting it, was going to be a real 'bastard'. With the lights turned on, and clear signage, they navigated their way around the floor with relative ease. However, in darkness, in smoke, in heat, it would be like navigating a maze. A maze placed inside an oven whilst they were blindfolded.

As Reece made his way back to the main entrance he was pleased to see that his pump driver had set in two lines of hose to the street hydrant and twin lines of 70mm hose snaked their way to the dry riser inlet box. Above him, up on the third floor landing, the Sub Officer had detailed Deptford's crew of four to start up their BA sets. They were tasked to take a hose line to the floor above and seek out the fire. A team of two from Lewisham would back them up. Three lengths of hose had been connected together and plugged into the rising main. As the pressurised water filled the hose it twisted and turned in the enclosed space. It formed tight coils on the landing and the stairs, quickly filling the staircase leading up to the next floor. Deptford's Leading Firefighter led his crew as they lifted and dragged the hose line to the fourth floor. As they reached the half-landing before the final 'dog-leg' flight leading up to the top floor, Lewisham's crew picked up the hose and waited for Deptford's crew to move forward. All their BA tallies had been handed to the firefighter nominated as the BA control officer. He recorded their time in, but more importantly wrote down, and would monitor, the two crews' calculated time out.

The two outer doors, at the head of the stairs, were cool to the touch. There was a gap between the inner and outer doors. The space between was full of smoke. As Deptford's crew discovered, the inner doors were warm to the touch. Lugging the hose they moved into the 'fire' floor, their hose preventing both sets of doors closing shut again. Thick smoke now filled the head of the staircase. The Sub Officer needed to have a quick look so, without BA, he did. As willing hands lighten the weight of the hose the Sub crawled up the staircase as the acrid smoke came down. Immediately his eyes started streaming and he was coughing by the time he reached the top floor. The last of Deptford's crew was half a dozen paces in front of him yet all he could see was the outline of a pair of fire-boots. The heat forced him down to the floor. He shouted to Deptford's Leading Firefighter:

"Can you see anything yet?"

A garbled reply came back, spoken through the BA set's full facemask.

"Nothing yet. But it's bloody hot in here!"

The Sub Officer could not maintain his position any longer: he had to retreat. Coming down the staircase, he told the pair from Lewisham to open the windows at the head of the staircase. It was impossible for him to stand as he told them to tell Deptford's crew that the BA entry control point was going to be moved to the ground floor entrance.

With the upper windows opened smoke billowed out into the night. The force with which it exited told its own story to those that knew what to look for. Deptford's crew were crawling in almost flat on their bellies. They were about five body lengths in front of Lewisham's pair. What few electric lights that were on made no difference to the visibility. It was, for old-timers, like crawling through a thick London smog of the 1950s; not that any of those on the fourth floor had been born then. The firefighters who were trying to locate the fire where only in their early to late twenties.

Reece was trotting up the main staircase as a spluttering Sub Officer came down. The tears flowing down his blackened face had cut a path on his smoke-stained cheeks.

"Whatever it is Guv, it's bloody hot and it will be difficult to find."

"OK," said Reece, as he spoke into his radio calling up his pump driver. He instructed his driver to send a priority message, making pumps eight, breathing apparatus required. With no sign of the missing Ernie he also told his driver to add "Persons Reported" to his message.

On the fourth floor the two BA teams were encountering great difficulty in moving forward, particularly Deptford. The intensity of the heat and thick smoke tested both their skills and endurance. Progress was painfully slow. Simple snags and obstacles demanded considerable exertion. The spaces between storage cages and the storerooms confused their ability to orientate themselves. Their saving grace was the single line of hose which marked their progress in and, more importantly, their route back to the exit. Whilst they had not found any fire they were being constantly punished by its effects. They saw nothing through the dense smoke. There was no trace of a flame.

They had managed to crawl another metre forward when the skin on their exposed ears started to blister. One was feeling the onset of heat stress, only he didn't realise what it was. The Leading Fire-fighter reluctantly had to turn about and the crew started to make their retreat, leaving the hose line in position. Their smoke-stained helmets no longer yellow, evidence of the extreme conditions that they had endured. Even their BA facemasks were transformed by a coating of carbonised smoke. Others would have to continue where they had left off.

As the exhausted BA teams started to make their exit, Reece knew where he had to be. Standing on the third floor landing, with the smoke forcing its way down to meet him, was not the place to be. His eyes were smarting as he made his way to the front of the building ready to direct the reinforcing crews. He had a plan; now he needed the extra crews to implement it.

Bleary sets of eyes read the teleprinter call slip to the eight pump fire as crews mounted their machines. One particular crew had only returned 45 minutes before from their three-hour relief stint at the Croydon blaze. Blue flashing lights and bright headlamps cleared what little traffic there was on the road that time of night. Powerful diesel engines had the fire engines travelling in excess of sixty miles an hour as they converged on the scene of the South London fire. Adrenalin started to course its way through the reinforcing firefighter's veins, heightening both their senses and the anticipation for what lay ahead of them.

A request for eight 'pumps' delivers more than just eight fire engines. Special appliances, emergency tenders, a hose-laying lorry, and breathing apparatus control vehicle (BACV) and the Brigade's major control unit (from the Lambeth headquarters) are automatically sent on. Certain senior fire officers are ordered, others are notified. Some have a specialist function; one of them must take command. Who Reece might hand over to, he had no idea. At this moment in time he did not even care. He was in command, something he maintained until formally relieved of it.

He checked on the exhausted BA crews as they exited. One individual looked the worse for wear. In fact he was almost collapsing. Before getting a briefing from the Leading Firefighter he told the young BA firefighter: "Go and sit by Lewisham's pump."

He detailed another firefighter to assist the distressed firefighter out of his BA set:

"Sit him down, remove his tunic and cool him down with some water. As soon as the ambulance arrives get the crew to check him over. If he gets worse, tell me immediately. Understand?"

Then, turning back the BA team, he listened intently to their report before saying:

"Well done lads. Get your cylinders changed and be ready to recommit. This is going to get worse before it gets any better."

Time seemed to stand still as Reece waited impatiently for the reinforcements to arrive. But it didn't, of course, and certainly not where the fire was concerned. It was consolidating its hold. Deptford's pump and his own pump-ladder were the first 'make-up' crews to arrive. Crews that Reece not only knew but trusted. They were quickly followed by the BA Control vehicle from the Lewisham Divisional headquarters, crewed by its two junior officers: a Sub Officer and a Leading Firefighter.

Reece's plan was to seek out and attack the fire on two fronts. Crews would be committed via the main staircase and the rear fire exit. East Ham's emergency tender crew were detailed to pick-up from where Deptford's crew had left off. With instructions to add an additional length to their hose line, Reece wanted them to have greater range on the fire floor. Deptford's pump crew, wearing BA, were to back up the ET crew and provide a covering jet for them. New Cross's crews were instructed to make a forced entry into the fourth floor and get a hose line to work from the fire escape. They were then to commit a BA team to search for and attack the fire. Reece's Sub Officer covered the rear of the building. There was no discussion; they all knew what to do and what was expected of them. Reece realised that there was little hope of finding Ernie alive if he had been on the upper floor. Nevertheless, he reminded them that Ernie was still unaccounted for.

There was a controlled sense of urgency as the firefighters went about their allotted tasks. Some did not need telling. The two staff officers, manning Lewisham's BACV, certainly didn't. They were already going about their tasks. One was setting the vehicle up as the control point whilst the leading firefighter collected the nominal roll boards from each of the fire engines. Others would be brought to them until the major control unit arrived and took over but until then the BACV crew had its work cut out.

BA control procedures had been brought about because firemen had died, both in London and around the country when, once, firemen did not have to check in before entering a building in BA.

197

London had led the way in getting better, safer, controls put in place in the late 1950s. They were vital to BA safety. Reece now ensured that they were being put in place. With a Stage One control point required for the fire escape, and a Stage Two (that required a BA emergency crew to stand by) for the main entrance, his bases were initially covered. But he knew things might change unexpectedly.

Considering the dire conditions, East Ham's ET crew made remarkable progress. They had reached the jet at the end of the hose line, the one Deptford left on the top floor. The Sub Officer, leading his crew, opened the branch to reassure himself that the hose line was charged. Deptford's pump crew hadn't been slouches either. They had brought up a second line of hose and were about 6 metres behind East Ham.

On the opposite side of the building, firefighters, wielding a combination of large axes, crow bars and a sledge hammer, were making a concerted effort to destroy the hinges to the fire exit doors. The secured fire exit was designed to let people out, not let them in. Without any external door handles or a door lock to break open the only alternative was to take the doors off their hinges. After four minutes one pair of hinges gave way, soon followed by the other. Hot thick smoke poured over the heads of the firefighters. They had to stoop low on the fire escape and, for the first time, flames were seen. Reece was informed that they had gained entry and they found the fire.

Greenwich's two fire engines were the last of the eight pumps to arrive. Reece dispatched them to the fire escape with instructions to get another jet to work and to put a BA crew of four into the building and attack the fire. Reece was concerned about his water supplies as he had now four jets at work. He instructed the staff Sub Officer to contact the hose-laying lorry crew, by radio, telling them to set into a large capacity water main when it arrived and relay water to the site. Finally, Reece sent an informative message sent back to Control saying what they had and what they were doing about it.

The duty Divisional Officer was passing Lewisham fire station when he intercepted the informative message. He had been sent to take command.

With two jets at both entry points Reece thought that, with luck, the crews might hold this fire. However, his experience told him to remember the adage of 'Murphy's Law', which typically states: *Anything that can go wrong, will go wrong*. He was also mindful that unless swift progress was made it would need more than eight fire engine to put it out. It was then that Murphy's Law came into play!

Fires follow physical laws regardless of whatever Murphy might have to say about it. The ignition temperature is the temperature at which something catches fire and burns on its own. The ignition temperature of paper is 233° Celsius, or 451° Fahrenheit if you speak in 'old money'. The temperatures had risen to such a level in the burning storeroom and the immediate vicinity. A flame front spontaneously ignited; its range included where East Ham's Sub Officer was crawling along the floor. He saw it coming towards him even through the thick smoke. He did not have time to turn and run, neither did the firefighter immediately behind him. Those on the fire escape were more fortunate; the flames did not reach them.

Deptford's Station Officer was leading his BA crew. His reaction was instinctive as he directed his covering jet to protect East Ham's ET crew now only a couple of metres in front of him. When he heard the sound of a distress signal unit being sounded his next action was calculated, but one that broke normal BA rules. He sent one of his men out alone to report what had happened, before he and the two remaining firefighters moved forward to assist and protect their colleagues.

The Sub Officer lay, unmoving, on the floor. One of the ET crew had turned the jet onto spray and it provided a limited protective water curtain. Deptford's jet was aimed at where the flames had come from. Survival reflex had kicked in with East Ham's ET crew as they tugged and pulled their Sub Officer back towards the exit. The other firefighter was in obvious distress, but his self-preservation instincts overcame his acute pain from his burns.

Immediately upon receiving the report from the lone BA firefighter Reece had made pumps 15. The emergency BA crew of two simultaneously started up their sets. They did not wait for their tallies to be filled-in before running up the stairs together with Deptford's firefighter to see what needed to be done. Reece had confirmation that no one was injured at the head of the fire escape and was informed that both jets were being directed at the fire.

The sound of the urgent shuffling down the staircase told its own story. With little grace, but great care, the Sub Officer was being carried, whilst the man who was directly behind him was being assisted down. The Sub's neck and ears and wrists were badly burnt. His skin was already sticky and peeling where the flames had scorched into his flesh.

The duty Divisional Officer had arrived and parked in the street. He was the only senior officer to have arrived by this point. It was as he was putting on his fire gear he heard Reece's priority message over his car radio. He knew his command would be short-lived as an Assistant Chief Officer was required to take charge of a fire this size. Unfazed, he booked in with the BA Control vehicle and walked over to Reece. As he did so the major control unit arrived. It would take its crew a few minutes to get set up in preparation of taking over.

Reece gave the senior officer, a man he knew and respected, a concise brief, including details of the injuries to the Sub Officer and the firefighter from East Ham. The Sub Officer was unconscious. He had suffered serious burns, and was now in an ambulance en route to Greenwich Hospital. The other firefighter was being given first aid for his burns and waiting for a second ambulance. The Divisional Officer assumed command and told Reece he was sticking to Reece's plan of attack. Since no other senior officers had arrived Reece was ordered onto the fire escape to take over there until relieved.

More pumps arrived. Water supplies were supplemented via the hose-laying lorry. A second stage two BA control point was set up at the fire escape and main BA control procedure was implemented. Hose lines were increased and firefighters, in BA, pushed slowly and cautiously into the building to attack the fire at close quarters. The era of former London 'firemen' having to endure vile smoke and noxious fumes at fires was long behind them: hazards which had exposed many to risks, and which in time would, and did, take its toll on their health. Cancers and other respiratory disease featured all too often on the death certificates of these once brave 'smoke-eating' London firemen.

Reece was subsequently relieved of his duty by an Assistant Divisional Officer, someone he didn't know. Reece was now just another white-helmeted Station Officer among many white helmets in attendance. He had gathered up his pumps crew and together they donned their BA sets and waited by the control unit for deployment. They did not have to wait long as long tongues of yellow and red flames reached up into the night sky. The wired glazing on the rooftop lantern light finally succumbed to the intense heat. Reece was ordered onto the fire escape and told to relieve Old Kent Road's crew working inside on a jet.

Assistant Chief Officer Bill Watts was London Fire Brigade old school. He would have been called a 'smoke-eater' once by firemen. He was only months away from his 60th birthday and the mandatory retirement age required of all senior and principal fire officers. He had intended retiring much earlier, moving West to his beloved Devon. However, the sudden, unexpected, death of his wife, Doris, had caused a change of plan. He had stayed with the family he knew, the Brigade.

Bill had always intended to join the fire brigade, then World War II got in the way. Entering the Royal Marines in 1941, at 18 years old, his talents were quickly recognised and he spent much of the conflict serving in the Royal Marines (RM) Special Service Brigade, its elite fighting group. By the time he walked into the Lambeth LFB's Headquarters at the end of 1948 and seeking a job as a fireman, the two senior officers conducting his interview first asked him to confirm he had left the RM with the rank of a sergeant? Next they congratulated him on being awarded the CGM (Conspicuous Gallantry Medal) for gallantry in the field. His interview was over. He got the job.

By 1958 he had been promoted to Station Officer serving, in the former 'B' Division, at Clerkenwell fire station. Simon Reece's dad had been one of his firemen and were close friends outside of work hours. Later Fireman Reece (Snr) transferred south of the Thames. It was Bill Watts, now in senior rank, who broke the news to the young Fireman Reece that his dad had suffered a fatal heart attack whilst on duty.

Bill's station management mantra was: *The southpaw is mightier than the sword*. The odd problem with a mouthy or workshy members of his watch was resolved behind closed doors and down in the stations' basement. After a few months Station Officer Watts ran a trouble-free 'ship'. His twenty-year Long Service and Good Medal was awarded a year late. It added red and yellow to the impressive array of colours on his Assistant Divisional Officers' uniform medal ribbon, which also included the silver laurel leaf of the King's Commendation for brave conduct that had been awarded for his rescue of a colleague at a warehouse fire in West London when he was Sub Officer at Fulham.

Chief Officer Joe Milner had arrived in 1970. Joe observed Bill Watts in action at a major fire. After that Bill became Joe's staff officer at Brigade Headquarters, and given their military backgrounds, the pair became firm friends. When Joe left under a bit of cloud in 1976 Bill was in charge of his own Division. "Somewhere in the suburbs," he described it. Despite his increasing years his razor-sharp intellect, his wit, humanity and integrity combined with his operational experience and skill placed him at the top of his principal officers' tree. It was no surprise that in 1978 that he was elevated to become the Brigade's Third Officer and the Assistant Chief Officer Operations. He was the firefighters' officer. He knew their job inside out and was good, very good, at doing his. He was a man who fitted his role perfectly, a round peg in a round hole. As he was driven, at speed, through the streets of South London in the early hours of Monday morning he knew this is what he did best: fighting fires and commanding those who fought them.

Bill booked in at the control unit, letting his senses tell him how well the fire was being overseen. He took particular note of how the main BA control board was being handled. He spoke briefly to the Divisional Officer in command, and received an update of the situation. He formally took command and, as was his way, went 'walkabout', a walk around the fire-ground to see if what he had been told matched the reality of the situation. He had a powerful, youthful, stride for a man of his years as he made a circuit of the building and studied the fire-ground. He absorbed all he saw and that he heard. He spoke to the crews in encouraging terms and listened to an exiting BA crew's assessment of the arduous conditions inside. He was a believer in the value of intelligence from those at the 'coal face'. He arrived at his decision and made pumps 25. This was a major BA fire and he was not sure that the right level of organised relief crews, equipment and supplies were in place. But most important of all was that he had sufficient back-up if emergency measures had to be implemented.

Reece and his pump's crew were one of many BA crews, along with six jets, at work inside the fourth floor. Reece had been tasked to continue the attack on fires which had spread into the secured storerooms. They had found, and relieved, a crew working with a jet. They had managed to get through store-room doors but had not penetrated very far into the storage area.

Conditions in the enclosed space were hot, very hot. Humidity added to their problems as water from their jet turned to steam. It made for extremely punishing work. They struggled in the poor visibility as the smoke hugged the floor – this despite it venting from the fire floor via the open fire escape and the windowless rooftop lift motor room. These conditions, together with the arduous nature of their task, shortened the working duration of their BA sets.

Reece led his crew, his driver behind him, Simpson next and old George bringing up the rear. Each constantly checked their pressure gauges. Their air was limited. Before very long they too would be relieved or would have to exit. Already the driver's cylinder contents were lower than his companions.

The layout of the secure storeroom meant movement, and therefore progress was difficult. The team had to negotiate narrow spaces between stacked containers. A glow had been seen towards the rear and their jet was dragged into a position from where it might actually hit the flames if they were lucky. The exertion had taken its toll, the falling contents of the driver's BA set setting off his low cylinder warning whistle. The crew had no choice but to leave. With their jet left in situ as Reece led his team back towards the exit and the fire escape.

Unattached wires had already caused problems for others. The mass of rewiring cables, free of the plastic binding which had secured it, hung down in large, loose loops. George's 'dodgy' knee was giving him real gip. He was still bringing up the rear as they crawled back out. Suddenly he stopped moving forward. He could not understand why. It was as though someone was holding him back. As he turned to investigate the cause a bad situation got even worse! He found himself suspended in a spaghetti of wires. The more he tried to free himself, the more entangled he became. He could no longer see the soles of Simpson's fireboots through the smoke. The old firefighter was becoming increasingly worried. In fact, he was plain scared.

As Simpson crossed the threshold of the storeroom door she realised George was not behind her. She called out. Nothing! Not from him or those in front of her. In the time it had taken her to turn around and peer into the murk the two in front were out of sight. The sound of the pump driver's warning whistle indicated his need for a swift exit.

As George would have said had it been someone else: "That fella is in a bit of pickle." But he was on the verge of panic. "Stay calm, George," he said to himself, but it was not easy as he could not move his arms. They were pinned to his sides by the tangle of wires. As much as he tried, he could not lift an arm to sound his distress warning unit. But Simpson could and this is what she did as she reached George. That was then the 'shite' hit the fan. Controlled pandemonium broke out.

Not everyone working on the upper floor could hear the distress unit sounding. Those on the far side of the building certainly didn't, but Reece did. He had almost reached the fire exit door and realised, to his horror, that two of his crew were missing. He could only guess who had sounded the distress unit. But he did not believe in coincidences. His first thought was that the inexperienced Simpson had got herself into difficulty and George had summoned assistance. Reece ordered his driver out with instructions to tell the BA Control Officer where help was most likely needed, then turned around and headed back to the storeroom. As he did so his own low cylinder pressure whistle started to sound.

As New Cross's driver gave details to the BA Control Officer, the emergency BA team, who had seen the lone BA firefighter running down the fire escape, had already started up their sets. Above Simpson had felt, rather than seen, what the problem was. She reached into her fire tunic pocket and removed the black-handled 'Jack-knife' – the same type of knife that Boy Scouts would have once hung on their trouser belt. She opened it up. She had bought the knife after George had told her that any 'fireman' worth his salt always carried a good knife. It had been the only bit of advice that George had ever offered the new female firefighter, although he would never have let her get in harm's way.

As well as Reece, other BA teams, who heard the distress signal unit sounding, stopped what they doing and responded to the urgent summons for assistance. It was easier said than done. Whilst Reece knew where to look, the others didn't. The sound played strange tricks. Not everyone was heading in the right direction. For a while confusion reigned supreme.

Bill Watts, on hearing news of a BA firefighter in difficulty, had immediately gone to the BA control officer and then to the head of the fire escape. He stooped low but couldn't see further than a metre or two into the building. He heard both the sound of the distress call and the clamour of activity of those trying to find its source. Reece had already succeeded in reaching the pair. George's low warning whistle now added to the cacophony emanating from the trio on the storeroom floor.

Simpson's sharp knife made short work of the array of wires holding George captive. Others had come to George's aid now. For a while mayhem ruled. It was a battle between 'many hands make light work' and 'too many cooks spoiling the broth'. Finally, with George freed and on the move – his whistle forming a duet with his distress unit's wail – the three were guided back to the exit and fresh air.

Assistant Chief Officer Watts was relieved to see the trio making their way down the fire escape under their own steam. However, it was a brief diversion as he fought, and succeeded, in bringing order back to the attack on the fire. It would be other firefighters who finally extinguished it, but not before the fire had put up a difficult fight. Some 15 hours later the charred, and unrecognisable, remains of Ernie were discovered and removed. No one knew who it actually was. It was just assumed to be Ernie as he was the only one unaccounted for. It would be dental records and the stainless-steel screws in his leg that confirmed it to be the former war veteran.

Ernie was cremated, what little was left of him. New Cross's Red Watch provided both the Guard of Honour and the pallbearers who carried the old man's coffin. George and Lauren Simpson had both volunteered as pallbearers. Three weeks after the fire they gathered at the Hither Green Crematorium. The on-duty watch stood on the fire station forecourt, in their fire gear, as a solitary hearse drove slowly passed before hurrying on its way to Hither Green.

George and Lauren stood face to face, across the coffin, as they prepared to lift and carry Ernie feet first into the tiny side chapel. The Union Flag-draped coffin bore Ernie's campaign medals. George choose then to whisper to Lauren:

"You're alright, Simpson. You'll do."

It was the first time George had spoken to her since he had thanked her for saving his life. As they carried Ernie's remains past the standard bearers of his old regiment and the local British Legion Branch, Lauren felt the tears well up for the old man. But she also wore the faintest hint of a satisfied smile as she absorbed George's few whispered words.

(Fiction)

Just Another Call

By Garry Warren

I JOINED THE FIRE BRIGADE in 1984, almost, fresh from school. I say 'almost' as after my A-levels, and before starting in the Brigade, I worked briefly for Tesco in their distribution warehouse. But after my recruit course at Southwark training school I was posted to Shadwell Fire Station. It's deep in the heart of London's East End and only a stone's throw from where some of my family still live today. I've very fond memories of my five years at Shadwell, many stories yet to be told. However, Shadwell only had one fire engine. With just one appliance I felt I was missing out. I hankered for the experience of serving on a two-appliance or multi-appliance station. A visiting senior officer asked me, as the youngest and newest member of the Watch, what I thought of the job. Wanting to impress him with my enthusiasm I told him I loved it but wished we were a bit busier. (I think Shadwell were attending about 1200 calls a year at the time.) He frowned, looked at me sternly and said:

"Just remember, whenever you go through those doors, as exciting as you may find it, someone else is in trouble and is suffering."

I've never forgotten those words and they are probably the wisest thing any senior officer has ever said to me! However, undeterred, I pressed on with my request for a transfer. It was granted in 1989. I then took up my posting to the Red Watch at Homerton.

Homerton was one of three fire stations in the London Borough of Hackney. My impression of the area were similar to that of Shadwell, one of poverty and degradation. Unlike Shadwell, however, which was beginning to regenerate with the development of the riverside wharves and warehouses into luxury apartments, Hackney was still a long way off the process of gentrification, although that would happen in parts of the borough in later years. In 1989 there were still inner city estates here that were like ghettos, which, combined with no-go areas for the local police, made the atmosphere feel threatening and intimidating.

Homerton's Red Watch were great, a mixture of old and new hands. It contained years of experience to observe and to learn from. I was interviewed by the Station Commander, Liam Hackett, on my arrival.

"Keep your head down," he said. "Listen and watch what's going on and you'll learn fast; mess about and you'll be out on your ear."

Whilst part of me was a little put out at being spoken to like a raw recruit – I'd had served five years, after all – another part of me knew he was right. This was a far busier station and mistakes would not be tolerated. So with this in mind I settled in, listening, watching and learning. A few weeks after my arrival I was sent out on a night shift to another fire station. It's termed an 'out duty' and I was off to East Ham as they were short of firefighters. When I arrived I was detailed to ride the back of the pump-ladder. I jumped up on the back of the appliance to test my compressed air breathing apparatus set. This is where I met my fellow crew members for the shift. One, who was to be in the breathing apparatus crew with me, was a tall guy who introduced himself as Pav. The other firefighter on the back, a bloke, just nodded. Both looked very young. But the events of that night would ensure Pav and I remained friends for life.

"Just out of interest," I said, "how long have you two got in the job?"

Pav smiled. "A year for me and he's still on probation, got less than six months in."

This explained why I had been nominated as a BA wearer. Normally, the station's own personnel covered those positions and the stand-by ends up as BA control officer or some other task. Pav must have seen the look on my face.

"Yes mate, you're the man tonight!"

It was quite surreal. I had gone from being treated as the 'junior buck' at my own station to being the most experienced hand at the station. Fortunately, the Sub Officer who was in charge of us was a man with lots of experience. He was a large man, firm but friendly. Called Vic, he exuded confidence and that went a long way to making me feel better.

The evening went on as expected – routine tasks around the station, one or two minor calls – while we all looked forward to the evening meal. Food on fire stations was always good and I enjoyed the atmosphere around the mess table. The banter and jokes: no matter what fire station you went to, it was the same and I loved it. The strange thing about East Ham was there appeared to be two messes, one for the pump-ladder crew and another for the emergency tender (ET) crew. The ET guys were far more experienced, more highly trained and they liked you to know it! I didn't really care, I just wanted my dinner.

The '999' call came in as every emergency call did. London's fire stations still had proper call bells then. They were loud and obtrusive; the noise they made jolted you into action. It immediately pushed up your heart-rate, causing adrenalin to pump around your system. The station lights would come on automatically and illuminated your path to the appliance bay at night. If the call was a false alarm then the adrenalin would take hours to ebb away before allowing you to relax. This time it wasn't a false alarm. This time it was a call to a house fire. It's difficult to explain, but sometimes you just got a feeling about certain jobs, even before you arrived. This was one of those 'shouts'.

Somehow – call it a feeling in your 'water' – I knew it was going to be a serious fire, or a 'good working job' as my older colleagues would say. My memory is a little hazy on precise details but I remember it as an end of terrace house. It was typical of many built in Plaistow and East Ham. It was well alight, in fact 'going like a train'! As we pulled up, Pav and I pulled on our BA sets. We were about to dismount when I heard someone shout that two babies were inside.

"Get a fucking move on."

I grabbed my fire helmet, jumped down and started up my breathing apparatus set. You may have seen fire dramas portrayed on television and in action films. The action follows your hero, or heroine, into the burning building where, conveniently, the flame only burns around the edges and smoke vents through an imaginary chimney. You get to see every detail of what's going on. But in real life it just isn't like that. Fires give off smoke. Burning furniture gives off thick, black, horrible, impenetrable, sticky smoke. It is full of stuff guaranteed to spoil your day; a lungful of this stuff will ensure you don't wake up again. Add to that heat: 800 degrees in a house fire isn't unusual, with a 1,000 degrees possible at ceiling level. Everything sweats. The carpet sweats, the walls sweat and most of all you sweat.

Black smoke deposits sticky soot on your BA set face visor, making it difficult to see. Your torch light reflects back off the smoke, rather like car headlights in the fog. The layer of heat pushes you down, so most of the time you are crawling along on your stomach. A firefighter has to overcome the compulsion to run away and push themselves into this horrendous atmosphere, to rely on their training, knowledge, equipment and wits to survive.

Pav and I entered the house through the front door. The fire was on the first floor in a back bedroom. Heat and smoke were coming down the stairs. We climbed the staircase, me in front and Pav backing me up, both of us taking the strain of pulling the hose-reel up the stairs as we went. The heat pushed us down. We were on our stomachs as we crawled to the top. The staircase led us to a small landing and then down a few steps into another corridor. To reach the fire we had to turn left at this narrow landing and get down the other side. Visibility was now virtually non-existent! Only by laying my head on the floor, and peering around the corner, could I see the room on fire along the hallway. As we tried to push on along the landing the heat levels were become worse. Then, as we saw flame in the smoke, I opened the hose reel to protect us. Immediately I felt searing pain in my left hand. With my senses already at full stretch, I experienced a momentary sense of panic. I moved quickly back down the staircase. Here the temperature was a few degrees cooler, but in the process I kicked Pav's face mask as I retreated.

My hand felt like someone had stabbed it and was now rubbing the wound with sandpaper. I think I yelled out but the noise of the fire, the pump's engine running outside, drowned it out. (If you wish to imagine what it was like trying to communicate to each other in a fire before personal BA radios were the norm, retune your radio set to white noise on full volume, then run your car engine at maximum revs, whilst with your hands covering your mouth: then try and make yourself heard.)

Pav, understandably perturbed, didn't know what had happened. I couldn't make him understand what I was saying. I took a moment to gather my senses, looked at my hand but couldn't really what the problem was in the smoke. The initial pain subsided and all I could think of were the children that were reported to be inside. So tapping Pav on the head, I gestured that I was going to try again and for a second time stuck my head around the corner. I don't know if a window, or windows, had blown out or shattered but it didn't seem quite as hot. So still on our stomachs we wriggled along the small landing and down the steps. Striking the fire with our jet of water the temperature dropped rapidly. By the time we got into the room we were able to move forward at a crouch. In the dim light of our torches the bedroom was a scene of devastation. Everything was destroyed, charred black, walls running with condensation and water from the jet, toxic black residue was everywhere. If anyone was in the room they would be in a bad way. Other crews had now joined us and I had another look at my hand.

The skin across the back of my left hand was falling off. Blisters had started to form on my fingers and the pain came shooting back. I held my hand up and showed it to Pav. With his facemask pressed against my ear he said:

"Let's get out, the others can finish it."

(Now a quick aside about firefighters' 'protective' gloves. I know you're probably thinking, "Why wasn't he wearing his?" You would be right to ask the question. However, at the time we weren't used to wearing the issued gloves. When I first joined we were issued with 'debris' gloves. These were cotton-based gloves with a red rubberised plastic coating. The coating would melt whenever you touched anything hot! There's many a fireman who has left his gloves stuck on the side of a council metal paladin that had been alight. So although we had been issued with the new 'Firecraft' leather gloves, we were not in the habit of wearing them. Mine had been left on the fire engine, an explanation that was considered a valid excuse by those that investigated my injury.)

Normally the cool night air is always a relief after you've been in a fire. The water, and sweat, in your fire tunic starts to steam off. Getting your BA set off is, literally, a weight off your shoulders as your heart rate starts to return to normal. This time, though, I was aware I was shivering. I showed my injuries to the Incident Commander.

"Stick your hand under that pump outlet," he said. "We'll sort out an ambulance."

Putting a burn under running water is generally accepted as a good thing. However, not many people are aware that the water in a fire pump can get warm as it rotates in the appliance's centrifugal pump. I knew this and so did the Station Officer, but in my confusion and his pre occupied state we both forgot. Whilst the water was not boiling it was hot. Now running on the back of my hand it felt like I'd put it in a saucepan of scalding water!

Pav, who had been briefing the Incident Commander on what we had done came and found me. He helped me into the back of the ambulance and left me with the ambulance crew.

"I've just got to take some details," said the ambulance man as he wrapped my hand in a dressing. The pain was getting steadily worse away from any type of cooling. He was now glancing at the side of my head.

"How does your face feel?" he said.

"It feels just fine," I replied.

"OK," he smiled, but still looked a bit concerned.

I shared the ambulance with two civilian casualties from the fire. Both had burns to their hands and faces. They were in obvious distress and, where today it's one casualty to one ambulance, in those pre-paramedic days it was seen as imperative to get everyone into A&E as soon as possible. So three of us were taken in one ambulance to Newham General Hospital.

Sitting on a bed, in a cubicle, the nurses had given me a bowl of water to put my hand into while I waited for the doctor. I was blissfully unaware I had been injured anywhere else. I sat in that state of ignorance and no one told me anything different. A Brigade senior officer had now arrived. He was there to look check on my welfare and to report on my condition.

"I've bought your shoes," he said. "I got the biggest pair off the fire engine."

He had assumed that as I was a tall bloke – I'm 6 foot 3 inches tall – the biggest shoes must be mine. However, he was wrong! Pav is a good two inches taller than me and his feet are two sizes bigger! While we waited I told him about the two casualties that had been bought in with me, and also that I'd been told by the hospital staff that another casualty that had jumped from a first floor window had been bought in by neighbours.

"Did they get the kids out?" I asked him. He looked a bit perplexed and just said everyone had got out.

The doctor arrived and looked at my hand and saying that he didn't have much experience of burns, so went off to get a more experienced nurse. When they came back he proceeded to find out how deep the burns were by poking them with a probe. To this day the only visible scars I have are the bits he poked at!

Declaring that my injuries weren't too bad, he instructed the nurse to apply Flamazine cream to my hand and taped it into a plastic bag. His instruction to dry dress the blisters on my face and ears was the first time I realised I'd been burnt elsewhere! I had a large blister on the side of my face, where the edge of my face mask had been, and both ears had blisters hanging down like grotesque earrings. With the pain getting worse, I gratefully accepted the offer of painkillers.

My wounds dressed, loaded up with painkillers, and wearing Pav's clown-like shoes, I was driven back to East Ham by the senior officer, an Assistant Divisional Officer. After breakfast, with reports and paperwork being the bedrock of the Brigade, I had to write a full report about what had happened. Vic offered to get a senior officer to drive me home.

"No it's OK, I need to get back to Homerton first and then I'll drive home."

Vic tried to persuade me otherwise but I was not to be persuaded. I felt I'd been enough trouble. I said goodbye, got in my old car and drove out of East Ham's yard. Unfortunately, I had underestimated how difficult it was to change gear with a plastic bag full of cream on your hand and the journey back was not great. Indeed by the time I got to Homerton, the painkillers had worn off, every gear change was purgatory and I was in agony. I completed the last mile or so in third gear, coasting around the corners where I could.

My guvnor at Homerton was old school. A little bit mad, maybe, but a great character. He was a man he knew his job and was well respected.

"What the bloody hell happened to you? You're meant to put water on the fire not beat it out with your bare hands!"

He had a grin on his face as he said it and I like to think he was quite pleased that one of his blokes had shown he didn't mind getting stuck in. I went to sit upstairs with my mates while they had their own late breakfast and was asked, none too politely, to go and sit elsewhere as the blisters on my ears had begun to drip and it was putting them off their food!

I was now in too much pain to drive home and my Sub Officer, Steve Sawkins, offered to take me. Fortunately my wife, who was six months pregnant, and my two-year-old daughter were staying at her mum's in Ilford, significantly closer than our own house in Essex, and Steve took me there. My father-in-law was on the drive when we arrived. He looked shocked as I got out of the car covered in dressings. Steve reassured him.

"It's not as bad as it looks," he said.

I thought, "How the hell do you know!" My father-in-law ran indoors to tell my wife not to be alarmed and my daughter ran away, scared by the bag and bandages, and that was that.

I healed pretty quickly, as you do when you're young. A visit back to Newham General was delayed by an extra day because it was a bank holiday. Normally a Flamazine bag is only kept on for 24 hours, but mine was on for over 48 hours before I could see a doctor. The young nurse tasked with removing the bag from my hand nearly passed out as she cut it away and the smell from the mixture of sweat, plasma and Flamazine assaulted her nose. It was like holding your hand in a bucket of slime for two days. My hand looked like something from the black lagoon, swollen and covered in blisters.

Under instruction from the burns unit at Billericay, a senior nurse cut away the blisters. I nearly passed out! However, it was obviously the right thing to do as within a month I was back on duty and I never forgot to put my gloves on again... well, almost never!

As for the 'two babies'? Sometime later I met up with Pav and naturally the conversation turned to that night. I asked him the same question.

"There weren't any babies," he said. "Do you remember those two blokes running over us as we tried to get up the stairs?"

I had to admit I didn't; shock and the injury had clouded any other memories.

"They were the babies and it was their grandmother screaming 'my babies are inside'."

To her, even though they were both in their twenties, they were still her babies. I had travelled to hospital with them in the ambulance.

(Fact)

In Control

By Harry Simmons

IT WAS, VERY NEARLY, an early ending to a promising control room career. With only a couple of weeks into my basic training course as a Fire Brigade Control Officer my instructor, Dick Bone, was absent from the Control Officers' training suite at the Lambeth Headquarters. He had to take his station officer's examination which left us twiddling our thumbs, or so we all thought. However, our training squad was placed in the operational Lambeth control room for the day, alongside the established, and qualified, members of Lambeth's control staff.

Three decades before I first walked through the main entrance of the London Fire Brigade's headquarters building on the Albert Embankment to start my new career, the mobilising in the former London County Council area was conducted from four Superintendents' fire stations: Clapham, New Cross, Manchester Square and Whitechapel. It was where the dial 'O' or 2222 emergency calls were received. These controls could mobilise up to 12 pumps (a District call). The Control Room, on the first floor at Lambeth, would assume command of all incidents requiring more pumps (a Brigade call).

With World War II looming an underground Control Room was constructed at the Lambeth HQ. The existing four Superintendents' stations assumed a major role by becoming responsible for the mobilising of large numbers of fire engines, Home Office emergency appliances and the Brigade's own appliances. Requests for assistance from these areas were passed to the underground control at Lambeth for mobilising of the London region's resources.

Then in 1948 the nationalised Fire Service reverted to local authority control. The Lambeth Control Room continued, from its basement location, to mobilise the Brigade across the London County Council. This continued until the formation of the Greater London Council in 1965. The enlarged London Fire Brigade, consisting of 620 square miles compared with the 117 square miles of the former London County Council area, came into being. The vast expansion meant a re-appraisal of the brigade's communications system. A new Control Room was devised for Lambeth. At the time it was considered state of the art and was re-occupied in mid-1966. Her Majesty the Queen officially opened it in November of that year, which also happened to be the centenary of the London Fire Brigade.

Now to return to my opening paragraph, I was placed besides the Control Room administration telephone switchboard operator. The aim was to show me how to deal with non-emergency 'admin' calls. Throughout the morning I thought had I been doing OK. Then the guy looking after me got up and went off to his lunch. His last words were:

"You'll be fine, Harry. Just answer the admin calls and put the caller through. The extension numbers are all there!"

So armed with the confidence of youth, and with absolutely no experience, I set about the task with relish. All was going well until the Control Room Duty Station Officer came stomping out of his office. He was red-faced and very angry. I had earlier taken a call from a principal officer, a Deputy Assistant Chief Officer (DACO). He had requested his car and driver. I remembered the call and had put the DACO through to the driver's location as I had the extension number. Wrong! What I hadn't been told was if an officer phoned for his driver, you had to get the driver, *not* the officer!

After my successful basic training I was posted to Stratford Control in East London. It was here I initially became something of a Jonah: a 40-pump fire, a 25-pump fire and a 10-pump fire all within my first month. I had joined my watch on 10 December 1969, a night duty. I was told I was going to be taught how to operate the radio, which had the call sign 'M2FE'. There were four Control Rooms then: Lambeth (M2FH), Wembley (M2FN), Croydon (M2FS) and Stratford. My watch was going to be short-staffed over the Christmas period and I needed to be able to contribute. My tutor, Ron, went about showing me the ropes on the radio. He was, as it turned out, pretty successful at his job!

He was such a good tutor that I was allowed to go solo! It was literally an ordeal by fire as during the night duty I got the chance to be the radio operator during a 40-pump fire in Hornchurch. As was the custom, a senior officer was ordered from Headquarters to the Stratford Control Room. The Officer of the Watch at Lambeth Control tipped us off that a DACO was on his way. I was horrified when told the DACO's name. It was the very same officer that I'd kept waiting for his car a few weeks earlier! A short while later the door to control opened and in walked the said DACO, resplendent in full undress uniform, complete with cravat! (An image rather spoilt by his pyjama sleeves appearing at his jacket cuffs and his pyjama bottoms flapping around at his ankles.) It was a night I'll never forget. Something that had very little to do with the vision of protruding pyjamas. For when he was told that I'd only been in the job for a few weeks he placed a gentle hand on my shoulder, and with the words, "Well done, son." He made sure he spoke them loud enough for me hear but did not broadcast it to the rest of the watch.

In my early years at the Stratford Control the relationship between Control Room and Stratford Fire Station staff, who shared the same site, was extremely good. A number of the control officers ate with the operational firemen, I included. However, on one occasion this was sorely tested. Stratford was a busy station. It was rare for a night to be free of fire and other emergency calls. One such occasion was when I was 'acting-up' as a junior officer on another watch. It was common practice, in the early hours that the control watch was spilt and each half took a turn of having a period of 'relaxation' (a rest break).

I'm in the Control Room with the Station Officer and another control officer. The room is adjacent to Ferns Road that runs along the fire station. We have darkened windows that allows us to look out but no one can look in. It's a chilly, misty morning and Ferns

Road is lit by an old orange street light. The Control Room is quiet and we're all just a little tired. The Station Officer decides he'll have a look out the window, not that there's much too see. He sees what he thinks is smoke and an orange glow coming from a college building at the end of Ferns Road. He turns round and says,

"Turn Stratford out, 'Smoke issuing from Building, Ferns Road'."

So without further ado Stratford's pump-escape and pump are duly despatched. As the Fire Station crews turn out, our Station Officer decides to walk outside and wanders down the yard to have a look, and liaise with the crews, just as they are about to request the verification and the origin of call.

On being informed the call originated in our Control Room, a few (or rather a lot) of expletives filled the chilly air. The stop message "Alarm caused by low lying cloud reflecting in street lamps" was duly sent. Our Station Officer didn't eat on the station but unfortunately I did. When I went for my breakfast at 7.30 a.m. there were nine very unhappy faces. I'm surprised I didn't wear the bacon and eggs that morning.

I've always enjoyed a great rapport with the majority of operational personnel. Perhaps because I loved the firemen's banter and the social aspects of fire station life. My first watch at Stratford Control were considerably older than me, given I was still only a young lad. Anyway, I was allowed to socialise with all the watches at Stratford. There were only three watches at the time. My breaks were spent playing table tennis and having an occasional beer! On Saturday afternoons I'd would join in their volleyball or have a game of five-a-side football. Christmas was always a special time for fun and high jinks. Stratford was a work hard/play hard type of station and they did. In the 1970s, and during the reign of Joe Milner as Chief Officer, he would always visit a number of stations on Christmas Day and, for some reason, he would always appear at Stratford during the evening.

I had been invited over, as usual, to have a beer on the station. There was also a surplus of young Chinese and Irish nurses visiting from Whipps Cross Hospital. As they were on duty, at times, over the holiday period, and couldn't go back home, they were happy to accept the firemen's invitation to party. So everyone's enjoying the evening when one bell sounds, a fire brigade summons whenever a senior officer visits a fire station. There is no one in the watchroom, of course, because everyone's in the mess-room having a good time. There is a sudden sense of foreboding and panic. A senior officer is on station with a 'social' gathering in full swing! The dutyman disappears down the sliding pole whilst the Station Officer follows closely, taking the scenic route down the stairs and putting his tie back on. (Being correctly rigged when reporting to a senior officer was the order of the day.)

Meanwhile, firemen are frantically tidying up the mess and thinking up excuses as to why the off-duty nurses are on the station. A few minutes later the mess doors open and in walks a smiling Joe Milner, the Chief Officer. His pipe in hand, he continues to smile as a beer is swiftly placed in his free hand. Joe proceeds to walk round the mess-room and stops at the group I'm talking to. A young Leading Fireman has concocted his story and is sticking to it as he tries to introduce his (Chinese) wife to Joe, at which point Joe turns round and says: "It's alright, son, your guvnor's already briefed me," as he turns to the pretty nurse and starts talking to her in Cantonese!

In the early 1970s the Brigade's Control Staff changed their representative body. They left the Fire Brigades Union and moved to the Greater London Council Staff Association. Part of the change resulted in an alteration to their rank structure. The basic rank became a Control Officer III, followed by Control Officer II and a Control Officer I. With the closure of the old Lambeth Control Room in 1974 there was an increased staffing, and workload, in the three remaining control rooms. The rank of Area Controller was introduced and was in charge of each watch.

Stratford control room was located in the corner of the Stratford Fire Station. It was an area that was once storerooms in the former West Ham Fire Brigade. The room containing the control's communications equipment was in an adjacent room but only accessible from the station yard. When an equipment failure occurred – which was often, given the age of the equipment – a call was made to the GPO (before BT) for an engineer to attend, investigate and carry out repairs. The key to the equipment room was held in the control room office and had to be requested by the engineer. On this occasion when an equipment failure happened the GPO were contacted and an engineer requested to attend as a matter of urgency. When they arrived the equipment room key could not be found! A previous engineer had, inadvertently, taken it away with him. So what do you do when you have an emergency? You call the fire brigade, in this case Stratford's Station Officer. A couple of minutes later he arrived with one of his firemen. Enter Trevor. Trevor was asked to put his weight against the door to try and spring the lock. Trevor does as he's told! However, Trevor is built like a prop forward and as he puts his shoulder against the double doors they open, immediately followed by the door frame and Trevor. They all end up in heap on the equipment room floor.

In the mid 1970s the new Poplar fire station became the F Divisional Headquarters. The Staff Office at Stratford moved to Poplar and we inherited a larger locker room plus a rest room for control staff. The rest room overlooked the station forecourt at Stratford which at this time was having its appliance room floor re-tiled. So, for a short period, the fire engines were reversed and turned out through the backyard gates and not via the front of the station.

One evening a crowd gathers on the station forecourt looking alternatively at a bedding factory opposite the station and the station itself! The reason for the gathering, and the glances, were the flames coming out of the bedding factory and a fire station full of engines but nothing happening! A control officer in the restroom glanced out of the window and noticed the gathering and then the flames. He returned to the control and put in a call. Not one member of the crowd had bothered to use the 'running call box' – an emergency telephone box located at the front of every fire station to call the fire brigade. Stratford's firemen didn't see anything because they were in the mess-room on the opposite side of the station. The blaze ended up a ten-pump fire.

Fortunately, throughout my career, I've always seemed to get on with people. I always tried to judge changes in people's responses and attitudes in differing situations. Some of my bosses said I was a 'people' person. I just followed the example of my late father and treated people as I would want to be treated. I quickly learnt from the actions of one of my early watch officers how not to treat people. But at the same time I also learnt the art of mobilising from him and looking at, responding to, and remembering incidents for future reference.

There were some regular locations for emergency calls. One such location was on Leyton's Fire Station ground. It was called 'Shinwell's' and, if my memory serves me, it was an electro-platers. In days before mobile phones multiple calls to incidents were extremely rare, especially from remote or isolated locations. This evening we took a 999 call to Shinwell's. The normal attendance was three pumping appliances; however, the officer of the watch said, "Put six on it." Thinking he was mad, but too afraid to argue, six pumping appliances were sent. The first priority message back from Shinwell's was make pumps six! This situation had occurred before and after. It was much easier then to 'bend the rules' or rather adapt to situations with manual mobilising procedures before computer-aided mobilising and voice recording came into play. Rightly or wrongly I used such 'gut reaction', foresight or plain luck throughout my career.

It's the 1980s and I'm about to be promoted for a second time. My first promotion came in 1974. I remained at Stratford Control but was transferred onto another watch. The promotion process, prior to the introduction of the assessment centres, was by passing a written examination followed by a formal interview. I vaguely remember the interviews for my first two promotions. I had to report to the Brigade Headquarters General Staff office, on the second floor, and was formally introduced to the board by the staff Station Officer. The room was itself daunting. It was the headquarters' large, oak-panelled conference room. A massive oak desk separated the interviewee from the three uniformed senior officers conducting the interview. Around the table were heavy oak chairs which you could barely move. However, I must have made some sort of an impression as promotions followed!

On my second promotion I was promoted to Control Officer and headed off to Wembley Control in North-West London. Wembley had a different shift system to the operational staff, in fact Wembley had a different shift system from any other control room. The Wembley Control was co-located with the G Division staff office, the staff office being on the floor below. During my long career I enjoyed a good working rapport with both my operational peers and senior officers. My watch worked alongside the Brigade's Red Watch most of the time. Here I got to know the Red Watch Staff Sub Officer quite well. His name was George. He was easy-going, able, efficient and appeared to be unflappable.

One evening, when I was the 'officer of the watch', the Divisional control unit, with the Staff Sub Officer in charge, were ordered on to an incident on the Chalkhill Estate on Wembley's ground. Chalkhill Estate was quite notorious, being a badly designed 1960s council estate. It was scene of numerous minor and not so minor Brigade incidents. On his arrival George sent the radio messages for the incident commander and, by the tone of his voice, all was not well.

As is normal practice, when a serious incident is in progress and it is anticipated that stations will be empty for an extended period of time, stand-by appliances are sent in to such stations to provide fire cover. Normally only one fire engine is sent to a station but on this occasion I instructed that two appliances be sent to 'cover' Wembley. Coincidently both these stand-by appliances arrived at Wembley at the same time. Confused as to why two appliances had arrived they rang control to check which one was to stay. At the same time a priority message was received from the incident making 'pumps eight'. Both standby appliances were last seen heading to the incident. As the incident progressed we learnt that crews had carried out numerous difficult rescues, were required to manoeuvre wheeled escape ladders over grass banks and some of the appliances had become bogged down! No wonder the Staff Sub O was stressed.

Still at Wembley Control, and one evening, we receive a call from a member of the public to rescue a parrot stuck up a tree in West Hampstead. The caller is referred to the RSPCA, as the attendance of the Brigade was restricted unless requested by them to attend. The caller hangs up. An hour or so later the same caller contacts us again. It's darker now and the parrot remains up the tree. The RSPCA has declined to attend until the following morning. Once again the caller is referred back to the RSPCA and told the Brigade cannot attend. By now it's completely dark and we receive a call to a man stuck in a tree! As there is now a risk to life, a fire engine from West Hampstead fire station attends. On arrival the crew find a man up a tree attempting to rescue his escaped parrot. West Hampstead's crew get the man out of the tree but leave the parrot where it is. The man pleads with the crew to rescue his bird. The officer in charge decides to help but without putting the crew at risk. The parrot is brought to ground level by *'parrotchute'*, the crew giving the bird a 'gentle' soaking with the hose-reel tubing. The parrot, unharmed if a tad damp, was a valuable talking bird owned by the local publican of a Parliament Hill Fields pub.

By 1982 I'm on the move again. Assistant Chief Officer Gerry Clarkson, who later became our Chief Officer, promoted me to Area Controller (Training). I am now responsible for all aspects of Control staff training, from new control room recruits to control officer continuation and promotion training (plus a few other things thrown in). I have returned to the basement at Brigade Headquarters. The former Lambeth control room is now the Control Training Centre (CTC).

It was here I began to have direct dealings with Principal Officers. I had enjoyed a good working rapport with senior officers. I lost count of the number of times an Assistant Divisional Officer or Divisional Officer, returning from an incident, telephoned me with their thanks. Frequently I had turned them out in the middle of the night with no real grounds other than I was unhappy, or uneasy, with the happenings of a particular incident. Their attendance, more times than not, proved to be well founded.

In my dealings with officers, but especially the senior ones, I always remained respectful, I didn't want the extra hassle. Whilst I never publicly embarrassed them, I would ensure that my arguments or disagreements were aired in an appropriate way. Other than the Principal and Assistant Principal Controller at the Brigade HQ, I was the senior Control Officer at Lambeth.

During the 1980s the Brigade was preparing for the introduction of its first computer-aided control system. It had established a 'testing and development team', comprising mainly of control officers. The team would be responsible for training 120 plus control staff in the use of the new system. However, the team needed more training officers and an advert requesting applications was published in-house. By the closing date there were not many applicants. I had not applied. I was already the Control Training Officer.

But on the closing date I am duly summoned to a meeting with the

DACO, who is the project manager. He asks me why I've not applied for a place on the training team. I reply: "As a matter of principle." I had no intention of applying for a job that I can be ordered to do.

"Harry, principles have consequences," he replied.

He looked surprised when I said I was fully aware of the consequences. I had done nothing wrong in not applying for the position. His veiled threat was that he could post me to another control room in my current rank. There was actually a vacancy at Croydon Control and I would have no problem going there. I was prepared to serve in any control room, and the Brigade would have to pay me an additional travelling allowance. End of interview. The control project had a new member for its training team, me! I could be a stubborn individual but almost always respectful.

I spent eight, very happy, years, in charge of control room training. I trained a significant number of trainees who would become the mainstay of the new Control, including one who eventually became my boss!

In the late 1980s the project to centralise the control room set-up is nearing conclusion. Croydon, Stratford and Wembley Control, together with Operations Room, are set to close. The Brigade is to combine all its command and mobilising functions. It created the Command and Mobilising Centre (CMC), a brand new structure built where once the former bandstand and social clubs stood at the Lambeth Headquarters.

The change from manual control rooms to one computer-aided control was not particularly easy. The original opening date for CMC was 1984. Unfortunately, due to numerous technical problems, CMC finally went live in early 1990. However, only two control rooms, Wembley and Croydon, actually transferred to the new control on the go-live date. Due to industrial unrest, Stratford had been closed some months earlier by the Chief Officer, its staff compulsorily out-posted to other control rooms.

As part of the CMC training team I was actively involved with acceptance testing for the Marconi mobilising system. I believed the system was far from perfect and the staff not as well trained as one would have hoped as the system went live. That said, the former Greater London Council control rooms were well past their 'sell by date'. Its equipment could no longer be repaired properly and work-loads were increasing. This made the Brigade's manual mobilising less efficient and more labour intensive; hence the need for change.

The implementation team were actively working with engineers, employed by Marconi, and despite some fraught times and heated discussions good working relationships, and some long-term friendships, ensued. Some of those engineers went on to become Brigade employees, caretaking not only the Marconi system but a large amount of the Brigade's information technology systems.

The day to day stress on the individuals resulted in a regular end of the week drink at the pub, either the nearby Windmill or the Old Father Thames. The sessions normally ended with the LFB/Marconi challenge involving the preferred weapon of choice: glasses of Black Russian, a cocktail of vodka and coffee liqueur.

When the new CMC control opened, a five-watch system was introduced. I found myself back on shift work. It was not by choice but a seniority process that saw the six most senior Area Controllers given the rank of Senior Controller. Five were assigned watches and the sixth Training. But I had a good watch, full of likeable and, above all, competent people. By a quirk of fate my guvnor was the same person responsible for my basic training back in 1969.

I was on CMC's No 1 watch when an incident occurred that had an impact on both the Brigade and the fire service nationally. It was July 1991. A fire occurred in an East End secure storage ware-house in Gillender Street, Poplar, a fire that resulted in the deaths of two firefighters. Whilst not a particularly difficult incident as far as mobilising went, it caused me some personal concern. It was a Green Watch fire and my elder brother, stationed at Homerton on the Green Watch, was at the incident. In control we were aware of the fatalities but did not know the individuals' names or their stations. It was a stressful couple of hours. I could not contact the station for information for fear of being asked the question, "Why, what's going on?" It made me realise what goes through the minds of the control staff who are turning out their partners and sometimes their children to difficult and dangerous situations!

With the centralisation of controls in 1990 there followed constant, steady, changes involving control systems, shift patterns, staff changes, and working practices. Then, in 1994, following an inquest into a fatal fire in another UK fire brigade, we saw the introduction of a national initiative for fire control rooms. It was called the 'Fire Survival Guidance'. Prior to that the general rule to the public at risk from fires in property was 'GET OUT AND STAY OUT'.

The 'Fire Survival Guidance' is intended to be used when a person is unable to escape from the property and to keep individuals safe from fire and smoke until the fire service arrives at an incident. The guidance means building a rapport with the caller. It requires control operators to reassure the often frightened caller, to give advice on articles to prevent smoke entering the apartment/room, advice about opening a window to attract attention, keeping low under any smoke, and so on. While statistics probably indicate the overall success of the initiative. I had reservations about the processes from day one. Reservations that would eventually prove correct with tragic consequences and far-reaching effects on me personally.

I took temporary charge of CMC's No 4 watch. I did so until 1997 when another staffing and shift review was implemented. I was off again.

The implementation of London's computer-aided mobilising system was largely successful. Some people might think I have a biased view, considering I was part of the testing, development and training team, but I hope I viewed things objectively. The system, in the early days, was subject to unexpected computer crashes. But there was a live back-up computer and other built-in degradation systems. I was in charge when one of many such 'crashes' occurred. It was a Saturday night, but not just any Saturday night. It was 5 November: Guy Fawkes Night. As usual we were very busy. Extra staff were on duty and we were coping well. It was approaching 7 p.m. We had even managed to get our refreshments breaks under-way. Unlike crews at fire stations a control watch cannot sit down all together to eat; our meal breaks have to be taken in rotation. As the officer in charge I'm not actively involved in taking calls and mobilising fire appliances, I'm supervising. Then the alarm, indicating a computer failure has occurred, sounds. Controlled panic ensues! Control operators' screens are locked: they are unable to record call details from members of the public, nor can they record messages from incidents. So what happens…? Well, you carry on. Staff absent from the control room are recalled and manual procedures are implemented. All emergency calls and operational messages are recorded on paper, locations are manually identified, fire appliances manually selected, then ordered to incidents by telephone. The whole thing is very labour-intensive. Fortunately, my watch, supported by others on overtime, were very professional and carried on with good humour, handling over two hundred calls during the two hours it took to bring the computers back online. Looking back, I'm thankful I started when we didn't have computer systems and the manual stuff was second nature.

The reduction in control staff numbers, during the 1990s, was dramatic. Whilst most was negotiated, there was a threat of termination of contract prior to centralisation at Lambeth. Control staff numbered 196 prior to the closure of the three Command-based controls and Operations Room. On the opening of the new Lambeth Control, with a five-watch system, the numbers were reduced by 64. A further review implemented in 1994, but implemented in 1997, saw a further reduction bringing the total number of staff to 93. The reductions saw the implementation of a four-watch system, similar to the operational structure of Red, White, Blue and Green Watches, although the duty times and rota differed.

I was assigned the position of Officer in Charge of the Green Watch. This was the first time I had been permanently in charge of a watch since my first promotion 23 years earlier. I stayed in charge of Green Watch for much of the remainder of my career, albeit with a break of about five years. When the four-watch system was introduced everyone, except the Senior Controllers, were asked which watch they wished to go on, the majority making their choice based on childcare and other domestic issues. On the Green Watch I had worked with some before, others were new and a number I had trained. My task was to bring them together as a cohesive, effective and efficient control team.

Perhaps the most notable incident we dealt with occurred within minutes of the Green Watch reporting for duty on the morning of 5 October 1999. At 8.10 a.m. the switchboards within Brigade Control lit up with emergency calls. Callers were reporting fire and explosions at various locations in the Ladbroke Grove area of West London. Because numerous locations were given, several attendances were despatched to investigate and deal with the reported incidents. However, amongst all the confusion one call was received that said a train had exploded! It transpired that it was the commencement of the Ladbroke Grove railway crash. Sadly, 31 people were killed and hundreds left injured. I was proud of the way my watch dealt with the situation, especially as they were taking many of those calls from people, many distressed, and on the two trains involved. Our pride went to the LFB crews who attended and dealt, first-hand, with such a terrible accident resulting in horrific injuries.

At the start of 2000 there were genuine fears of world-wide computers crashes and untold disasters occurring as a direct consequence of the beginning of the new millennium! It never happened but I was to find myself on the move again. This time I was to take charge of the Brigade Control's Technical Support Group. The Group were a small team of Control Officers tasked with assisting with overseeing the development and updating of our communication systems. This included mobilising computers, switchboards and radios, plus implementing changes to the computer software in response to operational requirements and the provision of mobilising data. The work was varied but most often routine – that was, until January 2003.

I strived to carry my knowledge and experience into the Brigade's computer-aided control era, right from the 1990s into 2000 and beyond. I never use the term 'computerised control', because without the control officer the computer system will not work. It was never that clever. Any recommendation given by the system could be overridden and changed to suit individual circumstances. With the mobilising control now moved to Greenwich View Place, in South-East London, one of my watch had taken a call to a collapse of a ceiling in a building in West London. Two pumps and a fire/ rescue tender were meant to be ordered by the system. However, I intervened and gave instructions for more pumps, another rescue tender and the Urban Search and Rescue (USAR) equipment to be dispatched, my reasoning being that the incident was a 'collapse of ceiling' in a Mosque. The outcome was that a person was trapped under a substantial block of material and not just a plaster ceiling as the control operator first thought.

Throughout the 1970s and '80s people in the United Kingdom had become somewhat inured to terrorist activity taking place on our shores due to the bombing from the Provisional Irish Republican Army. The emergency services, but particularly the fire service, had got used to picking up the pieces with whatever equipment or training they had, however inadequate. By 2003 the world of terrorism had changed on an unimaginable level. The Sarin chemical attack on the Tokyo Underground System in 1995, and then the 11 September 2001 'Twin Towers' attack ('9/11') brought significant changes in its wake. The Brigade's work to provide better protection, equipment, resilience and training gathered pace.

In January 2003 we are back on duty, having returned from the Christmas break. I receive a telephone call to go and see my boss. He, the deputy Principal Controller, informs me that the Brigade are holding a London Resilience workshop in West Horsley the following week. I'm told to attend and get some idea as to the probable impact on control room operations. By that Thursday my one day has been extended to the whole week and it's residential. The Monday arrives, I'm at West Horsley, and there are numerous uniformed and non-uniformed officers, from various departments, plus one control room officer: me! The others are divided into working groups, each dealing with a large number of projects with a lot with implications for control and mobilising. I spend the week going from group, advising, guiding, and giving input but most of all taking it all in.

I enjoy talking with people, and what better place to do it than in the bar! Maybe I'd had too much to drink, but I said to a Senior Divisional Officer, "If you need a control officer on this project, I'm interested." The week comes to an end and I return to the routine of the Technical Support Group, and having briefed my boss about the workshop. I carry on as normal. Several months have passed by and I'm summoned to see my boss. He tells me I'm on the move again. That comment in the bar has come back to haunt me. Apparently a team, under the tag of Special Operations Group (SOG) require a Control Officer. One with the knowledge, ability and enthusiasm to advise and give guidance to differing work streams and produce mobilising protocols for new appliances and equipment. My next three years are spent working with both operational and non-uniform personnel, including the Brigade's medical advisor, emergency planning officers and scientific advisors, who are bringing to fruition the new equipment and training brought about by the London Resilience initiatives. (It was while working with this group I reached heady heights of an Assistant Principal Controller, albeit only temporarily!)

As a result of the SOG work I believe the London Fire Brigade was better placed, equipped and trained to deal with the aftermaths of terrorist incidents and, as a consequence, also better equipped to deal with other routine incidents such as major flooding, building collapse and hazardous material incidents.

I remain proud of my small part in bringing into service: the urban search and rescue equipment; the mass decontamination equipment; detection, identification and monitoring equipment; high volume pumps; and in producing writing procedures, which I hope will not be required too frequently operationally, but nevertheless assists in protecting both the public of London and especially the protection of our first responders. Those that are going in while others run out.

But even with a proven history of terrorist attacks in London and on the UK mainland more generally, there were many within the Brigade, even at senior level, who were cynical of the work we were involved in. The 'it's never going to happen in London' attitude existed in many quarters! Sadly, on 7 July 2005 four co-ordinated terrorist attacks occurred on the London's transport network, and, with their resultant deaths and casualties, they clearly proved it does.

The SOG were located in the Brigade headquarters building. When I joined the group our office was the former Lambeth Workshop's hose repair room. Being of a certain age I actually remember seeing hose repaired there when I started my career. In a quirk of fate, SOG were then relocated to the CMC building, my old control room! The control had relocated to a new site with its new mobilising system in the heart of Docklands, just south of Canary Wharf.

By 2006 my work within SOG is changing, my role diminishing. So I knew that I would soon be on my way. Besides, experience taught me that when your new boss says, "I'm not there to dismantle the group", the opposite normally applies. So I'm heading off to Docklands and back in charge of my Green Watch.

It's was good to be back with a group of people that I've worked with before, together with some new control room faces, but moves were afoot. It was also a difficult time domestically. But with the support of friends and colleagues I came out the other side successfully. However, control room policy was undergoing major changes. In Docklands the new mobilising system was working reasonably well and work was ticking over. Nationally, on the other hand, there were ongoing national major changes within control room organisation, something the Brigade supported. Work was underway to regionalise fire control rooms. The then Government had commissioned the 'Fire Control Project'. This was designed to reduce fire controls from 42 county and metropolitan control rooms to 9 regional control centres. London, although being considered a region in its own right, would be majorly affected. The project was, in the view of many, a cost-saving exercise, ill-conceived and not properly thought out. The vastly over-budget project was eventually cancelled; the buildings completed were not put into active service, except in London where the current Brigade Control is located, with yet another new mobilising system called 'Vision'.

In the Docklands Control Room, 2007/8 was a time of considerable change. The Brigade's principal management decided to go with the findings of a review into control room recruitment policy. For the first time in my long career, positions were not only advertised within the fire service nationally but externally in the private sector as well. Appointee interviews eventually took place. A completely new control room management group was appointed. One had no previous fire service experience; another was from a different fire service; there was one in-house candidate.

New management titles follow for me: Principal Operations Manager and Senior Operations Managers. Manager is the new 'in' word and replaces the apparently outdated term 'officer'. Subsequently, new titles are given to other control positions: Operations

Manager (Officer n Charge of the Control Watch), Assistant Operations Manager (to any other Control Supervisory Officer) and Control Officer for the remainder. Temporary incumbents went onto other control room related projects or returned to their base position in charge of a watch.

As for me, my Principal Operations Manager and I never really saw eye to eye. Call it a clash of personalities, or differing management styles, who knows? Whilst we did manage a civil working relationship, it was never the same as before. It was a broom that differed considerably from the previous Principal or Senior Control Officers I worked with. In hindsight, I would say that there were faults on both sides; I definitely take some of the responsibility. Maybe after years of accepting change (willingly in some cases, reluctantly in others), this was one change too far. I had always considered my career a vocation, not just a job.

Operationally only one incident stood out in 2007. It took place in that November. London had been awarded the Olympic Games for 2012. A massive regeneration programme, involving large swathes of east London, bordering Stratford, Hackney and Leyton, was underway. A vast number of commercial properties were being demolished and land cleared of contaminated soil. (Those of us brought up in East London in the 1950s and '60s will certainly remember the smells and sounds of the numerous factories, including chemical plants around the Carpenters Road area in Stratford.)

The control room is quiet. I'm in charge of the Green Watch. It's a pleasant day, sunny but windy. Suddenly the switchboards light up as numerous calls are received to a warehouse on fire on the edge of Homerton's ground in East London. Nothing spectacular, just your run-of-the-mill fifteen pump fire, aerials four, and a high volume pump required! But whatever is alight inside the derelict warehouse, it is punching out vast volumes of thick black acrid smoke. The smoke is visible from the control room and it's drifting, drifting towards us. We can smell it as it enters the air conditioning. So what do you do in situations like this? One option is to evacuate to the fall-back Control Room and operate from there. Unfortunately, to get there we have to drive towards the smoke. So we sit tight and rely on our operational colleagues to get things under control.

Thanks to their firefighting skills they did a good job and solved my problem.

We're entering 2009. Life is good and my domestic situation, which had been under pressure for a number of years, is in a good place. I'm looking forward to November when I complete 40 years of control room service. I am possibly one of the first control officers, if not the very first, to have completed a full 40 years' service with the London Fire Brigade. An achievement that will probably be surpassed in future years due to changes in the pension regulations resulting in an extended, older, retirement age.

However this year was destined to become a very bittersweet year. On Friday 3 July, an event occurred that will forever be etched on my mind. It was the worst two hours of my whole career. To this day, despite the numerous incidents I had been involved in over my lengthy career, it remains the case that I cannot shake. A statement I subsequently made to the Metropolitan Police would come back to haunt me. The media, including the BBC, covered it at the widely publicised inquest in 2013, thirteen or so months after my retirement from the Brigade. My personal fears over the introduction of the 'Fire Survival Guidance' procedures in 1994 had come home to roost. That fateful Friday in July was a warm, sunny, windy summer's day. Just before 4.00 p.m., multiple calls started to be received to a fire in a residential block of flats in Peckham. (That fire at Lakenal House, in South-East London, became the precursor to an even more tragic scenario in 2017 in North-West London: Grenfell.)

I was in charge of the Control Room, supported by two assistant operations managers (supervisor control officers). I had ten control officers on duty that day, taking calls, operating the radio system, dealing with stations and undertaking other ancillary work. There were two further assistant operations managers in the fall-back control room. But being located some five miles away, they took no part in the mobilising process, although they were able to monitor the main control room.

Due to the sudden increase in workload I recalled my control officers who were in the mess room on a routine break. The control complex also had a number of control officers working on day duties, who undertook other essential, but non-emergency, work. In an effort to cope with the incoming tide of emergency and other calls I tannoyed for all available control officers to report to the control room with their headsets. There was a zero response! I'd had forgotten that it was a Friday afternoon in the middle of summer. The only people in the complex were my watch, a duty system's technician and a security guard.

Even as the officer in charge of control I cannot magic up extra control officers, no matter how much I wish to. So for the next few hours my watch work tirelessly, in the most distressing of circumstances, dealing with the very many emergency calls including a large number of 'fire survival' calls. Tragically, the incident resulted in the loss of six lives, including children. As a result of their unrelenting efforts, my control officers followed protocols and assisted in making individuals safe. Control staff I remain very proud of to this day.

It was apparent that all was not well at the scene. My two supervisors were engaged in passing vital information between my call takers and the radio operator to update crews at the fire, or to the control unit, to enable rescues to be made. What we were unaware of was that firefighters were constantly having to withdraw due to the conditions within the building. Fire was breaking out on the other side of the only access and exit from the building far from the original seat of fire. Fire was also spreading to floors both above and below.

The national press and, in particular, television news coverage had a field day over the 'stay put' part of the 'Fire Survival Guidance'. In my view control officers took a pasting. Were we right or wrong to give the advice we did? Regardless, we had no choice in the matter as it was Brigade policy.

The various lawyers attending the Inquest in 2013 each had their input. There were searching questions about the 'stay put' policy. In the following years I have looked back over those transcripts, listened repeatedly to the recorded calls of that day, and it's natural to question one's actions. My watch gave their all. Maybe not in the same way as the firefighters attempting to save the unfortunate people from the fire, but I certainly could not have asked more of them.

Tragically, there are powerful, and heart-breaking, similarities between the Lakenal House fire and the more recent, horrific, Grenfell Tower fire in 2017. Whilst Lakenal House had escape balconies installed, all led to the single central core with its lift and staircase entrance and exit, a feature common to both fatal incidents. For me, Lakenal House was unlike any other incident I had previously encountered. It left me with a feeling of complete and utter failure. I felt I'd failed myself, my watch, the Brigade and more importantly those poor souls involved in the fire. It is the only incident that caused me to lose many nights' sleep, both immediately following the incident and at the time of Inquest.

The full Inquest was a year after I retired. It was conducted in Brixton Town Hall and had already been ongoing for a few weeks before I was called to give evidence. I had been briefed by a senior officer and the Brigade's solicitor prior to appearing. However, nothing prepared me for the actual day. I was required to attend Brixton Fire Station, in SW4, where rooms had been set aside for the Brigade witnesses. One of my former supervisors had also been called but spent only a couple of minutes in the witness box. I was driven to the Town Hall and at around 11.00 a.m. walked into the witness box in the impromptu Inquest Court. After taking an oath I spent the rest of that day, and the morning after, giving evidence. What I wasn't, nor couldn't be, prepared for was the relentless and unyielding questioning by eminent barristers not only about the events of that day, but the whole policy of 'Fire Survival Guidance'. I have never felt so alone.

At lunchtime, on the first day, I had to sit on my own with only a court chaperone for company. At the end of that day I was formally warned I must not to talk to anyone about the events, nor have any contact with Brigade personnel – except for the uniformed officer who drove me back to the fire station. (Even then I was driven to the station in complete silence.) The next day again I could not speak with anyone from the Brigade until I had finished giving evidence!

I naturally consider the Coroner's Inquest an important part of the inquiry process. The Coroner was charged to find out who, and why; their role was to make recommendations to prevent similar things happening again. The Coroner found that the 'Fire Survival Guidance' was basically sound. However, it remains my view it isn't where building modifications (such as Lakenal and latterly Grenfell) are concerned. I feel, and fear, for the control officers who find themselves in involved in parallel incidents in the future.

But back to 2009 and summer is almost over. I know that Lakenal fire will hang over me for some time to come but I am looking forward to completing my 40 years' service on 17 November. The Green Watch are on duty and it's the anniversary date of me joining the Brigade. A nice coincidence, I thought. Little did I know what was planned? Told to "keep out of the way" by my Watch, I did. It was a delight to receive a number of kind messages, via email and telephone calls from people I'd met throughout my career. Messages and comments which made me feel very humble.

That morning my Watch presented me with an engraved tankard. It sits proudly with my other fire service awards and mementoes. Early afternoon and I'm called to an interview with my immediate boss. The 'interview' is a ruse to keep me out of the way to allow guests to arrive for an afternoon celebration. The guests included my wife, who had told me she was in meetings all afternoon and could not be contacted, my brother – now a retired Sub Officer with 30 years' service – off-duty control officers, other officers I'd served with, and together with non-operational and administrative staff I'd met along the way. This was the Green Watch at its best, and afterwards a visit to the local hostelry had to be made.

I later received my 40-year memento (an engraved whisky decanter) at a special Brigade award ceremony at the Southwark Training Centre, along with other control officers, operational personal and non-uniformed staff, who were all receiving their well-deserved 30 year service awards.

It's 2010, and the Lakenal House fire is still haunting me. I don't feel particularly happy working in the control room environment any more. There's talk of the control room moving (again) to the new 'regional' control site in Merton. Do I want this, the move? Do I want to do night duties anymore? I make my decision. One that sees me retire on my 60th birthday in January 2011.

On that day, again, my Green Watch came up with the goods. They organise the most unbelievable retirement 'do' at the Poplar rowing club. It is a night my wife and I will never forget after a career lasting 41 years and 2 months. I will never forget the Green Watch. They got me through the last 18 months of my career. I was asked, during the evening, was it after giving evidence in the Lakenal Inquiry that I decided to retire? Until then I really hadn't thought too much about it. In truth the reasons were many, but looking back to that horrific day in 2009 I knew I did not want be a control officer anymore.

(*Fact*)

The Fire Investigator

SHE THOUGHT SHE HAD seen it all. Until today, that is. Sammie was the product of the new world order – well, of changing times in the London Fire Brigade anyway. Whilst the macho generation of firemen, who had once poured scorn on ever more women 'firefighters' being recruited into the Brigade, had largely been driven underground, there was still the odd look or the pointed comment that said, "Prove yourself." Which is exactly what Sammie had done. It is a fact that Sammie had grown up having to prove herself. With four older brothers, and only catching a fleeting sight of her dad, in-between his frequent stretches as a guest of HM prisons, she had little choice. Gifted with a quick brain and the ability to use it, having excelled at school she was headed off to university when the Metropolitan Police's Fraud Squad referred her dad's latest money-making scam to the Criminal Prosecution Service. They had the ability to seize all his assets if he was to be found guilty yet again!

Confiscation might well be an essential tool in the prosecutor's toolkit, something that deprives the offenders of the proceeds of their criminal conduct, but it also left Sammie and her Mum high and dry. The family, five-bedroom home had been acquired from the profits of her dad's criminal enterprises. The house went for auction. Sammie's mum downsized, straight into a squalid two-bedroom flat in back-street Hackney. The four brothers rallied round, providing moral support but Sammie's mum, already in frail health, took a turn for the worse. Within eight months Sammie was reunited with her estranged father at her mum's funeral. The pair never exchanged a word. In fact she never even looked at him.

At 23 Sammie had completed her firefighter recruit training. She was the latest probationer to join the Blue Watch at Clerkenwell Fire Station. Despite the 'PC' policies of the London Fire Brigade (LFB), and all the 'huff and puff' that came with the Equalities Act, in a quiet corner of the firefighters' locker room, and out of earshot of the office staff, one person's quip was another's insult. Sammie found herself on the receiving end of a comment that not only challenged her sexual orientation, but one that said it was her sex that gave her preference over her far more able male counterparts in the selection process for the LFB. Sammie's reply was as short as it was decisive. Something that took her protagonist totally by surprise.

With a speed and agility that demonstrated that her years spent in an East End boxing club had not been wasted, she floored the utterer of the comment with a single blow and, with a seamless turn, prepared to do the same to his giggling mate. The crash against the metal locker reached the ears of the Sub Officer who was passing the locker room. By the time he poked his head around the door Sammie, looking relaxed, was helping the firefighter up off the floor. He was holding his bleeding nose and had managed to get himself back up onto one knee.

"What's up?" asked the Sub.

"I asked Sammie to demonstrate her boxing skills," said Sammie's antagonist.

"I didn't know she had any," replied the Sub.

"Neither did I," said the firefighter, pinching his bleeding nose as he continued: "It was my fault entirely, Sub – I never moved quick enough."

Sammie might have just landed a lucky punch; she never said. However, she certainly struck a chord with the Watch and, in particular, the antagonist who became her greatest ally. Not much got past their Station Officer who, it was said, had been at Clerkenwell Fire Station forever. He was in the twilight of his career, although seeing him in action you would never think so. He was both physically strong and possessed a razor-sharp intellect. Something that an unwary visiting senior officer, who was just out to impress and relying on his rank, found out to their cost. It was during the next tour, and whilst waiting for the police to arrive at a suspicious fire, the guvnor took Sammie to one side.

"You can't always punch your way out of trouble you know," he said in soft tones. "But on this occasion it seems to have worked." He gave Sammie a knowing wink as he moved away to talk to the rather bored looking police officer who had just arrived at the scene.

Sammie's progression up the promotion ladder was not meteoric, not least because of the changes that the LFB had introduced. Training 'inputs' were deemed old hat. They were yesterday's concepts. It was only 'outcomes' that mattered now. In fact, they always were, as the proof of the pudding had always been in the eating. The new national fire service's 'role map' was rolling ever onward. The new Integrated Personal Development System (IPDS) was the only way ahead. But the system had its detractors, not least because of the lack of resources the Brigade directed at it and which were so vital to make it work.

These were not the only changes for those who had started their careers as 'firemen' to assimilate. Another new concept sweeping in was the 'Dynamic Risk Assessment' (DRA). Basically, it allowed anyone on the fire-ground to make a decision regarding any dynamic development or situation that was likely to cause harm or imminent danger. So, for example, if there were people hanging out of a window, of a building on fire and who required a 'snatch' rescue, a DRA might delay the rescue until other measures were put into place, such as additional breathing apparatus (BA) or using additional personnel or equipment. Alternatively, if a BA crew, working inside a burning building, believe it to be too hot, their DRA action may be to withdraw. Many thought the DRA a load of old bollocks, an excuse by some not to fire-fight; a wimp's charter. Old hands said DRA went by a different name back in the day. It was called 'common sense' but what did the senior hands, those with the experience and time in, know?

Sammie's rise to Leading Firefighter rank saw her stay at Clerkenwell but on a different watch. It coincided with her advancement in another arena too. She became the Fire Brigade Union (FBU) station representative. A committed socialist, she had always shown a genuine interest in the Union. With rising tensions in 2002, and the retirement of the previous Union rep, she was the Station's natural choice to take on this role. Unlike the national strike of

1977–78, the legacy of this dispute would be a rift between those that managed the Brigade and those on the fire station's frontline.

When the military were brought into the fray in the late '70s, to provide emergency fire cover, generally there was no animosity shown by the striking firemen. However, this time round it was different. It was bitter. It was personal. A number of ugly confrontations took place in and around the Brigade and Sammie led from the front. Hers was a regular face on many of the flying pickets. Her right hook was as powerful as her leftist leanings and for one particular strike-breaker he found his jibe cut off mid-sentence as Sammie's fist rearranged some of his front teeth.

In June 2003, the dispute ended with firefighters accepting a pay deal worth 16 per cent over three years linked to changes in working conditions. This was the same year, with her Sub Officer's promotion confirmed, that she found herself serving south of the River for the first time. Her five-year Open University degree course, in Fire Sciences, had also come to an end. She passed it with Honours. With all the intense degree coursework and exams at an end she was left twiddling her thumbs. She craved something new to challenge her, especially if it concerned the causes of fire.

An Arson Task Force, whose aim was to reduce arson-related deaths, injuries and fire damage, had brought together the Fire and Rescue Service with police and government departments. It had been formed prior to the 2002 strike. In London the Brigade had instigated an Arson Reduction Team, whose role was analysing and addressing the extensive problem of arson in the capital. It consisted of a police officer and a fire officer from each of the 33 London boroughs. Their brief was focused on 'all things arson'.

Determined to stay watch-related, and after the strike somewhat distrustful of senior management, Sammie wished to continue to learn her craft at a fire station. However, her talents were soon recognised and, reluctantly, she agreed to become a Fire Investigation Team (FIT) reservist and to cover leave and sickness on the Clapham FIT team.

The Brigade's fire investigation teams were increasing their public profile. For many years the FIT teams had attended fires after the firefighters had put the fire out. Fire investigators worked closely with the police to find out how deliberate fires were started. New initiatives had seen FIT teams use specialist equipment and innovative techniques to determine the cause of fires. They could even call on fire investigation dogs, trained to sniff out accelerants such as petrol. It was whilst working one such 'doubtful' fire in Stockwell that Sammie had met a detective sergeant stationed at Brixton nick. He was now her flatmate and partner

Sammie never did become a Station Officer; the LFB had seen to that. 'Ranks' were changed to 'roles'! The general belief at station level was that increased pressure was being generated to 'civilianise' the Brigade. There was no actual proof, but neither was there an overwhelming harmony between many of its senior 'managers' and fire station personnel. Maybe it was always thus? Many of the old school 'Station Officers' and a few Subs, like Sammie, bemoaned the changes. Her own Station Officer, now designated a 'Watch Manager', summed up the feelings of many of his contemporaries one evening when he said to Sammie:

"Effing Tesco's and banks have bloody managers. I ain't seen the military, who are not slow to modernise, introduce platoon managers or managers of the Fleet!"

But it was a lost battle; and anyway the fire service had a history of changing titles. It had just not done so for a while.

Sammie's elevation to a Watch Manager (A) – a Station Officer in old money – was a bittersweet experience for her. She was sad to leave her Clapham watch, but the prospect of returning to her beloved Clerkenwell clearly excited her. The farewell bash at Clapham was held at her favourite watering hole. It also highlighted another of Sammie's attributes, her ability to hold her drink. Generally, it is accepted that females tolerate alcohol less well than a male. Not in Sammie's case. Whatever the physiological reason, Sammie drank her Watch under the table. Then again, none of them would see her later talking to God on the big telephone in her Hackney flat (a flat that no longer looked so squalid; in fact the properties there had become very sought after).

Sammie was at Clerkenwell Fire Station late on a Saturday afternoon in August 2011. An urgent teleprinter message had been circulated to all stations warning that 'Civil Disorder' procedure was in operation. The 2011 London riots had started.

The next day Brixton, Enfield, Islington and, in central London's

Oxford Circus, looting, arson and violence took hold. By the Monday morning London again appeared quiet, but that evening areas across London were affected by more widespread looting, arson and violence. Significant outbreaks occurred in parts of Battersea, Brixton, Bromley, Camden, Croydon, Ealing, East Ham, Hackney, Harrow, Lewisham, Peckham, Stratford, Waltham Forest, Woolwich, and Wood Green. The riots were unprecedented in modern times. It challenged the Metropolitan Police and it certainly challenged the London Fire Brigade.

Ordered into the affray Sammie lead her crews with distinction, even making it into the local East London rag as the following week's headline praised Clerkenwell's firefighters for successfully saving a parade of shops in nearby Hackney. Some of Sammie's contemporaries considered her and her Watch a bit 'gung-ho' when it came to her firefighting tactics. But her judgement was sound and her Watch had respect for both her firefighting skills and leadership ability.

Two years later and Clerkenwell was once again back in the London news headlines. The Mayor, Boris Johnson, had decreed that fourteen London fire stations must shut. It was all to do with funding the LFB and the consequences of stringent cuts in Government grants to Local Authorities. Each of the affected stations waged hard-fought campaigns to save their stations, but it was an uphill struggle. One that most were destined to lose as ten stations closed. Sammie's old station, Clapham, bucked the trend and successfully fought off its enforced closure. Sadly, Londoners could not be mobilised in sufficient numbers to change the political decision to reduce London's fire cover by almost ten per cent.

It was a cold January morning in 2014 that Sammie finished her night shift at Clerkenwell for the very last time. It was an emotionally charged moment as the seconds ticked down to 9.00 a.m. and the end of the shift. Today there was no day watch to take over the reins. Both national press and TV crews were jostling for position on the forecourt of the fire station. Inside it was filled with those that who had served at Clerkenwell over the years, many of whom had long since retired. Men who had seen the worst that fire can do, men who had witnessed death and destruction but who had kept their pain to themselves – until now, as some broke down in tears. Their anger, mixed with pain, spilled over into the street. Some had to be restrained as the station was secured and the appliances, no longer Clerkenwell's fire engines, were driven away. Sammie's old guvnor, from when she first arrived at the station, had driven up from his West Country home through the night. He had wanted to say so much to Sammie but this former decorated soldier was too overwhelmed, his sadness robbing him of the power of speech. He just stood, ramrod straight, holding Sammie's hand as the tears flowed down his face. His grief, at seeing such an iconic station disappear, was there for all to see.

Sammie was transferred into the Brigade's Fire Investigation team following the closure of Clerkenwell. She had been a regular stand-by on the team and followed the progress of her arson cases even when she returned back to her normal watch duties.

Individuals had, for centuries, used fire maliciously to destroy either what doesn't belong to them or to cover some other misdoing. They wilfully set fire to property with the intent to cause damage. It was, and remains, a serious crime. It is called arson. Previously under British law, and during the early 19th century, setting fire to domestic and commercial premises, and "any stack of corn, grain, pulse, straw, hay or wood", was punishable by death. Arson was such a serious offence that it could incur a life sentence or trans-portation. By the early 20th century society was less concerned with property damage than it was about crimes against the person. So as cities grew and expanded people living together, in close quar-ters, raised new fears about murder and assault. But while punish-ments for arson have become less severe over time, fire-starting still captures the public imagination. It challenges the authorities.

Today, psychiatrists and criminologists say people start fires for excitement, profit, to take revenge, covering up other crimes and because of mental illness. Arson is very accessible. Fire setting requires little effort. It requires few tools. In fact, the arsonists' tech-niques have changed little in modern times.

A short distance from Sammie's Fire Investigation base a fire was already moving through a house. It was a two-storey, tradition-ally built, terraced house in the back streets of Islington. The flames had spread along the downstairs walls, bursting through doorways, blistering paint and floor tiles and igniting furniture. Dense smoke pressed up hard against the ceiling before it banked back down.

It seeped, unstoppable, into each room via cracks and crevices before exiting from openings in the windows and staining the early morning sky.

Billie, a 29 year-old, lived a few doors down. Returning from her night shift, and strolling down the road, she had smelt the smoke. Fearful for her own home she started to run. That was when she saw the flames and a man standing on the front path. He was wearing only a pair of jeans, his chest blackened by soot, his hair and eyelids singed. He was shrieking.

"My children!"

His three children, one year-old twin girls and two year-old Amber, were inside the blazing house.

It was Billie who called the Fire Brigade whilst another neighbour, roused by the screaming, raced out of his house to help. He picked up a brick and used it to smash the children's bedroom window on the front ground floor. Fire suddenly flashed through the hole. He broke another window. Flames burst through that too. Beaten back by the intense heat, he retreated into the street. The neighbour would later tell the police that the man in the jeans kept muttering, 'My babies!' before finally falling silent.

"It was if he had suddenly blocked the fire out of his mind," commented the neighbour.

Billie felt the intensity of the fire just standing on the pavement. Moments later the windows of the children's ground floor room exploded. Flames rolled up the front of the house. Within minutes of the 999 call the first fire engine arrived. Then a second. The half-naked man ran at them shouting that his children were in the room where the flames were coming from. The officer in charge sent a priority radio message requesting additional appliances and that 'persons' were reported.

Whilst some firefighters grabbed hoses and directed water on the blaze, others put on their breathing apparatus sets and entered the hallway under the cover of water spray from their hose-line. Instantly they were enveloped in clouds of superheated steam that mixed with the smoke. Another crew raced around the rear of the house where they discovered that the back door was blocked, on the inside, by a tall refrigerator.

The man, who had been looking on in a daze, suddenly became

hysterical. A firefighter had to restrain him before he led him away towards a fire engine and where he tried to calm him down. The man, now sobbing, explained that his partner had gone to work the previous evening. He had been awakened by the fire. His efforts to locate, and rescue, his children proved fruitless. He had only just escaped the burning hallway.

It was the first crew in who found the children. A lone firefighter emerged from the smouldering house cradling a young child in her arms. As the unmoving child was being given CPR, the man ran back towards the house. He had to be physically held back, a firefighter receiving a black eye in the process. With the man handed over to the police he, and the unconscious child, were removed by ambulance to hospital under police escort. It was there he was told that his child was dead. Her name was Amber. She had been found in the parents' bedroom. The firefighters had then discovered the twins lying on the floor of the children's front bedroom, their bodies severely burned. Post mortems would show that they had all died from smoke inhalation.

Sammie was already on scene when the police surgeon arrived. It was the surgeon who pronounced the twins dead. Sammie had commenced her preliminary investigation, eager to determine the cause of this fatal blaze. Her know-how reminded her that a fire 'talks' to you if you listen. She was joined by the duty Inspector from the local Islington police station. They had met previously at other incidents and he was impressed by something she had told him. "Fire does not only destroy evidence – it creates it."

After the crews had made up the gear and returned to their stations Sammie moved systematically through the charred house. Starting from the least damaged areas she worked her way down, taking photographs and making notes as she went. She was like an archaeologist mapping out an ancient ruin.

At the back door she observed there was just enough space to squeeze past the refrigerator obstructing the door. The air smelt of burned rubber and molten wiring. Ash covered the floor. It had mixed with firefighter's water to form a slurry that was sticking to her fireboots. In the kitchen/diner she noted only smoke and heat damage: a clear sign that the fire had not originated in that room. The hall corridor, which passed an under-stairs cupboard, led to the parents' rear bedroom, then the children's front bedroom and ended at the front door.

In the rear bedroom, where Amber's body had been found, most of the damage was from the smoke and heat, suggesting that the fire had started further down the hallway. As she continued her search, stepping over fire debris and ducking under wiring hanging down from the collapsed ceiling, in the hallway she found deep charring along the base of the walls. Gases become buoyant when heated: flames, ordinarily, burn upwards. However, here she observed that the fire had burned extremely low down. There were also peculiar charring patterns on the floor, shaped like small puddles.

Sammie's mood darkened. She continued to follow the 'burn trail'. A path etched by the fire. A path that led her from the hallway into the children's bedroom. The beam from her torch illuminated more of the irregularly-shaped char patterns. She knew a flammable liquid, doused on a floor, will cause a fire to concentrate in these kinds of pockets. The intense fire had burned through the carpeting, the lino, and right into the timber flooring. The metal springs beneath the twin's cots had turned white from heat. A clear indicator, thought Sammie, of the extreme temperatures within that room. The children's floor contained some of the deepest burn scars, something she knew had been hotter than the ceiling. Given that heat rises, her findings were sounding warning bells. "This is not a normal fire. It is suspicious. Very suspicious"

Next she examined a shard of glass. One from the smashed windows. It had a characteristic crazed glass look, something that she recognized as a key indicator of a fire that had burned 'hot and fast'. It was all pointing to the fire being fuelled by a liquid accelerant, thus causing the glass to fracture in such a fashion. "This is a bloody crime scene," she muttered to herself. She traced out the burn pattern in her mind's eye. A distinct burn trail led through the lower part of the house. It went from the children's bedroom into the hall corridor and led to the front door. She scanned the walls for soot and burn marks, looking for marks that resembled a 'V'. The bottom of the 'V' would indicate where a fire possibly began. Sammie recorded a distinct 'V' in the main corridor. Examining the burn patterns, she identified three places where fires had likely originated: in the hallway, in the children's bedroom, and by the front door. She arrived at a clear conclusion. This fire had been intentionally set by a human hand.

She explained her findings to the duty Detective Inspector, someone Sammie knew through her partner. Then followed a procession of CID officers, each one higher in rank than the preceding one. Sammie repeated her conclusions to each one in turn. She had concluded that someone had poured liquid accelerant throughout the children's room, even under their beds, then poured it along the hallway and to the front door. The fire created a barrier that prevented anyone from escaping. The refrigerator, she suggested, had been moved to block the back door exit. The Metropolitan Police forensic team were now on the scene. They collected evidence of burned materials from the house. It was confirmed, following analysis at the Metropolitan Police's forensics laboratory in Pratt Walk, Lambeth, that they contained the presence of a liquid accelerant. It was their chemist who identified that one of the samples contained a mineral spirit. The type of liquid found in charcoal-lighter fluid.

This house was declared a murder scene. The man who had been standing outside the house – the only person, besides the children, known to have been in the house at the time of the blaze – was arrested. He was still at the hospital where he had been admitted for observation.

It was not long before the police uncovered a disturbing profile of the man. He had a history of drug and alcohol abuse and Social Services had the children on their 'watch list' register. However, despite all the indicators to the contrary, they had not been deemed at imminent 'risk'. There were reports of violence against his partner too. But no charges had been brought as she had twice withdrawn the complaint.

Sammie eventually made it home. Her other half had progressed upward in rank too: he was a Detective Inspector. The arrested man was being held at his police station. During the evening he highlighted details of the extended interviews that had taken place during the day.

"The bastard said he never knew Amber was in his room. He said, 'Maybe she had already passed out by the time I stood up and rushed out, or perhaps she came in after I left'," he told Sammie.

During the intensive police questioning the man insisted that he tried to reach the children's bedroom.

"I couldn't see nuffin' but blackness. The air smelled the way it did when the microwave had blown up some weeks before. Burning wire and stuff like that."

He contended that when he did finally make it into the children's bedroom his hair caught on fire.

"God, I never felt anything that hot before," he asserted.

He stated that he patted out the fire in his hair, got down low on the ground and groped about in the dark.

"I thought I found one of them but it was a doll."

Finally, unable to bear the heat any longer, he had crawled, and stumbled, down the corridor, which was now in flames, before he fell out the front door, gasping for breath.

When asked how the fire had started he said he wasn't sure. He and his partner used electric space heaters to keep the house warm. One was in the children's room. Sammie's initial findings, which the police held, plus her written statement, showed she had inspected the heaters, and although they were damaged by fire, her photographs showed their switches in the 'Off' position.

The arrested man insisted that the fire was caused by some electrical fault. Pressed by the Detective Chief Inspector, who was leading the interview, if someone might wish to hurt his family the man had replied that he couldn't think of anyone that "cold-blooded".

"Sure, me and the missus have the odd ruck," he said. "But we've been together for four years now, and yes we sometimes would get into a fight, even split up for a while."

When pressed about Amber, he said, "To tell you the honest truth, I wish she hadn't woke me up."

At last his story started to unfold. He previously had stated he wasn't even aware that Amber was in the room. The police were convinced he had killed his children. Sammie's findings confirmed the floor had a liquid accelerant poured onto it and therefore the fire had burned low. The man could not have run out of the house the way he had described without burning his bare feet. The hospital's A & E doctor's report stated that his feet were uninjured: not even a scorch mark.

"His whole story was one of pure fabrication…" Sammie's partner explained, but without any sense of satisfaction. "He just talked and talked and all he did was lie. From everything you found out, and from what our own forensic team have confirmed, this piece of shit lit the fires as he was retreating. Torching the children's room first, then the hallway before he legged out the front door. That is why the bastard scorched his face and singed his hair. But there's no clear motive and no life insurance policies are involved."

The man's partner was adamant that although he had hit her he had never abused the children.

"Our kids were spoiled rotten," she had said later, and under oath, standing in the witness box.

It was after the trial, and the Judge's order for a psychiatric report, it concluded the man was a sociopath. A man without a conscience. Someone whose abuse of his partner had climaxed, almost inexorably, into triple murder from a desire to hurt her.

Sammie gave her evidence at the Old Bailey during the man's trial. Despite her intense cross-examination, that lasted a whole day, she held her ground. She presented her evidence with conviction and a professionalism that impressed the jury. It certainly impressed the Judge who commended Sammie in his summing up. The QC, leading the Crown's prosecution case, concluded in her final submission to the jury that the accused was "a sociopathic individual who deemed his children an impediment to his lifestyle." It was an argument that convinced the Jury who returned a unanimous Guilty verdict. The man was given three consecutive life sentences. There were no celebrations.

Whilst annotating the case file, after the trial, Sammie hoped the bastard would never make it to the end of his sentence. If there is any justice, other inmates would see to it he got his just deserts.

(Fiction)

Yesteryear's Fires: King's Cross Underground Station

ON THE EVENING OF 18 November 1987, a fire broke out at King's Cross St Pancras tube station, a major interchange on the London Underground. At King's Cross, as well as the mainline railway station above ground and subsurface platforms for the Metropolitan line, there are platforms deeper underground for the Northern, Piccadilly, and Victoria lines. There were two separate escalator shafts leading down to the Victoria and Piccadilly lines. The fire started under a wooden escalator serving the Piccadilly line. At 7.45 p.m. it erupted in a flashover into the underground ticket hall. The fire would kill 31 people and injure 100 more.

At about 7.30 p.m. several passengers reported seeing a fire on a Piccadilly line escalator. Staff and police went to investigate and on confirming the fire one of the policemen went to the surface to radio for the fire brigade. Four fire appliances and a turntable ladder were dispatched at 7.36 p.m. The fire was beneath the escalator; this made it impossible to get close enough to use a fire extinguisher. There was water fog equipment but underground staff had not been trained in its use. The decision to evacuate the station was made at 7.39 p.m. using the Victoria line escalators. A few minutes later the fire brigade arrived and several firefighters went down to the escalator to assess the fire. They saw a fire about the size of a large cardboard box and planned to fight it with a water jet with firefighters wearing breathing apparatus.

By 7.42 p.m. the entire escalator was aflame, producing super-heated gases that rose to the top of the shaft enclosing the escalator, where it was trapped against the tunnel's ceiling, which was covered with about 20 layers of old paint. As the superheated gases pooled along the ceiling of the escalator shaft, all those old layers of paint began absorbing the heat. The ceilings had been repainted several times in the past without removing the old paint. (A few years before the fire, the Underground's director of operations had suggested that all this paint might pose a fire hazard. However, painting protocols were not within his purview and his suggestion was widely ignored by his colleagues.)

At 7.45 p.m. a flashover occurred. A wall of flames came up from the escalator shaft, filling the ticket hall with intense heat and thick black smoke. It killed or seriously injured most of the people in the ticket hall. The fire trapped several people below ground; they escaped on Victoria line trains. Several policemen, with an injured man, attempted to leave via a platform, but found their way blocked by locked gates. These were later unlocked by a station cleaner. Staff and a policewoman trapped on a Metropolitan line platform were rescued by a passing train.

Thirty fire crews, over 150 firefighters, were deployed. Fourteen London Ambulance Service ambulances ferried the injured to local hospitals, including University College Hospital.

Of the 100 people taken to hospital, 19 were serious injuries, some critical. London Fire Brigade Station Officer Colin Townsley was in charge of the first pump fire engine to arrive at the scene and was in the ticket hall at the time of the flashover. He did not survive, his body being found beside that of a badly burnt passenger at the base of the exit steps to Pancras Road. It is believed that Townsley spotted the passenger in difficulty and stopped to help her.

Assistant Divisional Officer Cliff Shore was the station commander at Euston fire station. He was first senior officer to arrive at the King's Cross fire. He was later awarded the MBE for his work that night. The following are his words:

"From the time that I received the call I had an uneasy feeling about the incident that was to follow. This feeling was compounded by the presence of smoke some three-quarters of a mile from King's Cross and the heavy traffic build up. I was forced to park in York Way and was unable to see the blue flashing lights of the appliances due to the density of the smoke. When I got to the scene I was confronted with two persons in a collapsed condition. I immediately got two firefighters to render first aid. On initial reconnaissance dense smoke was coming from three entrances in Euston and Pancras Roads, and the concourse of the main line station was rapidly filling with smoke. I was unable to make contact with any officer and quickly realised that a serious and chaotic situation was in progress.

I assumed control and made pumps eight, ambulances four, persons reported. I was desperately short of officers and men to carry out all the tasks that were needed. I was informed that two members of the public had been found inside and that four members of the Brigade were missing. The heat coming from the entrances was extremely intense. It was obvious that there could be large numbers of people involved, therefore in my planned rescue attempts and attack on the fire from three different entrances, I was forced to put firefighters through punishing conditions. It was therefore conducive to have experienced BA crews with a minimum of a junior officer in charge and probationary firemen not to be included as part of the crew. A short time after I took command I was present when Station Officer Townsley was brought out and with a negative response from the ambulance resuscitator, and with three other members of the Brigade still missing, I feared the worst. When I was relieved of command I was able to get below and immediately the true horror of it all started to unfold when I came across eight bodies. I was most relieved to reach two of the missing members of the Brigade, who had been cut off since the flashover, both of whom were uninjured. I returned to the main area of fire, and satisfied that it was now under control, returned to the Control Unit and reported this to the Officer in Charge.

I would like to commend the work, dedication and heroism of all the members of the Brigade at this incident, which I feel was attributable to many more lives being saved, and I feel most proud to have served with those involved."

The fire was declared out at 1.46 a.m. the following morning.

At the time of the King's Cross fire the fire kit worn by London's firefighters consisted of thin yellow over-trousers, a woollen tunic and cork helmet, which left much of a firefighter's neck and ears exposed even when wearing breathing apparatus. Their PVC protective gloves would have been more at home in the garden. As a direct consequence of the King's Cross fire, improvements were made to firefighter's personal protective equipment: the combed-helmet was replaced by Kevlar headgear and some Fire and Rescue services later opted for a design that encloses the ears. Padded over-trousers and more substantial tunics, with collars, were also introduced.

Many heroic acts took place that horrific night. Not all were recorded and placed in the public domain. The London Fire Brigade convened a special Honours and Awards Board to consider the actions of its firefighters at that fateful fire. It concluded that Station Officer Colin James Townsley, attached to Soho fire station, be posthumously awarded the Chief Officer's Commendation following the King's Cross fire. He was the Officer in Charge of the initial attendance, riding Soho's pump-ladder. He and his crew had made their way down to the station concourse, at the head of the escalators. Here activity at the station appeared normal, although a small fire was apparent about one third of the way down of the right hand escalator. Ordering his crews to rig in BA and get a jet to work, he sent a priority message, "Persons reported". The resultant, and unexpected, flashover tragically leaves questions as to what exactly happens next as to firefighting operations, but his own escape was delayed to assist a badly burned young woman along the St Pancras subway. As a fit and strong man he would have certainly reached safety but for his courageous and selfless act of helping another. For heroism, supreme humanity and outstanding leadership he was subsequently posthumously awarded the George Medal.

Assistant Chief Officer Joe Kennedy (North East Area HQ), Assistant Divisional Officer Clifford John Shore (North Area HQ), Sub Officer Vernon Ronald Trefry, Firemen Paul Henry Hale and Robert Edward Moulton – all attached to Soho Fire Station – were awarded a Chief Officer's Commendation, the highest London Fire Brigade honour.

ADO Clifford Shore was subsequently awarded the MBE

(Gallantry). Firefighter Moulton was awarded the Queen's Gallantry Medal, whilst Sub Officer Trefry and Firefighter Hale were each awarded the Queen's Commendation for Brave Conduct.

The Chief Officer's Letter of Congratulations were also awarded to: Station Officer Peter Kenneth Osborne of Manchester Square Fire Station; T/Sub Officer Roger William Bell, T/ Leading Firefighter David Charles Flanagan and Firefighter Joseph James Boland, Manjit Singh of Clerkenwell Fire Station; Firefighter Stewart Button, John Edgar, David Charles Priestman, David Robert Smith and Steve John Bell, all attached to Soho fire station: Station Officer Alan Pryke of North Area Staff and T/Station Officer Roger De Monte North East Area Staff.

Firefighter Button and Edgar were subsequently both awarded the Queen's Commendation for Brave Conduct.

A subsequent public inquiry into the incident was conducted by Desmond Fennell OBE QC. He was assisted by a panel of four expert advisers. The inquiry opened at Central Hall, Westminster on 1 February 1988 and closed on 24 June, after hearing 91 days of evidence.

Smoking on underground rolling stock (trains) had been banned by London Underground in July 1984. Then following a major underground fire at Oxford Circus station, in November 1984, the smoking ban was extended to include all underground stations in February 1985. However, smokers often ignored this and lit cigarettes on the escalators on their way out. The inquiry found the fire was most probably caused by a traveller discarding a burning match that fell down the side of the moving staircase onto the running track of the escalator.

London Underground were strongly criticised in the report for their attitude to fires underground, underestimating the hazard because no one had died in a fire underground before. Staff were expected to send for the Fire Brigade only if the fire was out of control, dealing with it themselves if possible. Fires were called 'smouldering'. Staff had little, or no, training to deal with fires or evacuation.

In a House of Common debate into the Fennell report findings and its recommendations Frank Dobson, the then MP for Holborn and St Pancras, made the following comment to the Minister of State for Transport, Michael Portillo:

"The inquiry, although absolutely necessary, was in itself an additional cruelty for many who had to give evidence. It forced them to relive the horrors of that night, and also subjected their every action throughout the crisis, minute by minute, to the harshest, most clinical public scrutiny. Something to which few of us would like to be subjected even for an afternoon at the House of Commons, where nothing more than our reputation is at stake.

I found it a humbling experience to read how my ordinary fellow citizens reacted when faced with a fearful combination of fire, fumes, smoke, darkness, noise and panic, all of it below ground. In that heat and horror many ordinary people performed extraordinary deeds, saying afterwards that they were only doing their jobs. No words of praise or admiration from me, at least, can do justice to, for example the firefighter, Station Officer Colin Townsley.

When Colin Townsley arrives on the scene he goes down to the booking hall, reconnoitres down the escalators and instructs other members of his watch to go back to the surface to order more pumps and bring breathing apparatus for themselves and for him. He himself stays down there, in that dangerous, horrible place, to urge passengers to get out. The flashover fire occurs. The booking hall is engulfed in flames – flames so hot that they melt aluminium. Colin Townsley gropes around in the dark, and picks up a woman who is badly injured and burned. He makes for an exit where light and air would represent life to both of them, but the fumes poison him before he reaches safety. The report says, in its prosaic way: his was a heroic act. St John's Gospel says: Greater love hath no man than this that a man lay down his life for his friends. Colin Townsley laid down his life for a stranger.

Constable Hanson of the Transport police, although himself very badly burned and injured, risked his life to save more people, more strangers. We should remember that to the members of the emergency services the risk of injury and death is an ever-present part of their workaday world. When a catastrophe occurs, the rest of us run away, but the people in the emergency services run towards it.

The Fennell report rightly makes it clear that the fire and the shortcomings in the response to it were not the fault of the people working at King's Cross that night, nor were they the fault of those working in the emergency services that night. But the fire should not have occurred and, having occurred, it should have been dealt with more promptly and more effectively. The responsibility for any failure lies with the managements of London Regional Transport and the emergency services, with those who laid down the priorities to be followed by those managements and with those in Government whose job was and remains to secure the safe operation of all our railways. At the pinnacle of that pyramid of responsibility is the Secretary of State for Transport."

Footnotes on the King's Cross fire

For 16 years, he was simply 'body 115'. Then in 2003 the mystery victim of the King's Cross fire was finally identified as Alexander Fallon. The small, unnamed grave in a corner of a north London cemetery had held on to one of the last secrets of the King's Cross fire. But the mystery of body 115 (named after its mortuary tag number) was solved. Forensic experts from the British Transport Police confirmed that the remains belonged to 72 year-old Alexander Fallon, a homeless Scot. No one knows what the pensioner was doing at King's Cross station just after 7.30 p.m. on that November evening after the fireball swept up the wooden escalator and into the ticket hall, killing him and 30 others.

According to his family, Fallon's life had begun to unravel 13 years earlier when his wife died from ovarian cancer. He sold their house in Falkirk, and in the early 1980s headed south to London where he began sleeping rough. He kept in touch with his four daughters – two of whom were in Scotland and two in the US – with the odd letter and phone call until 1987, then nothing. But Fallon was just one of thousands of missing people in London, and police officers trying to identify the badly burned remains had little to go on. They knew they were looking for the family of a man who was 5ft 2in tall, a heavy smoker and had recently had brain surgery. But they believed the victim was in his 50s or early 60s, ten years younger than Fallon.

Sadly, tragedy visited the same underground station again in the terrorist attack on London on 7 July 2005. A bomb exploded on a train in the tunnel between King's Cross and Russell Square. The London Fire Brigade rescued victims trapped below.

When, following the London Tube bombings of 7 July, it was revealed that radios used by most blue-light emergency services still did not work underground, despite recommendations made 20 years earlier in his report into the King's Cross fire, Desmond Fennell drily observed: "If the Americans can communicate with a man on the moon, then it seems extraordinary that the Brits cannot get a system going down to people 20 yards beneath the surface."

(Fact)

Firefighter Jack Waterman

BY RIGHTS JACK WATERMAN should have been dead hours ago. His comment, "I was born lucky I suppose," fell well short of the experience he had just lived through.

The sun was already up, London's early morning sky a pale, watery, blue. The criss-crossed pattern of white vapour trails, from the early morning flights overhead, gave an indication of just how many aircraft could be stacked high over the capital at any one time. Jack peered out of the appliance window as they headed back south over Tower Bridge. He looked up at the jet aircraft, like tiny phantoms, but which today he thought could just as easily be angels.

He and the other two firefighters, in the rear of the fire engine, had removed their fire-helmets. They were glad of the cooling breeze. It was coursing up the Thames and after their long, hot, vigil, they were grateful of the refreshing chill in the air. Plumes of smoke were still rising from the Wapping fire, a fire that had taken them from their slumber many hours earlier. Such large fires were not so common in the London Fire Brigade these days. Ron Brooks, their fifty-four year old senior hand, gleefully reminded them yet again that back in the 1970s, when he started, big fires were a frequent occurrence. They had had a taster of what it was like 'back in the day', but even Ron had never attended anything quite like this. As for Jack's actions, well they had witnessed nothing short of a miracle.

From Jack's perspective, things had always turned out all right for this cheerful Bermondsey lad. The lad with the white flash in his head of thick black hair. Jack loved where he worked at Dockhead's Fire Station, even if he didn't stand a chance of ever getting on the housing ladder in an area where both his grandfather and his father had lived and worked.

His grandfather had been a docker, although it never really provided regular employment. When he got a job unloading, or loading, ships in the docks it wasn't always secure. His father had seen even less of the docks, his five-year apprenticeship coming to an abrupt end when the last of the London's docks closed down. Jack knew both men were bitter. His grandfather had taken his bitterness to the grave; his father less so now, especially since his youngest son, Jack, had become a London firefighter and was working in those once-familiar south London streets.

Despite Jack's family moving to the Addington council estate, after his father's enforced change of career, he had stayed with his Nan. She was a formidable woman who rented her Druid Street home. Jack had grown up in streets that had, in more recent times, gone from poor to posh. However, his Nan had always managed to keep Jack grounded. A lifelong Labour supporter, and an original Suffragette, she had nurtured her grandson's own socialist beliefs. Her peaceful death at 92 had finally forced Jack to move away, the house reverting back to its anonymous landlord.

Jack's intelligence and his many life skills, gained after five years serving in the Royal Marines after he left college, had opened up a number of lucrative career opportunities. But his best pal Dean had joined the London Fire Brigade two years earlier and suggested to Jack:

"This is the job for you, mate. You should give it a try."

So he had and he loved his job as a London Firefighter.

Despite the passage of time, and the insistence, of first, his Station Officer and then his Station Commander, Jack resisted all efforts to get him on the Brigade's career development programme – a promising path to promotion that, they said, lay ahead of him. But it was his socialist roots that took him in another direction, a direction that led to the Fire Brigades Union. He had risen through their ranks and was now a member of its London executive.

Departing that day for his night shift, from his suburban London home near the Kent border, had not gone well. Just before he left for work there had been another argument. The subject matter was the same as recent days: a possible national firefighters' strike, something that seemed increasingly likely. Not that Jack's wife wasn't supportive of him. She was immensely proud of what he did, what he had achieved and who he was. She loved her husband dearly. She shared his political leanings, just not as intently. But the demands of bringing up their three young children, all under five, took its toll on both. Especially now that the twin girls, whose unexpected arrival had come as a shock, had entered the 'terrible twos' phase. Then there was the matter of the unfinished kitchen, a refurbishment that Jack had started some months earlier. Despite being a talented craftsman Jack found the pressures of parenthood, the demands of his Union duties and love for his shift pattern was causing conflicting problems on the home front. Yet regardless of her sense of frustration, his wife, as always, kissed her husband goodbye.

"Be careful Jack," she said. She meant it too.

Driving into central London, via the A2, he thought that if the strike did come about, which appeared a certainty, at least he might be able to finish the bloody kitchen.

Steve Gilbert was a man who naturally collected responsibilities. It was not his fault. People would ask him to do things and he did them very well, he was that type of guy. Even at school he was a natural choice for the headmaster to make a prefect. A Boy Scout, he became a Queen's Scout, and now in his adult years ran a successful Scout group in Deptford. Tall and lean, with thinning black hair and a very long nose, he had applied, and failed, to become a London fireman in the early 1980s. His asthma prevented him from passing the Greater London Council's medical examination for employment as a fireman, so he had become a Special Constable instead. His beat, when performing his voluntary duties, was walking the chic, upmarket streets of Wapping and Shadwell. A few decades earlier a solitary policeman, or a 'special', would never have been seen walking those particularly rough London streets.

Whilst Wapping's street names remained unchanged the expensively converted wharves and warehouse attracted a very different occupant from the past. These upmarket people wanted the law to protect them and their valuable properties in streets were not overly busy. In truth, Steve thought, not many of those he passed on his patrol even noticed he was there. The "Good evening, officer" was absent. Although he did get a polite "Thank you" from a City gent, a smart-looking man he held a car door open for as he struggled to slide in the box of Moët et Chandon champagne onto the back seat of his top of the range Mercedes.

In an area where its resident population remained relatively small, and who lived in exclusive apartments and penthouses, Steve nevertheless felt he had an important role to play. Yes, there could be occasional risks – for example, a random individual taking umbrage with an officer of the law, albeit a 'special'. For him it was a responsibility he believed was his duty. It was fate which found him on duty that particular night.

What the Wapping building had once been was of little consequence to the foreign investment company developing the site. It stood on land in one of the richest pieces of riverside real-estate north of the Thames. It was a prime site. Work had already started on the extensive rebuild when the developers were served with a court order from the City of London. It brought the work to a sudden, and expensive, halt. Archaeologists had overturned the refusal of the company to allow a dig. They had been awarded a three-week window to explore and excavate the site. A number of significant artefacts from the early Roman period had been found in an exploratory dig. Given the finds, there was every possibility that the dig would get extended. For the faceless individuals, those behind the investment company's façade, this was less than impressive news. Two were fuming. Unless building work restarted very soon they would be out of pocket by millions of pounds. They were not the sort of people you wished to confront or offend. They had planned to sort things out.

There was nothing exceptional about the start of the night shift for the Dockhead firefighters. Normal checks, normal routines and the normal firefighters' banter. No one pushed Jack for an insider's news of the likely strike. When he had something to say he would tell anyone keen enough to listen. But he never had any difficulty in attracting an audience or selling the FBU's case. He was a powerful and a measured orator. The station was 100 per cent FBU across all its watches. Not because they had to be but because Jack was an excellent ambassador for the FBU's values and its beliefs. No one, including Jack, was looking forward to the strike. It was not an 'if' but 'when'. There was an inevitability about it now. Tensions were rising between non-union Brigade senior officers and the membership of London's FBU.

The fire alarm call was received by Mondale Security, a company which monitored many of the City of London's automated fire detection systems. The duty officer there simply cancelled the alarm, indicating it as a false alarm: something he had been instructed to do and paid handsomely for doing so. These were not the actions of Special Constable Steve Gilbert. He had seen the flames. Summoning the fire brigade, before requesting additional police support, he ran to investigate the fire.

Whitechapel's pump was already out on a call so it was their pump-ladder, Shadwell's pump-ladder and pump, plus Poplar's aerial appliance that were dispatched to Wapping. The arsonists knew their trade. By the time Steve Gilbert had moved closer, and with the four fire engines drawing ever nearer, flames were spreading after the incendiary devices had been remotely detonated by mobile phone. The second 999 call, from a penthouse apartment south of the River in Bermondsey's Shad Thames, brought Dowgate's pump-ladder out in support.

Shadwell's Station Officer was in the final year of his 33 years' service. He was in charge of the first attendance and no stranger to East London blazes. He told his driver to pull in behind Whitechapel's machine, whose acting Sub Officer was relieved to see this particular 'guvnor' standing there. The Station Officer had no hesitation in making pumps ten as he set about directing the attack on the rapidly spreading ferocious fire.

There was a flurry of firefighter activity. Breathing apparatus sets were readied, hose lines laid out and water supplies augmented. Access was hindered by the narrow streets and the halted building works. The archaeologists' dig made the firefighters' life difficult since the intricate excavations had to be negotiated. Thick, choking, smoke started drifting down over the whole area as other fire engines started to arrive.

Shadwell's Station Officer knew his craft. His initial actions were clear in his mind. He communicated them to those around him in short measure. His own crews established a breathing apparatus (BA) entry control point and undertook a preliminary reconnaissance. Shoreditch's crews, led by their Sub Officer, made a similar foray into the building via the second floor mezzanine. They discovered smoke-filled passageways and heat – lots of heat. The Sub Officer reported, via his BA communications set, several seats of fire, his crew being forced lower and lower as the heat levels rose ever higher. Given other circumstances, a more restrained attack on the fire would have been consider appropriate. However, the reports of two missing security guards spurred the firefighters into greater efforts. They were putting themselves in harm's way.

The dry rising main had been charged at street level. The Poplar and Bow crews had worked miracles to get two lines of hose to work on the east of the building. They reported fire both in front and above them. Whilst a lot had been achieved in a short space of time, it was still not enough. The fire had the upper hand. The duty Station Commander intercepted Shadwell's Station Officer's second priority message to "Make pumps 15" as he turned into Wapping's Thomas Moore Street.

There was a controlled urgency in the actions of the firefighters. Crews inside moved forward slowly, some more slowly than others as conditions quickly deteriorated. Crews waiting in BA were ready to support, and relieve, their colleagues as they exited sweaty and fatigued. The smoke-stained BA face masks told their own tale: a tale of harsh, difficult conditions being experienced by those inside the building.

Dockhead's pump-ladder and pump were ordered to the fire on the "Make pumps 15" instruction. It was only a short distance to travel from their fire station south of the river before parking at the far end of a line of fire engines. Further down the street, Jack Waterman noted the Divisional Officer talking to a Station Officer and a Station Commander by the Brigade's main control unit. As they walked towards the control unit to book-in, it was Ron Brooks who piped up, "What are they trying to do? Talk it out?" Dockhead's crew were eager to get in on the action.

The sudden explosion caused pandemonium. The Brigade normally responds to them; it has limited experience of already being at the epicentre when one happens. The detonation sounded like a salvo of artillery fire. Its percussive sound pulsated around the surrounding streets. Some of those on the excavation's periphery were blown off their feet. Others had the sound of ringing in their ears, the smell of burning filling their nostrils. What had been organised chaos, with firefighters attacking the blaze, was transformed in an instant. The scene had been utterly distorted. It took a few seconds for the enormity of the event to sink in, experienced officers and crews alike trying to absorb what had just happened. This was when their training, and trepidation about their comrades' safety, kicked in.

The notoriously gruff Senior Officer, based at Shoreditch Fire Station, was a former Assistant Divisional Officer. He had been promoted to that rank before the term 'Station Commander' had been introduced in the 1980s. Now he was one himself, re-designated as a Station Commander. He was none too happy about being designated as the Control Unit Officer by the youthful duty Divisional Officer who had taken charge of the incident. With mayhem raining down all around him, the Divisional Officer looked much less self-assured than when he first arrived. In fact, he was totally bewildered by the turmoil that now confronted him. He was disoriented and nonplussed, unable to order his own thoughts let alone direct the actions of those around him.

The crotchety Station Commander had no such difficulties. He made a number of rapid decisions and took immediate action. He ordered a message dispatched stating what had happened and that crews were probably involved. Some might even be trapped. He made pumps 25 and requested four additional fire-rescue tenders whilst declaring a "major incident" at Wapping. He balanced ordering an immediate evacuation of the premises with the demands of initiating any rescues and searches required. He chose the latter. Despite taking on the mantle of incident commander he sent the messages in the name of the Divisional Officer who, at this time, he still felt the need to protect.

At those fire stations forming the next wave of attack, concerned firefighters looked at the ordering slips. They read, with incredulity, the possibility of firefighters, their comrades, being caught up in an explosion. Adrenalin started to course its way through their veins, heightening their senses, preparing them for the horrors that might lie ahead. Blue flashing lights and halogen headlamps cleared what little traffic there was on the road that time of night. The drivers of the reinforcing pumps and additional fire rescue tenders determined to get every ounce of power from their diesel engines. Fourteen additional crews converged on the scene in the East End of London, many travelling in excess of 60 miles an hour.

At Wapping, police officers, paramedics and fire crews, who were standing outside the site, rushed forward to do whatever they could. The walking wounded were swiftly assisted to safety. Some were just shocked, others clearly injured. Several had to be supported by colleagues, others required more intensive medical treatment where they lay. Two required urgent resuscitation. A semblance of order was being established but it was limited. A triage area was created. Urgent orders and commands directed the rescue efforts. Some of the rescuers were injured themselves but put their pain and discomfort aside as they fought to locate and render aid to their wounded firefighter colleagues.

Despite the flying debris, the chaos caused by the explosion, the predominant thought of those firefighters inside the burning building was:

"What the f*** was that?"

In most cases, but not all, it was followed by the thought: "It is time to get out." Ironically, it was the building that saved the majority of those still inside. The explosive devices had been strategically placed in the archaeologists' excavations: their aim, to destroy the reason for the development's delay. A combination of ancient stone and London rubble was flung in every direction, creating missiles that had the ability to kill or maim. The first principal officer to arrive ordered the site's evacuation. But with many crews still trying to get in to help, other crews trying to get out of the building on fire, confusion reigned. Tempers were lost. Harsh words were exchanged as orders were disobeyed, with some firefighters refusing to leave the damaged areas unchecked.

Jack Waterman and Ron Brooks watched as the two police officers had run forward to help the injured firefighters. They looked on, in total disbelief, as the two just disappeared from view, seemingly swallowed up by the ground beneath their feet. Jack and Ron were now running too. Ron grabbed a line from the nearest appliances as he chased after Jack who had jumped down into the excavation works and was peering into an apparent 'sink-hole'. As he neared the edge, crumbling debris fell into the widening pit. Jack threw himself flat on the ground to stop himself falling in. With only his head and shoulders poking over the edge he looked down for any signs of life. All he could see was the rising dust cloud although he thought he heard a pained groaning. At least that's what he told Ron as he prepared to take a closer look. Ron, who was holding onto Jack's feet, quickly tied one end of the rope around Jack's waist and the other around his own. He watched as Jack crawled over the edge and slid, head first, into the gaping hole.

Jack was eating dust. It clogged his tear ducts as he edged further into the hole. He had no idea what he might find at the bottom, but the groaning sounded real enough. He headed in the direction of the noise. It was a slow, painful, process as he clawed his way through the rubble. His torch beam gave little illumination in the dust-filled gloom. He had taken on the appearance of a ghost as fine particles covered him from head to toe. His mouth dried up. He attempted to spit but the dust absorbed what little spittle he produced. His progress was measured in centimetres as he scraped along the uneven surface then squeezed his way into an opening, always following the sound of groaning. He forced his way into a small chamber that had formed in the fallen masonry. He found himself in a space about half his body length. His outstretched hand touched something or someone. However, they neither moved nor made any sound. Jack had to listen hard for any sound of breathing. The groans he heard, weaker now, were still ahead of him.

Jack dragged himself into the constricted space, pushing rubble aside with each move. Filling all the available space he felt for a pulse on the body at his side. He found one. It was weak and feeble. The man remained unresponsive. Jack's hands moved down the length of the unconscious policeman, his hand involuntary withdrawing as he touched the jagged broken bone sticking out of the man's thigh. He then found the rubble covering the other leg. It pinned the man to the ground.

Jack attempted to call out to the other policeman. He wanted to reassure him that help was at hand. His first shout failed, dust clogging his throat. It was impossible to reach the second man without moving the first. Jack knew he could not do what was required unaided so, putting himself into reverse, he pushed his way back out to the base of the collapse.

As Ron looked down he hardly recognised the apparition as it emerged from the hole. The image immediately reminded Ron of the images of New York Fire Department firefighters in the aftermath of 9/11 and the collapse of the Twin Towers. Jack's eyes, his only feature that stood out, looked bloodshot and sore. Jack's voice was raw as he shouted up what he found and what was needed. By now Ron was no longer alone. He had help at his side. Dockhead's crew, and one of the fire rescue crews, were waiting in readiness and impatient to assist.

The first rescue took almost an hour. Some of the fallen masonry had to be made safe. What appeared as a disused tunnel wall had to be supported and secured. Progress was painfully slow. Access remained extremely difficult. Jack had crawled back into the tiny space first. He was followed by others. The more bodies that fitted into this poky space the warmer everyone got. Those behind Jack, toiling in this claustrophobic atmosphere, worked furiously. Finally, and after a paramedic had crawled in and administered pain relief to the unconscious man, the first of the policemen were released from the rubble's hold. His exposed and bloodied bone bore testament to the severity of his injury.

His recovery, back up to ground level, was no easy matter either. The danger of a further collapse of earthworks and falling masonry was ever-present. With nothing else available that could fit in the available space, the policeman had a section of a scaffolding board slid beneath him. It made for an improvised stretcher. With Jack pushing and another firefighter pulling they managed to get the man out to where he could be transferred on a proper stretcher. As Jack re-entered the tunnel, crawling on all fours, he scurried towards the second policeman who lay some distance ahead.

Steve Gilbert drifted in and out of consciousness, his legs crushed as far as Jack could tell. Using his bare hands, Jack worked for the next hour in the dimmest of lights, and increasingly foul atmosphere, trying to release Steve. His fingers raw and bleeding, Jack was now stripped to his waist. Portable lighting was directed along the shaft. It made the task, if not easier, then slightly less problematic. There was hardly room to swing a cat in the space, let alone move the entombing pieces of rubble. Piece by piece, lump by lump they were passed back along the human chain of firefighters who fed them outside from where they were hoisted up in buckets.

Ninety minutes after the start of the rescue Jack's working space was reduced by half. An air-ambulance doctor had joined him. Those behind Jack had to withdraw whilst the doctor and his medical kit made the perilous crawl into the confined space. He had to climb over Jack's back to reach the casualty. It took a few more precious minutes for the doctor to make his initial assessment, which wasn't good. Steve was likely to lose both his legs, if he didn't die first, unless he could be brought out to safety soon. To make matters worse some of the stone walling was starting to totter. The area was becoming increasingly unstable. The heavy plant that had been started up and working overhead sent vibrations through the ground. Orders were swiftly given and the machinery stopped moving. Everything now moved by hand.

Bent double, the doctor managed to squeeze into the space next to Steve. After administering morphine he inserted an intravenous drip and monitored the worrying vital signs. He fully appreciated the pressures the firefighters were working under but told Jack anyway:

"You really do need to hurry up."

With the last of the debris removed, willing hands moved Steve Gilbert along the length of the collapse. In order to extricate Steve, Jack had to take the weight of the tottering stones on his back whilst first Steve then the doctor moved past him. Jack was the last to exit. The tottering stones finally collapsed after Steve, in a stretcher, was being hauled up to safety.

After nearly three hours of hot, gruelling and exhausting work the task of extricating the two policemen, in near darkness, was over. Both had been brought out alive. The job of keeping them that way now rested with the doctors and the medical surgical team of the nearby Whitechapel Hospital.

All the while the fire had continued to burn. Amid the commotion, and resultant mayhem that the explosion had caused, Shoreditch's Station Commander remained clear-headed and resourceful. He had also stayed in charge of the control unit crew, retaining a sharp understanding of everything that had to be done and their relative priority. He was a positive asset to the unfolding drama and in stark contrast to the Brigade's incident commander, an Assistant Chief Officer, whose haughtiness won him few friends. 'Pompous' was the polite 'P' word used about him; most firefighters just called him a 'prick.' The Assistant Chief's adenoidal tones only highlighted the gulf that existed between the two men as Shoreditch's Station Commander briefed him, his gravelly East London accent telling of the number of firefighters injured and the successful recovery of the two policemen. He also reminded his superior:

"We need to get back to attacking the bloody fire, Sir!"

In fact, it had not entirely been forgotten. Some crews, once they had been accounted for in the roll call, had been instructed to contain the blaze. With order slowly being returned, it again became the main focus of the firefighter's attention. The grumpy Station Commander – who had started his LFB career wearing black leggings, carrying a bicycle lamp, wearing a black cork helmet and issued with a belt and fireman's axe – was in his element. His was the era of Melton tunics, silk neckerchief and red PVC gloves. His individual leggings gave him a wet arse in minutes and little, or no, protection from any object with a sharp edge to it as it penetrated and tore into the plastic fabric. His early years were spent fighting fires crawling on his hands and knees, and frequently even lower on his stomach. Breathing apparatus was only carried on the pumps back then and not wearing it did not mean you weren't expected to get stuck in. He would exit fires soaked, either from sweat or his overall trousers and underpants wet through. He had served his fire-fighting apprenticeship in a different age. But he brought his skills onto any fire-ground he attended in his senior rank.

Today's firefighters wear greatly improved fire kit, kit that gives them better protection. Although things had certainly changed, the Station Commander's attitude hadn't. New procedures had come hand in hand with the new kit, driven by lessons that had been learnt the hard way. Some had come at the highest of prices, a fire-man's or a firefighter's life. But his standpoint towards firefighting hadn't changed much. It was something that had won him the respect of his peers and station personnel alike. He was believer that you still had to get in to get it sorted. You were there to fight the fire, not surround it and drown it.

With Brigade personnel injured, some seriously, the Chief Officer had no option but to attend the incident. It would be the very last fire he would attend as Chief Fire Officer. His title was to change to that of 'Fire Commissioner'. Not that the injured fire crews, heading to the nominated hospitals, or those attempting to bring the blaze under control could give a damn what he was called. To them he remained a distant figurehead. Someone detached from the reality of their job. He had made no public statements in support of his own firefighters regarding the FBU's pay claim. In fact, it was rumoured he was seeking private security firms to provide 'scab' fire cover if the strike materialised.

The Chief did not take command, something he rarely did, but he was impressed by the succinct briefing given to him by the Station Commander in charge of the control unit. Especially so when informed that they still needed to get a grip on the blaze! The Chief listened intently but said nothing. He just nodded his understanding as he stepped back out of the control unit.

It was a non-smiling Assistant Chief Officer, the incident commander, who strode back into the control unit. His angry, nasal, tones made him almost inaudible following his discussion with the Chief. Shoreditch's Station Commander was relieved of his control unit duties.

"You are the sector commander on the south side. Let's see what you can do there."

Which is what he did, providing his brand of fire-ground leadership. The crews responding positively to his instructions and the vocal encouragement from someone who once would have been termed a 'fireman's fire officer'. His combative style was directed at the fire, not the crews fighting it. Neither was he overzealous or trigger-happy in the tactics he deployed. There was an innate sense, felt by the crews, that they were being led by a competent and supportive officer. They responded in kind. His reputation as fire-ground officer did not disappoint. To some of the junior officers and firefighters who had never met this upfront, blunt, Station Commander, he earned their immediate respect.

Jack never saw the fire extinguished. He and the other Dockhead crews were relieved. Brief statements were taken by the senior officers drafted in to commence the major accident investigation. No easy task when the site was an active crime scene too.

The incident commander never did congratulate Jack for a job well done, but plenty of others did. Dog-tired, drained, and with throbbing raw fingers, all Jack wanted was a hot shower back at the fire station.

There never had been much love lost between the Brigade's principal officers and Jack. Both viewed their respective worlds very differently. There had been little doubt regarding the outstanding bravery of many individuals that night, including members of the police, the medical services and paramedics. Still, it was no surprise, despite the range of subsequent bravery commendations awarded to members of the Brigade for actions above and beyond the call of duty, that Jack's nomination for a national gallantry award found little favour with the head of the Brigade. But the local 'City gent' whom Steve Gilbert had previously helped turned out to be a man of some considerable influence. In fact he was the City of London's Police Commissioner. He ensured that justice prevailed where Jack was concerned. His name would be added to the very few in the British Fire Service to be nominated for the George Cross and to be still be alive when he received it.

The Lord Chamberlain's confidential letter dropped through Jack's letterbox in November 2002, the very day the UK firefighter's dispute started. The FBU members voted, overwhelmingly, to take strike action in their attempt to secure a better pay deal. For Jack the medal was all rather embarrassing. Whilst his colleagues watching him that night said, "He deserves a bloody medal," Jack didn't feel he earned one such as this. He had done what others would have willingly done. Steve Gilbert disagreed. He came along to Dockhead's picket line in a wheelchair. He had insisted on visiting Jack and thanking him personally for saving his life. He brought with him the heartfelt thanks of the other police officer who was still too injured to travel.

It was some time later that Jack was invited, accompanied by his wife, to attend Buckingham Palace for the presentation of the George Cross by Her Majesty the Queen. He was required to attend in uniform. But with the strike still in full swing Jack choose to delay the award date. He mused, wishing to cite in his reply that the last thing he wished to see at the Palace gates was a FBU picket line! That was one line that he could not have crossed. So he sent a more diplomatic reply instead, suggesting it would be preferable to wait until the strike was over. It was something that the Queen never mentioned when she pinned the George Cross medal on Jack's chest.

The final chapter to this tale are the investigations, the most serious being the extensive police investigation which governed the other various inquiries into that night's explosive events. It was followed by the results of the Health and Safety Executive's investigation after the removal to hospital of nineteen firefighters and two policemen injured in the arson and bomb attack. Finally, there was Brigade's own ill-conceived discipline inquiry into alleged procedural failures by those who put themselves in danger to save others.

The criminal charges against the culprits, who were all brought to book, ensured that no members of the Brigade were punished on account of their actions. But it was some while before the Brigade matters were resolved: a legacy of a bitter strike, one which saw the gulf widen between firefighters and their non-FBU senior officers. Jack realised, in the wake of the strike, that radical changes were coming to the LFB. He wondered where they would all lead.

(Fiction)

First Night Duty

HE WAS A FUSION of excitement, anticipation and trepidation. It was his first night duty at the fire station, the date 22 September 1966. At 27 years of age he did not think those emotions applied to him but clearly they did. Since leaving school at 15 the East London man had had a number of jobs. "Just keeping the wolves from the door," he would say. But none had given him this sense of exhilaration or pride – emotions he was experiencing as he strolled up to the fire station's entrance following the bus journey from his Hackney home to this unfamiliar part of North London. For Alec it would be a night he never forgot.

He was pinching himself. It all seemed to have happened so quickly, but of course it hadn't. He had seen the advertisement to join the London Fire Brigade at the end of last year, just before Christmas 1965. He had been laid off yet again from the Millwall docks. This time it was feared they were to be laid off permanently. The LFB poster had said, "It's an exciting life with the London Fire Brigade." Alec had not given it much thought before; joining the Fire Brigade, that is. The salary of just £1080 a year was much less than he had earned at the docks, but he hadn't heard of many firemen being laid off work so he wrote off to the address shown – The London Fire Brigade (P), Albert Embankment, London SE1 – and waited for a reply.

He did not have to wait long. He was invited along to the recruit's selection day at the Brigade's Training School in Southwark Bridge Road in surroundings that had a distinct Victorian feel. This was due to the fact that is exactly what it once was: the former Victorian Metropolitan Fire Brigade headquarters. Its buildings now formed the Brigade's Training School. It was here he did his recruit tests. He knew what to expect. He had gone along to the Kingsland Road Fire Station and asked about them. Performing the firemen's lift and carry, over one hundred yards, never even brought him out in a sweat but the chill of that January day might have seen to that. The education tests proved no obstacle either, nor did the medical examination at the GLC's County Hall. It was the interview, conducted by two senior fire officers at the Brigade's Lambeth headquarters, which had caught him on the hop.

Having confirmed his name as Alec Beaucanon and his home address, Alec was ready to spew out all the prepared reasons for wanting to join the London Fire Brigade.

"So you're a boxer?" asked the more senior of the two officers, who looked as though he had been through a few rounds in the ring over the years.

"Yes", replied Alec, wondering where this question was going.

He soon found out as the officer, with far more 'scrambled egg' on his epaulettes than the other, who only had three pips, started his interrogation about Alec's boxing history. It was a history which started in a boy's club in the City Road. It would take Alec to the ABA's London championships three years later. He had won. It was the arrival of his baby daughter that, in part, was the reason he never turn semi-professional. His boxing talent had left his youthful looks remarkably unmarked despite his numerous fights.

"Thank you Mr Beaucanon, that is all," said the smiling officer as he closed Alec's file and picked up the next interviewee's paperwork. "You will be contacted about our decision."

Alec rose and left the office. As he closed the door the other officer looked as bemused as Alec about the interview questioning!

"We never asked him why he actually wanted to join the Brigade," said the Assistant Divisional Officer, the man with three pips.

The more senior man had, in his youth, been a 'Golden Gloves' boxing champion. He turned to his colleague, saying:

"Of all the sports boxing is one of the most physically demanding. It requires a blend of power and quickness, combined with excellent overall conditioning. Boxers are continually perfecting their craft as they move up in rankings to face tougher opponents. We need firemen; he has many of the qualities we are looking for. What he doesn't know we will teach him. Subject to his references, he will do, you mark my words."

It took a few weeks for Alec's two references to be returned to the fire brigade headquarters. Then another week before the headquarters' typist reached the details for Alec's letter. As she read through the officer's decision she never even looked down at the typewriter keys as her fingers swiftly typed out the offer of a job as a London Fireman. The letter instructed him to attend Southwark and commence his training as a recruit fireman in June.

For a few years in the 1960s London was the world capital of cool. *Time* magazine had dedicated a whole issue to London: the Swinging City. Commentators wrote about London and all things hip and fashionable. London began to look more futuristic as high-rise buildings and inner-city motorways changed the look of its streets. Just down the road from Hackney the first phase of the new Barbican development had been completed. To Alec's wife, coping with their toddler daughter in their dilapidated council flat, London did not look cool at all. The plans to shift London's docks downstream to Tilbury was seeing her whole world fall apart. Since Alec had sent off his application letter to the Fire Brigade the only money coming in was his dole money. Her hands were shaking as Alec passed her the letter that arrived with a London Fire Brigade franking mark on it.

"Go on, you open it," said her husband. "You will bring me luck."

She did and read aloud the contents of the letter. Suddenly their future seemed a whole lot brighter.

"Maybe," said his joyfully tearful wife, "we might even be able to apply for one of them Fire Brigade flats that they let the firemen live in. Like the ones at the Kingsland Road fire station?"

"Who knows?" said Alec. "Nineteen sixty-six is certainly a year we will remember."

They did too for many reasons, not least England winning football's World cup on 30 Saturday July. But music was a huge part of their daily scene too. While Liverpool had the Beatles, their London sound, in 1966, was a mix of bands including The Who, The Kinks, The Small Faces and The Rolling Stones. It was music that helped cheer an otherwise difficult time as they listened to the 'pirate' radio stations, stations like Radio Caroline, and Alec's favourite, Radio London.

Alec's recruit course was during the summer of '66. It started at the beginning of June. There was a buzz about Southwark, something he noticed as soon he walked under the arched entrance of the training school. The new recruits, Alec's intake, stood out like a sore thumb for the first couple of days as they went round in their civvies. Their instructor, a former Royal marine with 15 years' service in the Brigade, clearly believed he was still in the marines as he barked out his orders from their very first meeting. Alec's squad of ten was a mix of ex-squaddies, matelots and others. They were all older than him except two fresh-faced young lads.

The instructor's 'sergeant major' antics had little impact on the ex-servicemen. They had seen it all before. It might have been a breeze for them, but for the two teenagers, both only just 18 years old, it was all a culture shock. Alec could not be sure but he felt there was heartless side to his instructor as he gave the two youngsters a relentless teasing compared to the way he deferred to the former servicemen.

Within those first weeks, in their blue overalls, uniform caps and leather fireboots, they were all skidding into position across the cobblestone drill yard, pushing 50-foot wheeled escape ladders along and rolling out the heavy canvas hose. They jumped on and off fire engines, performing elementary drills which increasingly got more complicated as each week passed. At drills their instructor ran them ragged, especially the two youngest recruits. Wet through with sweat or soaked to the skin after a hose drill, they went for their morning or afternoon stand-easy, where they eagerly consumed bottles of milk and ate crusty cheese rolls whilst breathing in fag smoke in the recruits' mess-room.

The drills were interspersed with learning their technical notes, learning about building construction, pumps and pumping, hydraulics, foam and hydrants and the various subjects required of firemen. Weekly quizzes tested the absorption of a plethora of facts and figures about the length of this, the diameter of that or the weight of a particular item of equipment, plus how it was tested and when.

There was no let-up in their training. Whilst the squaddies took the early physical activity in their stride, one hit a wall when it came to hook ladders. He hated the idea of hanging on the outside of the drill tower, suspended by a narrow bit of steel that stuck out at 90 degrees to the hook ladder and gave the ladder its name. It was one of the two teenagers who came to his aid by volunteering to partner him in the two-man hook ladder drills. Whatever 'magic' this teenager used on the other man, it worked. His calming influence on the former soldier had them working as a team. It had other benefits too. Suddenly the two youngest in the squad were not treated as teenagers any more, even by the overbearing instructor. They were treated as equals, as men.

For Alec, and the others, there was also the more mundane parts of their course, like leaving a uniform cap on the cap rack whilst having stand-easy, then having to checking it was the right one after some silly sod swapped them all around! Finding the right cap was a tedious affair, especially with 60 identical 'uniform' caps on the rack. Alec was caught out more than once. It made him late for drill or class, which did not impress his instructor. Then there were the compulsory extra hours training on a Tuesday and Thursday evenings. Finally, each Friday followed a similar pattern: morning parade followed by scrub-outs and cleaning the whole of the training school before parading again, being paid for the week and then off home!

Alec valued every day of his training course regardless of what was thrown at him. He studied his technical notes. He kept his head down and watched and listened. In the second half of his twelve-week course, things moved up a gear. The drills got harder and more complicated. Recruits learnt to 'carry-down': carrying each other, using a fireman's lift, down the escape ladder. It was testing and potentially dangerous. Another recruit had fallen to his death performing this drill in the months before they started their training course.

A combination of different ladders were used together with their pump drills, the most complicated being when a 'first floor' ladder was tied to the top of a fully extended 50-foot escape ladder. This drill tested knot-tying skills and confidence. They would have to climb the near-vertical first floor ladder to the fifth floor of the drill tower before pitching a hook ladder up to the sixth. This was undertaken carrying a long line, secured in a leather harness, on a fireman's back. They would then haul hose up to the top of drill tower using the line.

Southwark's Training School did not only train recruit firemen; other firemen attended there too and undertook a range of practical training courses. One such course was the breathing apparatus (BA) course. Firemen who had served a minimum of a year attended the BA school and learnt to wear, use and test the Proto oxygen BA set. Alec had seen some of these firemen training as they shuffled and felt their way around the perimeter walls of the training school. Blindfolded and wearing their blue-bagged BA sets, they practised the skills necessary to move in smoke and darkness safely. Occasionally Alec saw the firemen exiting the smoke chamber, an underground maze and obstacle course. As they came out, either carrying items of equipment or a training dummy, they were shrouded in the chemical smoke forcing its way out of the smoke chamber at the end of an arduous training exercise. Alec was in awe of these real firemen. Seeing them standing proud, in their breathing apparatus sets, he looked forward to being one.

It was as though Alec's instructor had read his thoughts. He announced that the following day the squad were to go down the smoke chamber. There were excited mutterings as the squad left Southwark that evening, thrilled and full of anticipation for their first taste of real smoke.

The visit to the smoke chamber came near the end of their already extended training day. In fact, most thought the instructor was having them on or he had completely forgotten all about it. He had done neither. True to his word, he was providing some extra-curricular activity but after the Training School senior officers had left for the day. This was an unofficial lesson. Surprising as it must seem, firemen going into smoke during basic training was not something contained in their recruit training syllabus!

There was a conspicuous odour as they walked through the smoke chamber door: the aroma of decades of use of chemical smoke bombs, smoke canisters ignited by a fuse. The smoke chamber filled a multi-roomed basement area, an area divided into different sections. As the squad walked down the single flight of stairs into the chamber, the electric bulk-head lights threw out a strange orange glow, their original clear glazing obscured by the build-up of greasy tar residue from the training smoke. However, on this late afternoon, the recruits are to experience real smoke.

In the chamber the tang of smoke hung everywhere. To their left was a purpose timber built 'rat-run'. It comprised an elongated, narrow, enclosed obstacle course. Built on various, interconnecting, levels, it incorporated hazards firemen might experience in any building fire, including missing floorboards, ball-bearing rollers, small openings and vertical ladders. The configuration of the 'rat-run' could be altered by the BA instructors. By using a series of lockable hatches they ensured that only their selected route could be followed by BA firemen undergoing training exercises. Additionally, the design of the 'rat-run' allowed those inside only to move through it in single file.

"Right," said the instructor as he guided the squad towards the entrance of the 'rat-run', "through you go. There is only one possible route to reach the other end. Find your way out." Next, as he opened the access door, he said, "Right, Beaucanon you go first. Oh, and there are some dead-ends in there that lead nowhere."

Then as they all waited to enter, the instructor switched off all the lights. They were plunged into total darkness. No one could see a hand in front of their noses. The stench of the smoke-impregnated timber filled their nostrils. It was then the reality of this extra-curricular activity suddenly hit home.

Crawling through on hands and knees, or stooped low, they moved forward slowly and unsteadily. Some missed their footing, others banged their helmeted heads on low beams, two rolled back down the industrial rollers they were trying to climb. Alec took a wrong turning. He led them down a route only to find it blocked by a locked hatch! Confusion reigned as they groped and felt their way through the inter-connected galleries. Alec had to back up, causing a log jam, as those trying to move forward pushed against those trying to move backwards.

The instructor moved around in the blackness with a self-assured stride as he monitored their progress to the end of the 'run' before turning the lights back on. Some with sore knees, others with grazed knuckles were led into the adjacent room. About 20 feet by 20 feet, the room served as a 'search' area by those undergoing BA training.

In the centre of the concrete floor room stood a metal 'crib' piled high with waste sawn wood.

"Right you lot, stand back against the walls" said the instructor in a most unusually conciliatory tone. "If any of you has had enough smoke make your way out and wait in the drill yard," he continued, pointing to the metal door which opened onto the staircase leading up to the drill yard. "After I have lit the crib I will put some horse-hair stuffing on the fire. It's the same horse-hair you might find in a mattress, a settee or an armchair. Now just look and learn."

Their instructor never bothered to mention that smoke does two main things. It irritates the lungs and triggers mucus production and possible bronchoconstriction (asthma), if someone is prone to that condition. It also poisons the air because smoke is filled with soot and other debris. All the time a fireman is breathing in this toxic mix the fire eats up oxygen and produces carbon dioxide together with other gases. Depending on what is burning, those gases may include carbon monoxide, cyanide and hydrogen sulphate, to name but a few. However, that was not the way of things in the 'LFB' in 1966. Their instructor had been schooled by old school 'smoke-eating' firemen. The wearing of breathing apparatus was frowned upon at anything less than large fires. He was not about to change old habits, no matter what impact it had on the health of 'smoke-eating' firemen and the detrimental impact it had had (and would continue to do so) on their longevity.

Igniting the newspaper at the base of the crib the flames quickly set fire to the kindling as the instructor initiated a question-and-answer session about fire and its growth. The recruits had already learnt about the 'triangle of fire' in the classroom. Now they received a practical demonstration of its physical characteristics: how fuel, oxygen and heat joined together in a sustained chemical reaction. They watched the flame, as a heat source, ignited the additional fuel. Both convection and radiation currents ignited more surfaces. They saw the spread of the fire. As its plume reached the room's ceiling, hot gases collected and transferred heat, allowing any other possible fuels in a room to come closer to their ignition temperature.

Standing ten feet away the recruits felt the temperature rise in the confined space. The heat of the fire was reflected on their faces as their eyes smarted from the irritating wood smoke. Some started to cough.

As the fire in the crib burnt freely the instructor moved closer to the blaze. Taking handfuls of horse-hair from a sack he piled it onto the fire, almost smothering it. The nature of smoke changed immediately, as did the smell. No longer was it light, translucent, smoke with a blueish taint but an ugly thick brown smoke, smoke that obscured their vision. For those recruits who had smelled burning hair previously they recognised the unpleasant, sickly, odour. It was a smell that these recruits would, in the years ahead, become all too familiar with. It was the smoke associated with fires in private dwellings. The smell was noxious, it was pernicious.

The recruits saw, at first hand, the dynamics of smoke travel and its frequent fatal effects. They watched, through increasingly sore and stinging smoke-filled eyes, how the hot gases moved from hot areas to cooler areas. How the heated smoke, which was less dense, rose, then descended as it cooled. Inside the room the rising smoke and hot gases encountered the ceiling a few feet above the crib. It travelled horizontally, across the ceiling, forming a thick layer of heated air. When it met the walls it moved downwards where it engulfed the heads of the watching recruits who were forced ever lower. Most were crouched on the concrete floor when the first coughing fit started. It was soon followed by others. All were coughing bar their instructor who, seemingly impervious to the effects of the smoke, remained standing erect throughout.

If it were needed, the exposure to that smoke confirmed in Alec's mind that he had made the right decision as to his chosen career path. The Fire Brigade was far more than just another job. He was hooked, despite the fact he could still smell the obnoxious and repugnant tang of the horse-hair smoke all the way home. It seemed to have adhered to his nostril hairs and had left his throat raw.

Alec's final days at Southwark were filled with tests and exams. There were written and oral examinations plus combined practical drill tests and the individual scrutiny of knot tying skills and pumping abilities overseen by two senior officers. Finally, with his St John's first aid examination certificate presented, it was all over. He had passed out, albeit as a probationer fireman. All that was left was to discover where he was being posted to. His squad mates had all been allocated to LCC-LFB (now Greater London) fire stations. But not Alec; he was off to Tottenham Fire Station, which until April 1965 had been part of the Middlesex Fire Brigade.

On his last morning at Southwark Alec sat alone in the general office waiting for the Divisional van to pick him up and deliver him to Tottenham. He was feeling relieved but somewhat uneasy. Stories had filtered through to the Training School about the different treatment and reception given to new arrivals at a fire station. Alec wondered if he would be seen as one the lambs going to the slaughter. Not that he could not look after himself, but that was not the way he wished to start the next chapter of his adventure. But his welcome at 'J25' Tottenham that afternoon was both warm and friendly. However, this Day Watch were not Alec's new Watch. He was to start the following evening.

Alec was the first recruit in over three years. He was the very first London Fire Brigade recruit the station had ever seen. All his Watch, he soon discovered, were old Middlesex men. He was not the only new thing either. The station had only been open a couple of months. It shined like a new pin. The two-storey, brick-built fire station with its three appliance bays was the last fire station to be commissioned by the former Middlesex brigade. It had replaced the old Tottenham fire station that was opened in 1905. Back then Wood Green had its own fire brigade, with an engine-house in the High Road and old Tottenham station in Bounds Green Road. Absorbed into the Middlesex Fire Brigade after World War II the Middlesex crews and their three appliances were now housed in the GLC's station in St Loys Road.

"You're new and our first cockney," said a voice from behind Alec. "I'm Grant Richards," said the tall figure putting on his blue overalls by his locker. In fact they were bib and brace trousers, a legacy of the Middlesex issue to its firemen.

"Alec," he said as he held out hand to Grant, a man in his late 30s with a warm smile and a cauliflower ear.

"Do you play rugby?" asked Grant.

"No I box, or did until I joined the Brigade," replied Alec.

"Same thing really," said Grant. "Only we use a rugby ball and it's a bigger ring. Get your things and follow me."

The appliance room housed the three fire engines. It was where

Grant led the 'new boy' to his first roll call. The faces were those of complete strangers, people who he would get to know, some much better than others, and who would become his guides and mentors over the coming months.

At one minute to six o'clock the station bells rang six times and the firemen, in their fire gear, lined up between the pump-escape and pump for parade. Alex felt totally out of his comfort zone. Fresh from training school he was standing in the company of experienced firemen and he felt like a spare part! His thoughts were brought back into sharp focus by the Sub Officer. Standing in front of them he barked out an order.

"Parade – parade 'shun."

They all stood to attention, each man looking forward.

"Call the roll," said the Station Officer, a man in his 50s wearing his undress uniform, with a row of campaign medal ribbons over his left breast uniform pocket. The Sub Officer read from the prepared duty roster.

"Pump-escape: Sub Officer Pitts, Fireman Harris, Fireman Harvey, Fireman Beatty and Fireman Beaucanon. Pump: Station Officer Hogg. Fireman Richards, Fireman Wright and Fireman Crowe. Turntable Ladder. Leading Fireman Walsh and Fireman Watson."

The Station Office made visual inspection of his watch then made the briefest of an announcement to welcome Alec to the watch, telling him to report the station office at 6.30 p.m. before instructing the Sub Officer to dismiss the parade. It was the Sub Officer who guided Alec over to meet the rest of the pump-escape crew.

"Put your gear in the middle Alec and stick to these two like glue. They will show the ropes and run you through what's expected of you. I know this is all new but you are part of the crew tonight so look and learn. If you don't know something, bloody well ask."

With that he removed his own fire-gear and put it on the officer-in-charge's seat and his boots and leggings on the floor before he headed off to the station office.

"Hi, I'm Mike," said Fireman Harvey. "He's Colin," he continued, pointing to Fireman Beatty. "We check the machine over before we have a cuppa. You've got to see the 'old man' at 1830 so don't forget to wear your cap." Alec didn't notice the knowing smile.

For the next fifteen minutes the trio checked all the equipment in every locker of the fire engine. Some of it was new to Alex as the fire engines at Southwark Training School did not come fully equipped. Hose, ladders, branches and lines were about the norm for the recruits. While they inspected the equipment the driver started up the fire engine before checking the pump controls and that the 100-gallon water tank was full. As Alec was going about his checks he noticed the Station Officer seated on the back of the pump, testing his breathing apparatus set.

The mess-room, like most of the accommodation and the station office, was on the first floor. Alec had followed his crew mates up the stairs as they headed for their tea. As he passed each station call bell he was willing them to ring but they stayed silent.

Charlie Watson was the watch mess-manager and, as Alec would discover, he was the regular driver of the turntable ladder. In his 50s, his introduction to Alec was clipped and to the point.

"Pay up son. We pay by the month so you only got a full shift to pay plus your two night duties. You will owe for a full month from the start of October." With that Charlie returned to reading his *Evening News*.

Putting down his unfinished tea at 6.25 p.m., Alec went to his locker and got his uniform cap. Checking in the mirror he adjusted his cap and proceeded to the station office. He knocked on the door and walked in saying louder than he had intended:

"Fireman Beaucanon reporting."

The Station Officer looked up from his desk. Putting down his tea, he studied the new boy.

"OK Beaucanon, this is not bloody training school. You do not need to shout and you don't need your cap to come into the office lad!"

The Station Officer grinned widely as he formally welcomed Alec and told him for the next couple of shifts he would ride the pump-escape because they didn't have enough firemen to allow him to ride the back of the pump.

"There is no one to keep you under their wing yet Alec, but as soon as there is, you will ride the pump along with me. In the meantime the Sub Officer will be watching over you. On day duties we will talk again and I will let you know what is expected of you if you wish to get through your probation. I assume you want to get through your probation?"

"Yes Sir," replied Alec.

It was an uneventful early evening. Some drills and then station work. At 8.00 p.m. they went for supper. They all ate together but Alec noted the pecking order around the long mess table. The Station Officer sat at the head, the Sub Officer to his side. The others seemed to have set places and Alec was worried about taking some-one's seat when Grant said:

"Sit here Alec, and make yourself comfy."

Which he did until Charlie said:

"Move your arse, buck. You only been here two hours and you nicked my fucking chair"

The room erupted in laughter as Charlie took his rightful place and Alec found himself an empty chair.

Alec had been all waiting all evening for the call bells to ring: when they did he almost jumped out of his skin! At 9.28 p.m. the station resounded to the sound of ringing electric bells and all the station lights came on automatically. Alec found himself following the others along the corridor to the pole house. One at a time the firemen slid down into the appliance room. Alec later learnt that the person making the '999' call to the Wembley fire control room had been evasive. The only information the control officer had gleamed was "Fire in the timber yard, High Road, Tottenham, near the school." As Tottenham's two fire engines left the station, another from Stoke Newington Fire Station, which made up the attend-ance, headed for same address. Alec was all fingers and thumbs as he tried to do up his fire tunic buttons while the pump-escape sped its way through Tottenham's streets. Mike Harvey looked Alec over and told him not to leave his side. There was so much for Alec to absorb: the Sub Officer looking alert and ringing the engine's bell, the driver weaving through the evening traffic, whilst Mike and Colin put on the hook belts. All were taking it in their stride except Alec, who could not recall when he ever felt so nervous, not even when climbing into the boxing ring. As they proceeded he watched Colin looking up the nearest hydrants to the address given in the appliance ledger.

Alec craned his eyes for the slightest sign of any smoke or fire on the horizon. As they neared their destination Alec saw nothing; neither did anyone else.

Arriving at the address, Tottenham's engines stopped at the entrance of a timber yard. Alec noted the wide sign above the impressive double iron gates: Bamberger's, Ltd. Stoke Newington arrived from the opposite direction but reported no sign of any fire on their arrival. Two women, who were standing by the entrance, told Station Officer Hogg:

"There could not possibly be a fire in here as we have only just left the premises."

Hogg summoned the night-watchman over and with Tottenham's crews he proceeded to carry out a systematic and thorough search of the timber yard. Alec was amazed just how colossal the site was and the vast amount of timber stored there.

The crews covered every square yard and found no trace of any fire. Station Officer Hogg contacted the Wembley Control by radio and required the local telephone exchange to verify the origin of the 999 call. The exchange stated that it was made from a public call box some considerable distance from the timber yard. After satisfying himself that there wasn't any fire anywhere in the immediate vicinity, Station Officer Hogg radioed back to the Wembley Control Room saying it was a 'False Alarm'.

Returning to the station Alec's sense of exhilaration had turned to disappointment. Not a sign of any flame. Not even a whiff of smoke! He felt gutted.

While Tottenham's fire engines were driving back into the station the night-watchman at Bamberger's, who had accompanied the fireman, had another look round the site. Finally convinced that there was no fire anywhere he went for his supper in the yard's security hut. His duties included patrolling the premises at 90-minute intervals and he was required to clock-in at the various check points.

With some of Tottenham's firemen putting their beds down and others watching the telly, Alec was wishing the calls bells would ring. At the timber yard the night-watchman was summoned to the entrance gate by the enquiry bell ringing. A passer-by told him that smoke was coming from one of the sheds near the far end of the site, adjacent to the River Lea towpath. It was 11.30 p.m. When the night-watchman went to investigate he saw the flames and ran back to his hut to call the Fire Brigade. His was not the only call. At 11.44 p.m. the first of three 999 calls were received by the Wembley control room to a fire at Bamberger's.

Alec was not at calm as the others when the station bells started ringing. He could hear his heart thumping in his chest and his pulse was racing. The same two Fire Stations' engines were dispatched. This time an additional fire engine was sent from Stoke Newington. Alec heard rather than saw the first indication of a fire when Sub Officer Alan Pitts, his officer in charge, shouted out, "Holy shit!" as they approached the timber yard for the second time that night. He observed the huge, slow-moving column of thick black smoke rising over the timber yard set against the clear night sky.

Sub Officer Pitts directed the pump-escape driver to head into the yard, the night-watchman having already opened the gates in anticipation of their arrival.

"Two lines of hose lads," shouted Pitts.

Hose was laid out and fed by water from a nearby hydrant supplying the pump.

"Stay close to Mick and Colin, Beaucanon," ordered the Sub Officer as he led the attack on the fire.

Station Officer Hogg knew this was touch and go. They needed additional support and six minutes after the initial call he made "Pumps five". Hogg realised that was not enough when he looked into the building and saw fire spreading swiftly along the south wall and towards him. One minute later he made "Pumps eight".

With the arrival of Stoke Newington's two crews, a further line of hose was taken into the timber yard. Tottenham's firemen were already forward, and Stoke Newington's firemen were running in to back them up, when the flashover occurred. Flames, 20 feet high, ran along the complete length of the covered timber yard wall on its south side. It was heading directly towards the firemen and moving from the east to the west. Hogg saw the searing flames; so had his Sub Officer who, looking round for Alec, ordered the fireman back from the seat of the fire. They didn't need telling twice: the flames were moving quicker than they were. The flashover spread at such a rate that it reached their point of entry to the timber storage area before they were clear of it. The Sub Officer grabbed Alec and was dragging him along when Alec noticed that Colin had fallen over the abandoned hose line. He broke free of the Sub Officer's grip and ran back to help his colleague.

Heat scorched Alec's hands and face with each step he took towards Colin. Yanking him to his feet he saw ugly blisters forming on the fallen fireman's face and exposed neck. They ran for their lives. Three of Tottenham's pump-escape crew sustained burns to their backs. Alec thought his face was on fire.

Station Officer Hogg was relieved to see his men reach the entry point, clear of the intense heat and the singeing flame front. But he had little time to reflect or to check on their welfare, as the flames headed his way too. At 11.54 p.m. he made "Pumps ten" and ordered Fireman Harris, the pump-escape driver, to drive his engine out of the timber yard. The fire was spreading with extreme rapidity. It involved a large area, bordering along the back of private premises and running adjacent to the River Lea. Five minutes after his arrival Station Officer Hogg made "Pumps 20".

Those who had pulled back at the time of the flashover were ordered to break the hose couplings of the hose-lines forsaken in the timber stacks. However, it was easier said than done, due to the pressure still in the hose. It was Grant Richards who finally broke the couplings, at the pump's outlet, using a crow-bar. This enabled fresh hose-lines to be brought to bear on the fire, something the crew managed regardless of their painful burns.

As the first reinforcing appliances started to arrive Station Officer Hogg instructed a police constable to have the nearby houses evacuated whilst he directed the new fire engine crews to attack the fire from the north and west flank of the sites. With the arrival of Assistant Divisional Officer (ADO) River, from the divisional headquarters at Edmonton, command of the fire passed to him. But River only held the mantle of command for eight minutes as a more senior officer arrived who immediately assumed command of the rapidly growing fire.

Alec stood with the ambulanceman as Colin and the Sub Officer were treated for their burns. His own face looked like he had spent much too long out in the sun. Given this brief respite he was able to look about him for the first time since he had arrived at the fire. The timber yard sign said Bamberger's. It was a timber importing firm. He saw that the site covered a vast area, somewhere in the region of 500 feet by 450 feet. Along its western edge was a road. The Sub Officer told Alec that to the north lay a recreation ground and the River Lea. The rear gardens of private houses ran along the southern edge. The Sub Officer continued:

"They hold an enormous timber stock, mainly teak and plywood and veneers. Most brought in by barge on the River Lea. It's off-loaded by means of the electric cranes."

Alec had seen, on the earlier 'false alarm' call, the lorries and articulated trailers parked in one corner of the yard, whilst other lorries and trailers, laden with timber, were parked in the various gangways between the storage sheds. Much of the timber was stacked under the continuous roof of the Dutch barn construction.

"Finally," Colin chipped in, "by the River Lea's towpath are the 'dumb' barges. Several of these are usually fully loaded with timber and covered with tarpaulins."

As Alec looked up at the site, much of it was going up in flames – flames that were still spreading. As was the way with big fires, Tottenham's crews became just faces in the crowd. With over 100 firemen at, or heading to, the scene Station Officer Hogg and his men were tasked to assist with the protection of the private houses which were in danger of catching fire due to the radiated heat from the gargantuan blaze. Alec was now one of only four on the pump-escape as Mick Harvey's burns had necessitated his removal to hospital. As they made their way along the street they saw Charlie Watson arriving on the turntable ladder. Their Station Officer said, to nobody in particular:

"Old Charlie will think he is back in the Blitz with this lot going like a bastard."

Alec had never seen so much hose, hose that filled the street from side to side. Fire engines were hither and thither and he wondered how anyone could ever make order out of such chaos. But the Divisional Officer in charge was trying to. He had told ADO River to take responsibility of the fire-fighting at the rear of the adjoining houses to the timber yard. It was the ADO who told Tottenham's crew to get a couple of jets to work, through one of the houses, and attack the fire whilst, at the same time, protecting the surrounding properties. When Alec entered a house, next to the fire, he saw that the 24-ft high corrugated iron wall at the south side of Bamberger's was white-hot for the whole of its considerable length. Additional lines of hose were being brought through the houses and other firemen got jets to work to cool the corrugated iron wall. No sooner did the water hit the superheated metal than it hissed and sizzled angrily as vast volumes of steam were added to the noxious mix of smoke and other gases.

The Divisional Officer had established a control point at a nearby road junction. Even though the wind was moderate the fire was still spreading. Fires of such intensity create their own wind currents.

Two pumps crews had been ordered to gain access to the River Lea and to supply hose lines from the river. The occupants of the private houses, opposite Bamberger's, were warned to be ready for immediate evacuation. With a dire situation on his hands the Divisional Officer made "Pumps 30" 15 minutes after midnight. He also requested six radial branches (static monitor like jets that could throw vast quantities of water at a fire). The Massey Shaw fireboat was also dispatched to the incident from her moorings at Woolwich.

The Massey Shaw left her berth shortly after midnight. She proceeded up the Thames to the entrance of the River Lea on the north bank. Passing Silvertown, she entered Bow Creek before following the route of the Lee (as the River Lea is spelled when it nears the Thames). After the considerable widths of the lower reaches of the Thames the Lee seemed to close in on the fireboat as it navigated its way north to the Tottenham fire. By Homerton the fireboat's crew had no doubts where they were heading as the glow in the night sky was acting like a homing beacon.

The fire now involved the whole site. As it reached the six single-storey buildings hose-laying lorries were increased to three. The fire was being attacked on all sides. Holes were cut in the fences to the River Lea as firemen, using pickaxes and hand axes, passed lengths of suction hose through the openings and additional hose lines got to work. Across the recreation ground more lines of hose were laid out to augment the supplies to pumps. Fire engines were sent towards the towpath and, using water from the river, got jets to work on the dumb barges to protect the timber stacks.

A deputy Assistant Chief Officer took command just before 12.30 a.m. He made a swift assessment of the deteriorating fire situation, with its extensive area and continuing rapid spread, and sent an urgent message. "Make pumps 50."

Much of this activity was lost on Alec. He had been directing his jet into the flames. He wasn't sure that it was making much of a difference, something that was confirmed when his Station Officer came to check on the 'new boy'.

"Alec, that fire is generating so much heat that most of your water vaporises before it even hits the fire. The timber yard is lost, son, but we can make a difference to these houses. Keep going, lad."

With the subsequent build-up of reinforcing appliances more crews were allocated to each side of the fire. There were soon 15 jets on the south side preventing the spread to the private houses. However, there was still the danger from flying brands. These could set fire to houses in the surrounding streets and patrols were instituted to deal with any such outbreaks of fire.

London's Deputy Chief Officer was Frank Mummery. He was the former Chief Officer of the Middlesex Fire Brigade prior to the creation of the Greater London Council in 1965. This was his old patch. He had no hesitation in taking command and directing the attack of the fire, which was steadily increased. By 1.06 a.m. Mummery was able to send a message stating that progress was finally being made in containing the fire.

The fire was brought under control at 2.45 a.m. It involved nearly the whole of the 13 timber storage sheds, and eight lorries and trailers in the timber yard. It severely damaged the office building and the other single-storey structures in the yard. It was only by the strenuous efforts of firemen, and the crew of the Massey Shaw fireboat, that prevented the fire involving the petrol and diesel storage tanks or any of the nearby houses, although a few of those had suffered minor damage. A total of 44 jets, four radial branches and the Massey Shaw's massive monitor were used to extinguish the blaze. The would continue to pour water on the smouldering ruins for many hours to come

It was just after dawn that, first, Tottenham's pump-escape and then its pump were relieved and weary firemen made their way back to the station. There was no excitement, just tiredness and hunger. With Charlie still directing his turntable ladder monitor into the heart of the blaze it was left to Dolly, the station cook, to deliver their much needed breakfast. Even after a shower they still smelled of the pervading smoke. With red, sore eyes – after their tear ducts had dried up due to the excess of heat and the smoke – they sat and tucked into their breakfast. It was the Sub Officer who broke the tired silence around the table.

"Well Beaucanon, I have never ever seen a fire of that magnitude. It is something I will always remember and I know you will too."

Alec left the fire station just after 9.00 a.m. and caught his bus home. He would be back on duty again tonight, no doubt returning to the timber yard again, this time to damp down. He would do so for many more shifts to come. Sitting on the bus he thought of old Charlie Watson. He had returned from the fire just before the shift ended. He had seen Charlie standing in the appliance room and the senior firemen beckoned him over.

"A good night, Alec? We all started like you, lad. The older firemen taught me to button up my tunic and muck in. Old Sammy Francis told me, 'You don't need much in here son, just a bit of common sense and a lot of bottle.' Remember that Alec, and you will do just fine."

As the bus headed towards Hackney Alec caught sight of a newspaper headlines. "London's biggest blaze since the Blitz." Below the headline, and in bold print, the story continued, "Almost three hundred firemen, fifty pumps and many other specialist fire engines were brought into action at Bamberger's Ltd, an enormous timber yard in Tottenham N17 last night." Alec's still scorched, and pink, face cracked into a smile as he thought, "Yes, and I was one of them."

Walking through the door of his flat that morning Alec's wife was busy with their daughter. She looked up, smiled, and asked:

"How was your first night as a real fireman?"

"It was fine," replied the weary man standing in the kitchen doorway. "We only had one fire."

(A fictional tale based on eye-witness accounts.)

Remember, Remember the Fifth of November

by David Waterman

David is a South-west London fire officer. He is stationed at Battersea Fire Station. Here he reflects on what Bonfire Night means for him.

AS A BOY, GROWING up in south London, I remember being really excited in the run up to Guy Fawkes Night. The construction of the huge bonfire on a communal green near my home was something my friends and I took great pride in. Then on the night itself families from all over the local housing estate would gather to witness the fiery spectacle. I remember us kids, faces glowing in the heat of the blaze, watching the setting off of the inexpensive fireworks against the backdrop of that bonfire – fireworks that never really lived up to the expectation. But I loved it nonetheless.

Now, 40 years on, those memories remain fond but now feel somewhat naïve. I've spent the past quarter of a century as a firefighter. I serve the same community that I lived in as a child, but Bonfire Night has taken on a completely different meaning for me. It's fair to say that November the fifth is not as busy these days as it was, say, 25 years ago. Back then the London Fire Brigade had special mobilising arrangements which were regularly adopted on bonfire night to deal with the exceptionally high volume of calls.

But whilst things might not be as hectic nowadays, fireworks have become bigger, more powerful, and more dangerous. As a service we're dealing with incidents now with fewer fire engines and smaller numbers of personnel.

A couple of years ago I was standing in the wreckage of a bedroom having just extinguished the fire that was started by an errant firework, one which found its way in through an open window. Caught up in the net curtain it continued to burn, setting fire to the whole room. So serious was the blaze that it rendered the flat uninhabitable. The family were homeless until well into the following year. A young girl was sat on her bed when the firework entered her room; thankfully she managed to escape and raise the alarm. Things might have had a more tragic outcome had the curtain not impeded the firework's trajectory.

Last year, 2017, and a couple of two weeks before bonfire night an unpleasant individual, travelling in a van through the underpass at Clapham Junction, thought it would be amusing to aim a firework at a mother and her two children that were walking through the tunnel. The resulting explosion had mid-afternoon shoppers running for cover while the young mother fought to prevent what may have been life-threatening injuries. It was a truly horrific, mindless, act.

The unsocial use of fireworks as weapons is not uncommon. News reports frequently highlight the attacks on the firefighters themselves. Last year there was a spate of youths, in East London, attacking cyclists with powerful fireworks. The London Fire Brigade recommends that people should only attend official Bonfire Night events and to follow the Firework Code (the official guide on how to stay safe while using fireworks). These responsible guidelines are followed by the majority of people. Sadly, they are scoffed at by the type of immature, anti-social,individuals who believe it is acceptable to aim and discharge these legal explosives at innocent people especially, and it seems, women and children.

The potential danger of fireworks is not fully understood by some until it's too late. That danger was brought home 16 years ago in Holland when the Enschede fireworks factory exploded, killing 22 people, including four firefighters. The resultant fire and explosions injured over 900. Despite the lessons learned from that disaster, and the relatively robust laws around fireworks in the UK, this country experienced its own fireworks factory explosion in Southampton in May 2017. It took 13 fire appliances and 70 firefighters to extinguish that fire.

My partner loves fireworks. In fact, she insists we go to the locally organised event. She picks up on my reticence and reservations about attending and thinks it's simply me being miserable. I don't discuss the operational side of my job a great deal at home. I prefer not to relate the stories of the suffering of others. But if it helps prevent just one injury, and explains my reticence, I would urge anyone to consider the case of Donna Stringer. Donna, the resident of a care home in Barking, was almost killed when a rocket was fired from a car through the window of her bedroom. She suffered horrific injuries, including severe burns to her throat, arms, hands and chest. She suffered months of painful operations and had skin grafted onto her throat. For months she could only be fed by a tube. The two individuals responsible for that attack pleaded guilty at Snaresbrook Crown Court. One was jailed for six years, the other for seven.

As I said, I'll go to the firework display with my partner as I'm not working this 5 November. But I'll be glad when it's over.

(Fact)

Poles Apart

THE CROWD OF MOURNERS had finally departed. She sat alone in the deserted flat. Kirsty's dad had always loved a 'good funeral'. He had been to plenty over the years, mainly his former Brigade colleagues. Holding the photograph of her dad, Kirsty smiled wistfully as she told him,

"You would have loved your funeral, Dad, from the flag-draped coffin, to the Brigade's Standard bearer in his best Number 1's. Your Queen's Gallantry Medal was placed next to your Long Service and Good Conduct Medal on top of the Union Flag. Your mates all came along too. They certainly saw you off in style, Dad. They drank you under the table at your wake."

As she placed the two silver medals back in their presentation boxes she looked down at the array of cardboard boxes covering the floor. They were brimming with her dad's bits and bobs, just some of what he had ferreted away over the years. Then she noticed something that caught her eye. On the top of a stack of papers was a copy of a letter to the London Fire Brigade. A letter she had sent 20 months before.

Kirsty's dad had joined the London Fire Brigade in the days of the London County Council. His original LCC cap badge was mounted with his fireman's axe, a retirement gift from his watch at Shoreditch in east London. He joined when they were all referred to as *firemen*. He had seen some changes. In fact, he said the Brigade never stopped changing. He had seen the wheeled escape ladders go, hook ladders go and worn three different types of fire kits before he was pensioned off in 1986 with an injury pension. An accident at a fire had left him permanently disabled. The vacant wheelchair, in the corner of the room, reminded her of his struggle with pain in his last year. Not that she needed reminding just how much courage he had.

Kirsty had been born in a hurry, her mum's waters breaking on the ride bus to the District Hospital. She was delivered in the back of an ambulance. This was the 1960s and with three teenage children already she came along as a big surprise to her parents. They later told her she was the result of a romantic weekend with consequences. But they loved their youngest daughter as much as her older siblings: two sisters of 13 and 14 and a big brother of 16. Her childhood was idyllic. She lived an amazing life in an old renovated rectory near Sevenoaks that had been left to her mother in a will. Kirsty was considered a tomboy who would rather be playing at cowboys than nurses. She owned both a Barbie doll and a push chair but much preferred climbing trees and getting dirty. Expanding her frontiers were always encouraged by her parents. She simply had a ball.

Her teenage years were never that easy again after her mum died following a painful and short illness. Afterwards her dad went through a spell of drinking too much and her elder brother and two sisters just drifted away. Kirsty stayed with her dad. It all affected her academic studies but her sanity was saved on the sports field and in the swimming pool where she excelled. The problems at home involved Social Services at one point, especially after her dad started his drinking. But not for long. He got his act together for no better reason than he wanted to care for his youngest daughter rather than losing her too.

With a natural talent in drawing and design, after leaving school at 18, she spent three years at Goldsmiths Art College in South London. It was more fun than actual studying. After leaving college aged 21 she worked for a London graphic design company before striking out as a freelance designer with various advertising agencies. However, with little idea of what she really wanted in life, she always felt something was lacking.

Kirsty loved and admired what her dad had once done. What he had been, an ordinary fireman – although he told her plenty of times:

"There is no such thing as an ordinary fireman, they are all rather special."

Her dad had never shown any bitterness that his injury had brought his career to a premature end. As he frequently told his youngest daughter:

"Shit happens – get over it."

She held the view that all firefighters were heroes, leaders in the 'blue light' services. People who saved the lives of those in danger whether from fire, road accidents or a flooding disaster. Although when looking for similar views in the columns of the national newspapers, or in television news reports, she did not often find much to support her opinion about such bravery. Her dad would fume when a senior police officer stood in front of the press cameras praising the efforts of the "emergency services" when it was firefighters who had just saved a family from a house fire or prevented the loss of part of a city centre involved in a major fire.

"What is so bloody hard about saying the word firemen?" he would moan before changing the TV channel or discarding the offending newspaper in dismay.

Then in 1986, sitting with her dad watching Jack Rosenthal's ground-breaking television film *London's Burning*, the course of her life changed. Interested in the idea of becoming a London firefighter and given a recruitment leaflet at the local Jobcentre, she contacted the London Fire Brigade. It was a few days later that someone from the London Fire Brigade recruitment team rang. She was told of the new scheme and was offered a place. Called 'pre-entry training' she asked how much it would cost her. The pleasant lady, at the other end of the phone, told her: "We'll pay you."

Kirsty accepted there and then. Her dad had been genuinely delighted when she said, "Dad, I have applied to join the LFB."

There was no discussion, just that statement. It was a few days later that he said, "It won't be easy, you know."

Kirsty smiled and replied, "Whenever has our life been easy?"

Her mind was made up. Aged 23, she embarked on a complete career change. She really wanted this job, not because her dad had once done it but she wanted to work alongside a team of people who would respect her for what she was hoping to become, a firefighter. She also wanted to work and earn a wage that was equal to men.

Her dad had often told her of the exciting, unpredictable, physical and rewarding side of the work, even if he, occasionally, might have embellished the odd tale. But she wasn't under any false illusions either. She realised it could also be dirty, frequently dangerous and occasionally horrifying. Undaunted by the possibility of the sheer hard work she anticipated that it had its fair share of the mundane, with boring routine duties. She wanted to follow in her dad's footsteps. She got her wish. However, in the process she would discover that the pressures on London's women fighters considerably outweighed those on her male counterparts. Why? Simply because they were female. Respect, Kirsty learned, came at a price.

She attended the pre-entry training course in South London. Kirsty was one of 18 individuals to start and one of the 14 who stayed and finished it ten weeks later. They were a cross-section of Londoners, both sexes and including both black and white. The youngest was 19 and the eldest was 30. During the first day they were informed that the course had been set up because the London Fire Brigade had a serious recruitment issue. This initiative was an attempt to address it and increase the under-represented groups into the Brigade. Neither women nor Asian men had broken the 5 per cent barrier in the LFB's overall uniformed establishment.

Covering core subjects of Maths and English there was considerable emphasis on physical training. Kirsty found the course great fun but not overly challenging. At the end all 14 passed. However little did Kirsty, or the others, realise that it was a controversial course! It was only when undergoing her recruit training course that the instructor had a quiet word with the course participants. He advised that when, and if, they got to a fire station it was something they shouldn't shout about doing. It was considered by many across the Brigade as profoundly unfair. Pre-entry training would remain a contentious issue for many years to come.

With the course behind them they became potential candidates for recruit training. The 14 were required to undertake exactly the same tests (written, oral and physical) as any other hopeful firefighter recruit. There were no free passes or an easy route in. They either passed or failed the recruit firefighter selection tests. She passed, and unlike her dad who had trained at Lambeth as a recruit fireman in the 1950s, she reported to Southwark, the principal training venue for all the LFB's firefighter recruits. Walking through the Southwark Training Centre gates on her first day of training she felt very proud, but also daunted by the prospect of what was to follow. It was an unwarranted concern as she enjoyed her time at Training School, in fact she loved it.

Southwark Training School was running at full capacity. The 12 recruit squads were in various stages of their basic training: a recruit course that ran for 12 weeks, followed by two weeks of breathing apparatus training. They would all have to pass both elements to be posted to a fire station. Of the 138 recruits undergoing training, 132 of them were male. Kirsty, and five other women, made up the balance. It represented the norm of female firefighters across the Brigade. Kirsty never considered herself as a minority group, although she was clearly in one. She just thought of herself as another recruit firefighter. Thankfully, in the enlightened Training School environment, that was exactly how the recruit instructors and their senior officers saw, and treated, their charges too.

She could never have believed she could enjoy herself so much. She felt totally at home, undergoing her training to be a London firefighter. She was not found wanting in any aspect of her training. Surrounded by an excellent squad of 10 men she was one of two females who just got on with the task of acquiring the basic firefighter skills and knowledge that would be extensively tested at the end of the course. If there were elements of sexism at Training School she never came across it. She worked hard, excelled at what she did and came out with a glowing report. However, the same cannot be said for when she finally got to a fire station. Things changed.

Her posting was Lewisham Fire Station, in south London. She arrived on her 24th birthday. She soon realised that things were not the same as Southwark! For a start Lewisham was not your average fire station. It was the recently created South-East Command headquarters, originally built as a divisional headquarters station. Following the demise of the Greater London Council in 1986 the Brigade had gone through a radical re-organisation. Its 11 former Divisions became five new Commands. The Brigade was now governed by an unelected quango (for the first time in its history): the London Fire and Civil Defence Authority. The fire station still occupied the lower two floors and senior officers, headed by an Assistant Chief Officer, had their offices on the revamped upper floors. Some firefighters referred to being stationed at Lewisham as working in a goldfish bowl. Kirsty wonder if her posting to Lewisham was just a coincidence or it had some other meaning.

She was posted onto the White Watch, one of four different watches across the Brigade. Whilst there was no open hostility, and they did their best to make her feel welcome, there already had been a precursor to her arrival: a visit by a senior uniformed officer from the Brigade's 'Equalities' section. The White Watch were sitting in the television room, waiting for their 'informal chat'; when the officer finally walked in he looked like he had just finished school and was fresh from the sixth form. He was a young-looking officer who was clearly among the Brigade's up and coming 'movers and shakers'. Someone who, no doubt, would be a Chief Officer some-where one day. However, this adolescent, uncompromising Divi-sional Officer came with a clear message. One he was very keen to deliver. His simple communication was, in effect, to threaten them with the discipline code if Firefighter Kirsty Miller said or reported anything untoward about their behaviour towards her!

For her first two tours of duty Kirsty found it was like walking on eggshells. Whilst she drilled alongside her new male workmates, attended her very first fire, and went about her station duties, there was an obvious underlying tension. All the while she was trying to holding true to her training instructor's final words of wisdom.

"Listen and learn, Miller, keep your head down for the first few months and you'll do just fine. You have the making of a fine firefighter."

She didn't blame them for being cautious or keeping her at arm's length but after two weeks and she had had enough. Speaking to her Station Officer at the start of her first day duty of the third tour she asked if she might speak to the whole watch. He asked what about, so she told him.

"OK, at stand easy this morning," he said.

When she stood to speak the Watch were all seated around the mess table. She could feel her heart thumping. She felt faint. But she had put her head above the parapet and it was now or never. All eyes turned to her as she spoke.

"Now it's probably not escaped your attention that some of my bits are different from yours. I also have bumps on my chest where you don't, well most of you don't anyway! I am the first woman fire-fighter at this station. That might not please you. One because that we women are even in the 'job' and two that I am stationed here with you. But women firefighters are here. We are here to stay.

"I'm but a lowly probationer firefighter – that's firefighter, not female firefighter. I don't want, and don't expect, any special treat-ment. I don't want any favours. I certainly don't want any special treatment because I am a different gender to you. What I do want, and I won't get through my probation without it, is for you to treat me like any other probationer. I will listen. I will learn. I will benefit from your experience and will profit from your guidance. If I fail my probation it will be because I am not good enough to become a London firefighter. It will not be because I haven't tried my hardest to become one. So if I can't do what you do on the fire-ground, or on the drill ground or around the station, given the right guidance and training, I will walk away. It is as simple as that. All I am asking, in fact the only thing I am asking, is to prove myself to you."

She sat down. There was no round of applause. Some continued to eat their cheese rolls, others went back to reading the newspaper, but a knowing wink from the Station Officer told her that she got her message across. Only time would tell just how well it had been received.

Kirsty thrived at Lewisham and although her own Watch were good to her – in fact so were the surrounding watches of New Cross, Greenwich, Downham and Forest Hill – not all shared their enthu-siasm for Lewisham's only female firefighter. Some station watches made a judgement on everything she did. Rarely was it favourable.

It was after 11½ month's that Kirsty had her final probation-ary interview. Her Station Commander, Ken Cooper, had already recommended her for continuous employment in the London Fire Brigade, but it was subject to the ratification of the Divisional Officer 'Operations'. Her interview with this officer turned out to be more of an informal chat, which was his way on such occasions. Then as the interview drew to an end it all became much more formal. He was joined by both Ken Cooper and her Station Officer. "So this is what it takes when they sack you," she thought. "They gang up on you!"

Sat behind his desk, a desk that faced a wall (he was the sort that didn't need to hide behind office furniture) he stood to face Kirsty. Reaching for a foolscap envelope, two in fact, he removed what was inside the first as he said.

"Firefighter Miller, I am to inform you that your recent actions have been the subject of formal reports and a local inquiry. The findings have been considered by the Area Commander. He has arrived at his decision.

"Both you and your Station Officer have been awarded an Assistant Chief Officer Letter of Commendation for your actions at the 'persons reported' fire in Deptford High Street three months ago. You jointly rescued two young children from a serious flat fire in difficult and dangerous conditions and subsequently rendered month to mouth resuscitation. Tragically one of the children subsequently died from its injuries but that does not detract from your actions which were in the finest traditions of the Brigade. Congratulations to you both. I had previously spoken with your Station Officer and he requested the certificates be presented together. You will also be informed, in writing, that your appointment to the Brigade has been confirmed. Well done, Miller."

As he handed them both their certificates he told Miller that it was a double celebration and no doubt the Watch would capitalise on her achievements next time they all went out for an after-work drink. As they left the office Ken Cooper turned to Miller.

"Your dad would have been so proud of you, Firefighter Miller. You got here on merit, nothing else, and you seem to be following in his footsteps by putting yourself in harm's way."

Kirsty was just about to say "Thank you" when Ken Cooper continued.

"Your old man was the senior hand at Shoreditch when I was posted there after training school. He took me under his wing and taught me so much. A bloody good fireman too. I was sorry to have missed his funeral but I was at the Fire Service College in Moreton-in-Marsh at the time. It seems like father like daughter. Be proud young lady, but you still have plenty to do and lots to learn."

She had no idea that there was any connection between her Dad and her Station Commander. She was also very much aware that her pat on the back, for the job on Deptford's ground, was more by luck than design! Deptford's crews did not look kindly on women in the job. Her guvnor had told her to stick to him like glue as they pulled in at the blazing flat in Deptford High Street. So she did. It was why she was by his side as they crawled in on their bellies and found the two children in a back room. She left her tears to the privacy of her own flat after she was told that one of the children had died six days later.

For the next couple of years she got on with her busy life at Lewisham. After her probation was confirmed she became active with the Fire Brigades Union (FBU), she started to meet up with other LFB women firefighters too. In 1989 Kirsty became a founding member of the FBU's Women's Committee. Her desire was to give female colleagues a voice. For some it meant a voice that others found hard or choose not to hear, regardless of how loud the women shouted. She, with others in the Women's Committee, started to take on the 'white male dominated' Brigade management. They worked to give female firefighters their own toilets/showers and sleeping facilities and for 'porn' magazines to be banned from fire stations. It was not an easy task.

Lewisham Fire Station had been the exception not the norm when it came to facilities for its lone female firefighter. The size of the station helped, plus an Area Commander who did not wish to 'shit on his own doorstep' by having Kirsty struggling for basic facilities. He had ensured a degree of privacy as regards female toilet, washing and sleeping arrangements from day one. But Kirsty was aware of deep injustices within the system. She felt the need to right the wrongs. Frequently it proved to be an uphill struggle. She was often told that she had to be like a man to do the job but, as a committed firefighter, she had higher aspirations. She wanted to do it better. She wanted to change things. Things did change during her time in the job, some dramatically. But her private fear then was that any momentum the Committee may have been gained for equality was being lost.

There were plenty of examples for Kirsty to choose from. Female firefighters going to a station often struggled to find any facilities. The Brigade had made a powerful case to get more women to join but the local politicians wouldn't put the money in to support all the promises. They were not making it a workplace that could fairly accommodate women. Where they did, male firefighters would use the female lavatories and not in a respectful manner either. Other female firefighters were spoken to badly, only to discover, or realise, that no-one would do anything about it. It was intimidating for individuals to bring it up, male or female. It took a determined sort of person to do that in the predominately 'macho' environment. Frequently there was the problem of the pack mentality, for instance when one person starts a sick – or, at best, poor – joke and others get sucked in. Many women firefighters found it was easier to run into a burning building than to challenge work colleagues who had views contrary to good-manners and civil behaviour.

Then in late 1990 Firefighter Miller became Leading Firefighter Miller. She was posted to East Greenwich Fire Station on the same Watch. Her first day started with a flurry of activity. With the Sub Officer on annual leave Kirsty found herself in charge of the pump-ladder. As she called the roll for the Station Officer at 9.00 a.m. the station bells started ringing. The pump was ordered to a fire on Plumstead's ground. As it cleared the forecourt the bells started ringing again and she fully expected to be following the pump. The 'dutyman' (gender neutral terms were slow in coming) shouted out that the call was to somewhere different, a road traffic accident on the A102, the Blackwall Tunnel Southern Approach. It was on their ground. As the pump-ladder turned right into Wool-wich Road, Leading Firefighter Miller was informed that multiple calls were being received to the accident by their control room radio operator.

An articulated lorry had jack-knifed and been hit by several cars and other commercial vehicles. As East Greenwich's crew drew nearer what they saw confirmed that they had a serious inci-dent on their hands. At least one car was terribly smashed up; its passenger and driver did not appear to be moving and smoke was already pouring from the front part of it. Kirsty had been thrown into this chaos and she was fully aware that besides taking in the scene confronting them, her crew were also assessing their new Leading Firefighter's reaction to it. It was ever thus. Later she would examine her own coolness as she calmly took control of the situa-tion. She instructed her driver to make pumps four and requested an additional fire rescue tender. She asked for the police to control traffic and for two additional ambulances. She directed her crew's immediate lifesaving actions and quelling the car fire before it got more serious. She was well aware that her time in charge was limited but she ticked all the right boxes and prioritized the actions of the first rescue tender to arrive, even though she was outranked by the Sub Officer riding in charge of it. She passed over the salient information to Poplar's Station Officer when he pulled up. Firefighters and equipment filled the scene, ambulance crews worked hand in hand with the crews in the extrication of the trapped driver and passenger and treated other injured drivers. Command of the incident passed to the duty Station Commander and the Divisional Officer 'Operations' came on to monitor the situation. As the intense action started to subside and the last casualties were removed to hospital, the Divisional Officer called Kirsty to one side.

"Well done, Miller. Interesting start to your new role. Keep it up."

He was not the only one seemingly impressed. Any concerns the Watch might have had about their new female on the station, even if she was their Leading Firefighter, evaporated. Upon their return to the station she thanked her crew. It was later in the day that she finally got the formal welcome by the Station Officer, a short stocky Irishman who had a three Fs reputation: fair, firm and friendly.

"You did the business, Miller. Pleased to have you here. You have set the bar high, now just try to maintain it."

In the months ahead, and having passed both her Sub Officer's written and practical exams, Leading Firefighter Kirsty Miller was spending as much time at surrounding stations as her own, either on temporary detachment as an acting Sub Officer or standing by in charge of another station's pump ladder. There were few station White Watches that hadn't come into contact with Kirsty. Some experiences were better than others. But only the foolhardy would take on this articulate and athletic woman face to face. Even the hardened misogynists at fire stations had to admit Kirsty knew her job and could do theirs standing on her head.

* * * * * *

On Sunday 4 February 1996, a fire occurred at a supermarket in Bristol. It was a fire where firefighter Fleur Lombard lost her life. She was the first female firefighter to die in the line of duty in peacetime. Fleur was inside the premises and fighting the blaze wearing breathing apparatus when she and a male colleague were caught in a 'flashover'. (The fire was recorded as deliberate ignition and ravaged through the building whilst the shop was still open for trading.)

Fleur Lombard died shortly after two retained firefighters from Blaina in South Wales died trying to save the life of a child at a house fire. Kirsty thought people, both in and out of the fire service, would finally realise that not only do female firefighters do the same work as the men but they can die like them too.

Fire Brigades from all over the UK sent representatives to the fire-fighter's funeral. A contingent, headed by an Assistant Chief Officer, represented the London Fire Brigade. Kirsty was part of that contingent, but she would have attended anyway even in a private capacity. It was whilst sitting at Fleur's funeral service that she listened to the moving eulogy spoken by Avon's Chief Officer, Kirsty's tears showing the pride, and sadness, in being associated with Lombard's legacy. Then the Chief said: "Fleur joined because she loved the job, not to make a point." Kirsty's sadness was now mixed with something else, anger. It grew in the following days as his remarks were faithfully reproduced in many daily newspapers. Kirsty believed the man had sentenced all the women attending Fleur's funeral, and those dotted about the country, to the eternal game of "Is she, isn't she?" He had implied that females who joined the fire service were making a point. She wondered if that inaccurate accusation came in the same breath as those individuals accused of 'hidden' or 'political' agendas. She had no doubt that there were some who would have been accused of all three.

* * * * * *

Big changes came along for Kirsty in June 1996. Already a mother herself with a one year-old son, like many working parents, she was balancing work and family. Promoted to Sub Officer, she not only changed stations but watches and commands too. She was the new Sub Officer on Brixton's Green Watch, only she wasn't! Not anymore. 'Ranks' were considered 'old hat' and 'roles' had been introduced across the Brigade. It was the era of the managers.

Kirsty was designated a 'Watch Commander B'. Still the same rank markings, just a different label. But she was not the lone female at Brixton. They already had a woman firefighter on the Red Watch. Kirsty had meet her before and had been mightily impressed. Only wishing to be good at her job, she had regaled Kirsty with her tales of her firefighter selection interview. A single mother, Amber Platt had expected to be asked all the usual questions by the interview board: "Why did she wanted to join the fire service? Any relevant experience?" and so on. She did not expect to be warned that she could not "wear make-up or have nice hair in this job."

"So when I sat down," recounted Amber, "in front of the people interviewing me they asked, 'What will you do if you get married and have children?' I replied, 'I already have a two-year-old. And what's that got to do with it?'"

Amber just smiled as she recalled, "They didn't know what to say. I'm not sure many female candidates talked to them like that."

It came as no surprise for Kirsty to discover that Amber was Brixton's Union rep. Amber had written to the Brigade's in-house magazine *London Firefighter*. They publisher her letter word for word in the 'Dear Editor' column. It had caused quite a stir and it certainly made an impression on Kirsty, who was still working to advance the work of the Brigade's woman's minority group. She kept a copy of the article on the back of her locker door. Amber's letter had been spot-on when she wrote;

"Mary Joy Langdon was the first women to join a British fire brigade. She started on August 21, 1978 in the East Sussex Fire Brigade. Her arrival came with a huge fanfare of national news coverage, together with the Home Office announcement that females would be accepted into the fire service. It took another four years before London's first female firefighter joined in 1982, a whole seven years after the Sex Discrimination Act of 1975 first came into force and enshrined, in law, the rights of men and women concerning employment, training and education. The London Fire Brigade clearly took a while to catch up, but that is the nature of the beast. It's a reactive, not proactive, organisation. Now two decades later and where exactly has this progress got us?

Mine is a personnel response to the widespread feelings of many female firefighters who have seen an adverse reaction to us getting out act together. Our male counterparts appear to be complaining about the 'troublesome' women's minority group within the Brigade. I will try and explain the fundamental difference between what they have experienced and what I and many of my gender have experienced since stepping onto a fire station in recent years. No doubt we all would argue that we were equally keen, capable and eager to learn then. Many still are. However, the ill-treatment which many female firefighters have endured can border on cruelty. Something you cannot imagine happening you say, what happens on the fire station, stays on the fire station! Such things that, anecdotally, include swearing, name calling, insults and, in extreme cases, violence to women on stations. It is rarely mentioned. Sometimes it is subtle, other times it is called innocent 'fun'. Boys will be boy's stuff. Stuff that remains, sadly, still around today. It is both draining and it is wholly unwarranted.

In the recent history of the fire service, and certainly in this Brigade, female firefighters remain the new 'kids' on the block. Of course, a male recruit going to a station will be new too, but they are entering what is still seen by many of those serving, and by the general public too, as a *man's* world.

That first day at the fire station will always be tough no matter what life experiences you might bring with you. Newness brings with it trying to join in and learning to be accepted. The advice to a recruit, leaving training centre, might well be 'don't put too much pressure on yourself', but for anyone it's a steep learning curve trying to figure out how a watch works. What makes it tick? Whilst the now 'probationers' are not expected to hit the ground running, they do just that. They are riding a fire engine, albeit under supervision, and everything they do, or say, is observed and analysed. There will be mistakes along the way, it's inevitable. But in the case of the female firefighter they most commonly are attributed to their gender.

Trying not to ruffle any feathers is harder than it seems. It takes some time to absorb a station's culture, and they vary widely. In some cases the ethos is to pick on the probationer regardless as they are fair game for a 'jolly jape'. However, being a female appears to push the boundaries that bit further and in an attempt to see what she can take.

For the 'new kids' the probationary year (up to two years for an extended probation) should be equally challenging regardless of gender. Abilities as a firefighter should not be automatically doubted and yet they are frequently by those doing the assessing and report writing. Their unintentional 'macho' language (giving them the benefit of the doubt) makes life all that much harder as the solitary female vanishes in a watch's lineup of identical firefighter uniforms.

Trying to progress through this firefighter's learning curve, in the eyes of those that didn't want you there in the first place, brings forth challenges that only the most robust of individuals can survive. Checking things, or details, with other watch members, those with experience, can bring about unwanted comments. It adds fuel to the fire for those who will use every opportunity to undermine the abilities of those learning their craft, be they male or female. But the odds are, the labels stick more readily if she is a women.

Trying to act positively, when the cards appear stacked against you, tests the resolve of many. Yes, politeness is, of course, important. You're working in an environment where people feel ownership of being a firefighter even if the majority of senior hands, those with more than 15 years in, still refer to themselves as 'firemen'. You might even forgive yourself the odd *faux pas*, simply because you're not going to know how to do the job until you learn how to do the job, but you will be one of the few who do.

There will be female firefighters in the Brigade who say they don't recognise these situations or these attitudes. I wish we were all so lucky. My first posting was hell. But there was no way I was going to be the weakest link. After a difficult probationary year, and with my probation extended, I was posted to my current station. I struck gold and it was in an environment that would be the envy of many. I was on a watch where I was treated fairly, equally and without rancour.

Of course there has been progress over the past two decades.

The 'women's minority' group has helped in that regard and will continue to do so. As the 'old guard' ride off into the sunset, tomorrow's culture will become the norm. But until that happens we make no apologies for making a stand. We will tackle blatant discrimination wherever we find it and challenge those that deliver it. We are proud to be London fire-fighters and will strive to encourage other women to think of it as a worthwhile and meaningful career. Things won't change overnight, but we are moving in the right direction. That is something to be welcomed by fire and rescue services across the country."

Kirsty had rarely heard the problems faced by many of London's female firefighters better expressed. Amber told her the words might appear severe but they were the truth. It was the truth as it had affected her and many others who had spoken to her. Amber knew she was fortunate in being on such a good watch, with people that she stood shoulder to shoulder with when dealing with fires and other life-threatening emergencies. Kirsty thought Amber's obser-vations not only reflected the harsh realities but shone a light on the various experiences of female firefighters in the LFB.

* * * * * *

Kirsty celebrated her 33rd birthday at the fire station. It was 1998 and she had reported for a night duty. The mess-manager had got his wife to bake a cake. It was over supper that she discovered she was not only the eldest on the watch but was also senior in time served. Her 'guvnor' who was promoted at 30, and after only nine years' service, beat the watch's firefighter 'old hand' by seven months. Two of the watch were black, a couple of old hands both had ten years in, there was a probationer and everything in between. They worked hard and shared a laugh. They worked as team They trusted their officer's professional abilities and each other's. Kirsty considered it a gift. She loved coming to work.

It was six months after Amber's article saw the light of day that some of those female challenges came knocking on Kirsty's door. It's customary to expect that those in the 'blue light' services have the odd 'hair-raising' experience. Kirsty had more than her fair share, although none quite like this. Hair length or hair style appeared to be one of the main niggles with those initiating unwanted harrying. According to the LFB's 'Brigade Orders' (the Brigade's bible of policies and procedures), whilst female firefighters were allowed long hair, it had to be tied or pinned up. This was contrary to the requirements of male firefighters who were not allowed to have long hair, even if it was pinned or tied up.

Kirsty had been fair game for hair-related comments over the years. Some had complained to her face that she could grow her hair and they couldn't. Another favoured tactic was to get their officers to complain to hers. It had gone on and on. It was like water off a duck's back until her hair again became the focus of attention. Only this time it wasn't a firefighter doing the complaining.

The 'shout' had occurred in the backstreets of Clapham. A waste paper recycling plant, covered by metal corrugated sheds, had been set alight. Kirsty saw the pall of smoke as her fire engine sped along Acre Lane towards Clapham High Street. There was an excited calm among her crew, aware that they had a working job on their hands. Multiple calls had been received to the fire; four fire engines had been dispatched, two from Clapham and two from Brixton. Clapham's fire engines were the first to arrive, their officer in charge having no hesitation in making pumps eight.

As big fires go it was pretty much run of the mill. There was lots of hose, lots of water and some excellent work by Brixton's BA crews stopping the fire spreading to an adjoining shed; within 90 minutes they got it surrounded. As senior managers arrived to take command and with the fire under control, if not actually out, the crews prepared for the arduous task of breaking down the bales of smouldering waste paper to ensure every vestige of fire was extinguished.

That was when a senior manager took Kirsty off the fire-ground. Instructed to stand by the control unit, she waited for her crew to be relived and to return to Brixton, all the while giving the impression of being very calm and collected about the whole situation. She was anything but! On return to the station she immediately spoke to her Station Commander who, on light duties, had not attended the incident. A veteran of many a Brigade cock-up, Station Commander

Vaughan had developed two distinct responses to the moment of impact. If he was on the incident ground, with the eyes of watching senior managers upon him, he would tilt his fire helmet at a rakish angle and set about righting the wrongs others had generated whilst wearing an expression of exemplary calm.

Unobserved, as now, he was more likely to favour his second option, which was to freeze in the position in which the news had hit him whilst pinching his left earlobe between his thumb and fore-finger as he considered how to deal with the issue at hand, which was all about Kirsty's hair. She informed him she was instigating an official grievance. It was the start of a three-year battle, a battle she eventually won. It would bring about a change to the relevant Brigade Order, one that applied equally to both men and women.

During her time at Southwark Training School she had worn her long hair up when in uniform. Although it was a frequent topic of discussion she had always maintained the party line and conformed to the accepted standard of prescribed wearing of hair, then she had cut her hair short.

With the notification of her grievance the shit hit the fan. Phone calls were made and senior and principal managers started circling the wagons. In fact, principal managers would prevaricate and stall over the months ahead; anything to keep the status quo. She was not surprised to see the same senior manager who removed her from the fire-ground arrive at the station. By this time she had formalised her grievance in writing.

Kirsty was not a believer in coincidence although on this occasion she was prepared to make an exception. The senior manager before her was the very man who had hit on her at a retirement 'do' before her posting to Brixton. His offer of 'going out for a drink' was firmly, but politely, rejected. It was something of a setback for this 'lady's man's' ego. But as it was a conversation that only the two of them knew about, there was no point in bringing it up now. For Kirsty, a talented and articulate advocate of causes, this was an issue that needed sorting. She was in the mood to finally get the ball rolling.

The initial conversation did not go so well, for him anyway. Whilst her hair appeared to conform to the letter of the Brigade Order to her Station Commander, the senior manager asked if she could pin up her hair. Kirsty asked him to explain exactly why she had been taken off a fire-ground. "Your hair was deemed not to conform to Orders, it was considered a hazard." She then demonstrated that her hair was, in fact, too short to pin up. Following a telephone conversation his next course of action was to tell her that she would be placed on day duties and to report to Croydon HQ. She would remain there until the situation had been resolved.

Content with his decision, Kirsty just wanted the whole 'hair' situation settled. As she prepared to leave the station he made a series of phone calls. She never got to Croydon. When he finished on the phone he informed her that, in his opinion, her hair did comply. He qualified his statement by saying that her hair must have been uncombed and messy at the incident! He told her that if she wanted to go back 'on the run' she should first retract her grievance. However, if she felt she still had a grievance then she must submit an amended one. She did, and so it started.

The next interview took place immediately following her four days off. Brixton again was the venue. A more senior manager arrived this time. He, and a grim-faced Station Commander Vaughan (sitting in as a Brigade witness) were waiting in the Station Commander's office. Kirsty was on duty but not riding an appliance. With her revised grievance read out it was confirmed that Kirsty had requested Union representation. In fact Kirsty had used her off-duty time wisely and her 'friend' was Andy Lightwater, London's FBU Executive Council member, a hardened campaigner for more female firefighters in the Brigade and on equality issues generally. Kirsty and Andy had been in the same recruit squad together and had become firm friends over the years. There was no need for a private word with Kirsty when Andy arrived at the station as he was already up to speed. Suffice to say, there followed a frank and full exchange of views, the Station Commander secretly enjoying the advantage the pair were gaining on the senior manager and his growing sense of unease.

"So," said Andy, "it seems that the officer concerned about Watch Manager Miller's hair, who is not here to comment, amended his views later to say the hair in question complied with the relevant Brigade Order. It is disappointing that this situation has even arisen and your view appears that Watch Manager Miller should be satisfied with a verbal answer to her grievance. Well, that is not going to happen. This is not the first such occasion that a female firefighter has been removed either from the incident ground or from a drill yard because of the arbitrary judgement of a station or senior manager.

"The Station Commander, who was the eight-pump fire incident commander until he was relieved by a more senior manager, was sufficiently satisfied that Watch Manager Miller's hair was safe enough for her to enter an active fire-ground. His judgement was that the fire situation was not going to change for the worse and place Watch Manager Miller, or anyone else for that matter, in immediate danger.

"The hair, allegedly uncombed and messy, was enough to pose a problem, yet was safe enough before she rigged and was committed in breathing apparatus. Her own officer in charge was not concerned, even though he stood only a few metres away. She had worn her hair in the style you see before you now for the last few months. A style that was, apparently, acceptable to her Watch Officers, the Station Commander and even visiting senior managers, yet, strangely, appeared unacceptable to the person who removed her from the fire-ground."

Kirsty would have loved to put her four pennyworth in but she held her tongue.

Andy continued, "Clearly the Brigade Order does not give sufficient guidance to Watch or Station managers. Currently advice must be sought from Equal Opportunities Section and Training School. Then even there are differences in their interpretation of accepted practices."

The interview ended there. A now smiling Station Commander watched as the senior manager rose, closed his file and said:

"I'll contact you again."

He never did. It took eight months for the Brigade to be forced, by the FBU, to apologise and to admit the Brigade Order was to blame. It was another three years to make the hair policy equal for men and women. Even then, the Brigade took credit for changing it although a couple of other females claimed recognition for challenging the unequal rules. Maybe they did.

* * * * * *

In 2005 The Queen unveiled a £1 million bronze sculpture in White-hall to commemorate the role of women during World War II. The 22-foot high bronze sculpture depicting the uniforms and working clothes worn by women during the war. Kirsty was there, part of the inter-emergency services honour guard, paying tribute to the women of the past.

Kirsty was well aware that female firefighters are nothing new, only they were called 'firewomen' back then. During the Blitz of 1940–41 many of London's firemen and the auxiliary fire service was commended for their bravery and among that number were its firewomen. They undertook a range of duties including driving, dispatch riders, and control staff. The first two firewomen to be awarded gallantry medals (BEMs) were Annie Wilkins and Bessie Wulbern. They had been on watchroom duty during an intense enemy bombing raid and had remained at their post. One particu-lar London firewomen was Gillian Wilton-Clark (née Tanner) who received the George Medal for her exceptional bravery. Her particu-lar story, and the role women played in the Blitz with London's fire service, remain an important part of the LFB history.

Kirsty could not help thinking, as she watched the unveiling cere-mony, that 64 years on and with female firefighters still compar-atively rare, that their achievements remained largely overlooked by the media: a media which still talked about 'firemen' rather than 'firefighters' (a title the London Fire Brigade changed in the mid-1980s). She thought it ironic that during the War, with its mix of regular and auxiliary firemen and firewomen, as a collective they were simply referred to as 'firefighters'. Maybe events such as this would get people talking about how they describe fire service staff?

Gillian Wilton-Clark was one of the surviving George Medal recipients specially invited to the ceremony and who was presented to the Queen. When Kirsty got home she Googled Gillian Wilton-Clark's name. She found the details on the *London Gazette* website.

"Awarded the GEORGE MEDAL. Gillian Kluane TANNER (L/G, 35058, 31st Jan 1941, pp. 610.) Firewoman (Aux). Six serious fires were in progress and for three hours Auxiliary Tanner drove a 30-cwt. lorry loaded with 150 gallons of petrol in cans from fire to fire, replenishing petrol supplies, despite intense bombing at the time. She showed remarkable coolness and courage throughout.'

Intrigued, Kirsty dug further and discovered that on 3 September 1939, the day war broke out, a 19-year-old Miss Tanner drove to London in her front-wheel drive BSA car from her home near Cirencester, in Gloucestershire, to see what she could do to help. The Women's Voluntary Service directed her to the auxiliary fire service where she became a driver. Gillian Tanner had later written her own account of those times. Finding the link Kirsty read on and discovered this country girl, whose main pastime had been horse riding, was posted to Dockhead fire station, in Bermondsey, which she thought of as 'the slums'.

Gillian later recalled in a radio interview:

"There were two drivers allocated to Dockhead and I was the only one who had the heavy goods licence, so I had the canteen van and petrol lorry to drive. You had the petrol in two gallon tins and they were stacked on shelves around the lorry. I didn't think about it at the time, luckily.

They [the AFS] took over a lot of schools and made them sub stations and they all had their own trailer pumps – I remember going to one not far from Tower Bridge and we were pouring petrol into the engine and it was red hot. I didn't even think about the fact that one drop, and we would go up in smoke. You had a job to do and you got on and did it. I remember taking my fiancé back to Sandhurst, it must've been the first day of the Blitz, because when I turned round to come back I could see London burning from Sandhurst – that was when they bombed the Surrey Commercial Docks."

Gillian delivered petrol to fire pumps around Bermondsey while the docks were being bombed during one of the worst nights of the Blitz. Kirsty had felt humbled to have met such a lovely, modest, lady during the informal reception after the unveiling.

* * * * * *

Kirsty was due her 20 years' service award, the Fire Service Long Service and Good Conduct Medal, in 2006. She was running her own watch at Southwark Fire Station by then, having been promoted to a Watch Manager (A), something that would have been called a Station Officer in old money; a title she much preferred. She was also back on the White Watch. The medal presentations were held at London City Hall, home of the London Assembly. Watched by her partner and two children she proudly walked onto the podium when her name was called, the Commissioner shaking her hand before pinning the medal onto her immaculate new 'officers' undress uniform.

"Congratulations, Miller," he said. "I have heard a lot about you."

He never mentioned if it was good or bad as they turned to face the camera to have the obligatory photograph taken. Her local newspaper got wind of her presentation and asked for an interview. Uncertain, she agreed. Not only was it printed in the weekly community rag but taken up by the national press too. It made for good copy, apparently. After the reporter's brief introduction about Kirsty, her age, family and where she worked, Kirsty gave her take on her career.

"Although my late dad was a fireman I was drawn to the team-work, the physical fitness and how wide-ranging the job could be. Some people may see the fire brigade as just squirting water on hot stuff! It is so much more. The flexibility of the shifts appealed to me. When I joined, the biggest barrier was the lack of female facilities at fire stations. In the late 1980s the push to recruit female firefighters was little more than window dressing. Fire stations simply weren't ready to accommodate us women. There were no locks on rooms and an almost total lack of shower and toilet facilities. When a fire station did get them they could only accommodate one woman at a time!

I can truly say that I enjoy almost every aspect of my job, from tackling a fire to showing a group of children around the fire engine. No two days are ever the same. I enjoy the 'family' life of the fire station and love being a part of a watch. Shift work doesn't suit everyone but it suits me perfectly. My two day duties followed by two night duties followed by four days' leave allows me to spend quality time with my family.

The physical work never fazed me. You try bringing up two young children and doing a full-time job at the same time. It was clear to me that the Fire Brigade offered me the opportunity of both a worthwhile career and to do something positive within the community

It's not all about fighting fires and dealing with other emergencies either. There is the extensive fire safety work too. The number of fires we attend has actually reduced since I joined some 20 years ago. My work regularly involves doing fire safety work in the local area. Working as a London firefighter doesn't necessarily mean that I spend all my time working at a fire station either. For example, I work with others occasionally to encourage people from different backgrounds to consider a career as a firefighter. The firefighter's basic training is now about three months. It involves a great deal of study and physical exercise. So today's recruits need to be disciplined enough to study on your own and maintain a high standard of physical fitness.

Me, I love working in London. It is one of the most diverse cities in the world. It hosts millions of international visitors every year. So it's vital that London firefighters represent the different communities we serve. Having different people from a range of backgrounds increases our ability to connect with the public in what, for them, can be really stressful circumstances. But with women and some ethnic groups still under-represented, it remains work in progress. The fire brigade needs women and women need to demand what they require from the fire brigade."

Her last comments raised a few eyebrows in the higher echelons of the Brigade but speaking the truth had never been a problem for Kirsty Miller.

* * * * * *

It seemed like ordinary day duty in early 2011. However, Kirsty was convinced that there was some skulduggery going on amongst her Southwark Watch; she just couldn't tie down what it was. Then at morning stand-easy, as she walked into the station mess room, all became clear. There were far too many people in there for a start. She wondered why the Station Commander had kept her talking in her officer for the past hour, going over things of little importance. Now she knew.

Her friend Andy Lightwater was now the Assistant General Secretary of the FBU. He had joined the Brigade on the same day as Kirsty. Over the years they had never lost touch with one another, even though their career paths differed considerably. Now they stood side by side in the mess-room. Andy was there to present Kirsty with her 25-year FBU badge. They stood in front of the picture portrait of a young Queen Elizabeth II when she attended the Centenary Review of the Brigade at Lambeth in 1966. As Andy pinned on the badge he spoke to the packed mess room.

"You have all heard of Dorian Gray. I am certain Kirsty has, as I think she has taken a leaf out of Dorian Gray's book. Hidden in your locker must be a hideous portrait of you at your true age today! Meanwhile, unlike the dear Queen behind us, you have declined to age graciously. You are still smiling at us like the 23 year-old athlete, exactly as you did when we were running around like blue-arsed flies during our recruit training days all those years ago in the drill yards outside these windows. I would point out too that you fared better than the poor old Training Centre, which despite its multi-million pound refit is likely to be closed and sold off to the highest bidder!"

It was not the only presentation Kirsty and her White Watch received that year. Between 6 and 11 August 2011 thousands of people rioted in several London boroughs. The resulting chaos generated looting, arson, and the mass deployment of the Metropolitan Police. The riots were nicknamed the 'Blackberry riots' as many people used their mobile devices and social media to organise into gangs of rampaging youths. The disturbances had started on the afternoon of 6 August following the death of Mark Duggan, a local who was shot dead by police in Tottenham. Violent clashes with police ensued, along with the destruction of police vehicles, a magistrates' court, a double-decker bus, and many civilian homes and businesses, thus rapidly gaining attention from the media. As Kirsty reported for her night duty looting and arson was taking place in Tottenham. It spread to a retail park and involved nearby Wood Green. The following days saw similar scenes in other parts of London.

For those London firefighters on duty it was one of the most challenging post-war periods of concerted operational activity. It resulted in an unprecedented number of gallantry awards being bestowed to individual firefighters and fire station watch crews in its recent history. Ten firefighters were injured as the Brigade dealt with over one hundred major fires caused by the disturbances. Eight fire engines had their windscreens smashed and two fire cars were attacked. Private vehicles, homes and shops were attacked and set alight. At least one hundred homes were destroyed in the arson and looting. An estimate by the Association of British Insurers put the likely pay-out in excess of £100 million.

Kirsty and her two fire engine crews had been ordered to a fire in Peckham. Well aware of the civil disturbance and the need for caution, when they arrived the situation demanded immediate action. Southwark's crews took it. With a police officer seriously injured and his patrol car overturned and set ablaze, the flames spread to an adjacent shop. Protecting the officer until police rein-forcements arrived, they also tackled the shop fire, leading three people to safety in the process. Southwark's pump was one of those fire engines attacked. As a result of their actions Southwark's White Watch were presented with Commendations from the Metropolitan Police for their "bravery, professionalism and dedication to duty in assisting an injured police colleague during this major public disor-der". It was the last honour that would be entered on the Station's Honours and Award board which hung, in pride of place, in the Station office.

* * * * * *

The year 2014 turned out to be a bittersweet one. Kirsty knew the rancorous and unwarranted closure of Southwark Fire Station was coming. Station personnel, local political groups and community leaders had fought a hard campaign to save the Station. They had failed. Southwark was one of ten fire stations, the London Mayor, Boris Johnson, had ordered the fire authority to shut, together with a controversial plan to axe 14 frontline fire engines. The cuts were included in a new London Safety Plan drawn up by Fire Commissioner Ron Dobson in the wake of reductions in central Government and City Hall funding. It was the largest cull in London's fire cover since the 1920s.

The personnel from Southwark, and the other affected stations, were transferred to different locations. Most had their posting of choice, a few didn't. Kirsty had requested a return to Brixton and, much to her delight, got it. Station Commander Vaughan welcomed her back warmly. Later that year things went full circle. Her daughter started her training with the Brigade, although she never walked through the iconic Southwark Training Centre arch. In fact, the Brigade no longer even trained their own recruits! Training was 'outsourced' to Babcock's, in yet another cost saving exercise. Her daughter walked into an industrial unit in North London but Kirsty imagined she probably had the same feelings of pride and anticipation that she herself had experienced all those years earlier.

* * * * * *

Kirsty genuinely welcomed the appointment of the first ever female London Commissioner in 2017. She had met her a few times at 'Women in the Fire Service' events. It was previously called the 'Networking Women in the Fire Service', it being a voluntary, not-for-profit organisation, Kirsty had been active in it since its inception in 1993. She had been given the Silver Award by its National Executive Council for her outstanding contribution to promoting women in the fire service.

Recent changes made her realise she was poles apart from her dad's generation: a generation of 'firemen' in an era of wooden ladders and iron men. Kirsty knew hers were different times and with different rules, but, whether firemen or firefighters, they all shared a common bond, a common purpose. She was proud she was a London firefighter, proud of her daughter's career choice. She wondered what her daughter would make of her generation in the years ahead.

One of the new Commissioner's first high-profile public campaigns was to challenge the public's perception of the cartoon image of 'Fireman Sam', or rather the term. The new incumbent wished to see the creators catch up with the times and use 'Firefighter Sam' instead. Kirsty knew that language really matters, that language influences awareness and opinions. The Brigade still had a long way to go to address the gender imbalance between men and women applying to join the Brigade. "Did I make any difference?" Kirsty wondered. "Who's to know? Will the new Commissioner make a difference? Only time will tell?"

Knowing she still had another six years to serve to her 60th birthday, and a well-earned retirement, she hoped she would. She hoped, too, that other strong women would share in the success and experiences that she had had over the years and continue the fight for equality.

(Kirsty Miller is a fictional character inspired by the experiences of real London women firefighters.)

Note

As of the end of 2017 there were 300 female firefighters in the London Fire Brigade, or seven per cent of the total. It remains the highest percentage in the UK which, early in the same year, stood at only 3.1 per cent.

Old Dinosaurs...
We Are Who We Are...

DESPITE THE TITLE OF this book, I was actually a *London fireman*. Exactly five decades separate the two following accounts of fatal fires. The first, outlined below, was small, albeit tragic, and involves me. The other, described in the next section, is unprecedented in the annals of the modern London Fire Brigade. The term 'dinosaurs' is often used by today's firefighters to describe us 'old' ones: those who formerly wore a fireman's uniform and once served in the Brigade. The fact that the Brigade has changed, beyond recognition to yesterday's firemen, is without doubt. New kit, new ways, and a new order of things. But there are some things that have never changed. Fires are just as hot and potentially as dangerous as they always were. The other unvariable is the attitude of those on the frontline: the very people who ride the fire engines, and who put themselves in harm's way when duty calls.

* * * * * *

Brixton Hill, SW2

Do you ever wonder about that particular moment when you knew you took the right career path decision? Mine was about the decision to join the Fire Brigade. Not just the social side of the 'job', all the fun, the jolly japes and the larks. Not that these were always shared with those back home. Frequently they were kept strictly on the watch or confined to the fire station. But this is not the moment to which I refer, it's the other moment, the one out on the street. That moment that you would not wish repeated but you know was nevertheless affirming about your choice of occupation.

There is an iconic picture, in the photographic insert, showing two firemen from the Old Kent Road fire station (page 164). They are attempting to revive a child, on the pavement, with oxygen from a Proto cylinder following a serious fire at the Elephant and Castle. It is an image that always invokes that moment; my moment. I was but a mere, wet behind the ears, probationer fireman serving at Lambeth Fire Station. Tony Sowerby (like me another former Junior Fireman) was stationed at the adjacent Brixton Fire Station, also on the Red Watch. It was during a conversation with Tony, about our fire brigade days, that the moment came flooding back. A moment, in truth, I had pretty much tried to forget about.

It is 1967 and I am sitting on the rear of Lambeth's pump which had been ordered onto a fire call in support of Brixton's pump-escape and pump crews. It is a "persons reported" fire at Brixton Hill. I am a mere 'makeweight' on the back of that fire engine. I've no experience and very much the 'junior buck'.

Brixton's Red Watch were a *tour de force*. Old, steady, experienced hands. Some were ex-army and one was a former Royal Navy sailor. With almost two years' service, Sowerby was their 'junior buck'. Arriving at Brixton Hill at a serious house fire involving small children, Brixton's crews were fully committed. Lambeth's crew seemed to know exactly what was required to be done and set about doing it. I was left standing on the pavement like a spare-part!

The blackened, crazed, glazing of the first and second floor windows gave a clue to the extreme heat inside. One of Brixton's veteran hands was vomiting violently on the doorstep, another clue to the vile smoke that filled the house, as I walked up to the front door to peek inside.

Three firemen are wearing breathing apparatus, all the others are without. The house is full of firemen, firemen desperately seeking the missing children and fighting the fire. Then a sudden commotion coming down the stairs. Shouted orders, and some confusion too. Sowerby is holding a child. I am given another by a fireman who about-turns and heads straight back into the smoke-filled house.

Sowerby cradles the child in his arms. It is wrapped in something, I can't recall what. The face of the toddler I am holding is covered in grime and is smoke-stained. Neither child is breathing but neither Sowerby nor I wish to believe the children are dead. They can't be. We both start mouth to mouth on the children. Suddenly we find ourselves in the back of an ambulance being driven at break-neck speed, and under police escort, to King's College Hospital in South London's Denmark Hill. Neither of us stop trying to revive the unmoving children whilst the ambulance man, in the rear and monitoring our progress, attempts to hold us steady.

"Keep going, lads," he encourages.

The arrival at King's A&E sees an initial frenzy of activity. The children are whisked from our arms and rushed inside.

We seemed to wait for ages but in reality it was only a short time. The doctor's face told us what we didn't wish to hear. The two children never made it. He thanked us for our efforts, which doesn't count for much when you fail!

The police car returns us to the fire scene. There is a palpable sense of loss in the other firemen's faces. Their bloodshot eyes, snotty noses and blacked faces tells its own tale of their determined efforts to rescue those two children. Sowerby and I say nothing. Not to each other, not to anyone else either. We try to avoid the looks of the others. Brixton's guvnor calls us both to one side. A big gruff powerful man, he tells us we were already fighting a losing battle. We could not have done anything more than what we did. However, it was the nods and the wordless pats on the back from firemen I was in awe of which showed a compassion, a sympathy and benevolence that this 18 year-old had not seen or experienced ever before. You could see the genuine sadness in their eyes that their efforts had been in vain. But they left me feeling that they would do it all again in a heartbeat to try and save a life.

It was because of them (and so many more that followed) that this sticks as the moment I knew I had made the right choice. I wanted to a London fireman. It was a feeling that lasted for the next thirty plus years.

It is fair to say that I had one driving ambition when joining the London Fire Brigade, over five decades ago now, and that was to be worthy of the title 'fireman'. It was a rank we all started with but that one simple word carried with it so much more than just rank. The rank of fireman may, in the opinion of some, have been a humble one; but we who know the work which the fireman had to do, in all its guises, would disagree. They had to be able to climb up, get down, crawl in and use their senses when plain common sense tells those getting out to run faster. We learnt our tradecraft from people called *Firemen*, the senior hands who took and believed in this noble calling. Our proudest moment was to save a life. Yet we were also brimming with pride when told by the 'old' hands:

"We'll make a fireman of you yet!"

We are, of course, without doubt yesterday's people. We know the baton has passed onto new, younger, faces. Men and women who are in the frontline of our 'Blue light services' when it comes to all things fire and rescue. Today, when we speak of 'heroes and hero-ines' it is understood that we're dealing with individuals that have the power and drive to overcome their fears in an extraordinary way, regardless of the problems they may face. Today's title is 'fire-fighter'. Firemen of the past were considered heroes because of what they did. Firefighters today are proving they are equally worthy of the same respect and acclaim. There are two words that still instils pride in me. Pride in what I once did and what today's people still do. Those words are 'London Firefighter'.

The Grenfell Tower fire

AN UNPRECEDENTED FIRE STARTED on Wednesday 14 June 2017 in a 24-storey high rise residential block of flats in the Borough of Kensington and Chelsea, West London.

The first of 344 emergency '999' calls was received by the fire brigade control room, to an incident in the tower block, 54 minutes past midnight. The call directed London Fire Brigade crews to Flat 16, Grenfell Tower, Lancaster West Estate, W11. The three fire engines dispatched were North Kensington's pump-ladder (with Watch Manager Michael Dowden in charge), their pump and the pump from Kensington. The fire was on North Kensington's ground and as they left their station in Ladbroke Grove, Kensington was leaving their station in Old Court, Kensington High Street. As those engine crews arrived, Hammersmith's pump was also dispatched four minutes later from its station in Shepherds Bush Road.

With a fire confirmed in a fourth-floor flat, and considered serious, the officer in charge of the first attendance requested assistance. His priority message was timed at 1.13 a.m. and pumps were made six, plus an aerial appliance requested. With Paddington's turntable ladder sent, so were the first two fire control units. Five minutes later pumps were made eight. Although flames were showing at the external kitchen window, the fire was still believed to be confined to the room of origin.

But a disaster was rapidly starting to unfold. Unexpectedly, and bewilderingly, strange developments in the fire occurred. It was seen spreading outside the containment area and involving the metal clad exterior face of the tower – a tower which was now well alight! It was spreading upwards, and diagonally, at an alarming rate. At

1.24 a.m. pumps were made ten. This was followed three minutes later by "Make pumps 15 aerials 2". The mobilising Control Room Officers at Stratford hardly had time to respond to that urgent message before another followed. Less than two minutes later, Watch Commander Mike Dowden, still the Incident Commander, made pumps 25, plus an additional fire rescue tender.

In line with its operational protocols the Brigade instituted its 'high rise' procedure-fire survival guidance. The blaze was now an inferno: a towering inferno. An event so dire that no firefighter attending Grenfell had ever encountered anything similar before.

With pumps made 25 at 1.31 a.m., the calamitous situation, confounding both the rescuers, and those needing rescuing, was becoming clear. Many residents were trapped inside their flats, one would jump to their death rather than face the horror of the spreading flames. Others made frantic bids to escape. Many made repeated, desperate, 999 calls to the fire brigade 'fall-back' control room at Stratford. (The regular Control Room at Merton was undergoing a software upgrade that night.) However, unaware of the unstoppable rate of fire spread on Grenfell Tower, a fire which was illuminating the West London's night-time skyline, control officers, handling the most distressing of emergency calls, provided the standard policy advice. It was for people to stay put until rescued. This advice relies on the assumption that the fire service can contain a fire within the building's interior compartments, compartments built of non-combustible materials. But this impossible fire was spreading rapidly via the building's cladded flammable exterior.

As people died, trapped in the tower block, and others were rescued via the only means of escape, the central protected staircase, pumps were made 40 at 2.04 a.m. Twelve minutes later, and given the enormity of the rescue and fire situation being faced, fire rescue tenders were made ten so as to secure the maximum number of extended breathing apparatus sets at the incident. There has never been an incident requiring ten of these specialist crews in the history of the London Fire Brigade, not even at the Moorgate or Clapham rail disasters. In excess of 60 fire appliances were now at, or converging on, the blazing tower.

Dany Cotton was then the recently appointed first female London Fire Commissioner. She had already left her Kent home in response to the earlier assistance messages. She knew that in extreme situations such as Grenfell Tower, the local authority (Kensington and Chelsea) would normally dispatch a structural surveyor. But in the early hours of the morning one was not immediately available and Commissioner Cotton had to make urgent decisions about whether to commit her firefighters in the absence of that formal safety assessment. She takes up her account of that fateful morning.

"I did a dynamic risk assessment and we knew we were going to be doing things that were not following our normal procedures. Had we just followed standard fire brigade procedures, we would not have been able to commit firefighters in and conduct the rescues we did. That's very difficult for me. I'm in charge of London Fire Brigade, and I was committing firefighters into something that was much unknown and very dangerous. The assessment I made was that there was saveable life in that building at that time, and it was our job to go in. It was very difficult, it made me feel physically sick, looking at the building and knowing I had a hundred-plus firefighters in the building at any one time. The decision almost certainly averted an even greater loss of life. There was a massive risk to my firefighters, but you balance that against the fact that you join London fire brigade to save people's lives. We wanted to save as many people as we could. That was the bottom line."

Cotton went into the tower to gain an understanding of the nightmare confronting her firefighting colleagues.

"I could see the conditions when we went in, the severity of the fire. The debris was raining down on us. I knew I was committing them to an extreme situation, and in those situations things aren't always predictable and that was very frightening."

As Cotton entered the tower's downstairs lobby she was struck by her colleagues' demeanour.

"The one thing that was overwhelming for me was the calm professionalism of the firefighters; they were going into something that they knew was extremely difficult and challenging."

Despite the frenetic pace of activity, Cotton considered the fire crews were clear about their roles.

"It was very structured. It wasn't people running into the building. We have officers at different points to do checks, so we know who's in and who's out. When they came out they [the firefighters] were excessively tired, they were hot. They were working very hard in difficult conditions, but they wanted to go back in time and time again."

Daylight brought a new appreciation, and the dreadfulness, of the unfolding tragedy.

"It became increasingly difficult just looking at the building and still knowing there were people in there. The pressure we all felt to keep trying and doing our best was immense. I personally went round to loads of my crew. I was just saying, 'Drink more water, sit in the shade, take your fire gear off, cool yourselves down, get yourself ready to get back in.' It's absolutely essential for their ongoing health, to be able to deploy them again."

It is likely that the horrors of the Grenfell Tower blaze will linger in the minds of the firefighters attending that blaze for many years to come. The findings of the Public Inquiry is yet to be published but commentators consider London firefighters did everything humanly possible to rescue as many people as possible. But that does not stop the self-doubt, the feeling: *What if?* Cotton considers, "We could have done no more." Her view was had they tried to do any more it would have risked losing the lives of firefighters. Those waking up to the London disaster scene, broadcast live on breakfast news channels, were bombarded by graphic images and news bites.

"The walls of the concrete stairwell, where hundreds of residents made panicked evacuation attempts as the inferno erupted' have been turned black from the blaze."

"So far none of many victims have been identified."

"Detectives fear the identities of some of those killed will remain a mystery due to the ferocity of the 1,000°C fire that devastated the 24-storey block."

"Firefighters rescued sixty-five people, with seventy-four people confirmed by the NHS to be in six hospitals across London. Twenty of them in critical condition."

What became known is that a total of one-hundred and fifty-one homes were destroyed in the tower block and surrounding area. The fire ranks as the deadliest structural fire in the United Kingdom since the start of the 20th century, a time when detailed records began.

What was less widely reported, until the Grenfell Inquiry started hearing evidence in the summer of 2018, were the comments of individual firefighters. Firefighters caught up in this unprecedented blaze. However, some stories did filter out via social media and whilst I don't know the author of this particular story, suffice to say they are a serving London Firefighter. This is one firefighter's account of that horrendous Grenfell Tower fire, as they wrote it.

"As always we were woken with a start. The lights came on and the automated tannoy voice started shouting our call signs. It never fails to set your heart racing. Getting dressed I looked at the clock. I'd only lay down less than an hour ago. Time to see what we've got this time? Down the pole to the fire engines. I'm handed the call slip. 'Make pumps 25'... What! No... That's a big incident. Wait.... I don't know where this is? It's not on our ground. We have to look it up and then we're out the doors.

We arrived about 1.35 a.m. But due to the way cars are parked in the streets and the fire engines that are arriving with us we couldn't get closer than 4–5 streets away from the building. Other engines, closer, would be setting up water ready for us to use.

We could see this was bad immediately. The sky was glowing reflecting the rising flames. Leaving our engine we started walking quickly towards it. Picking up pace we carry our breathing apparatus sets (BA) on our back. Drawing nearer we try to read the conditions in front of us. Try to take in as much information as we can. How big is the tower? Where is the fire? Where is the fire going next? How's it behaving; how many flats are affected? Most importantly of all, how many people are still in there?

We are mustered outside the entrance. Parts of the building are already starting to fall off into the surrounding area. As we entered the 'Tower' the fire on the outside was raging from the top to the bottom. Walking up the internal staircase to the 'bridgehead' on the 3rd floor we are told to look at the floor plan. A plan that had been hastily drawn on a wall. We stood looking at it waiting at entry control to be given instructions. My BA partner (a new mother herself) and I stand waiting there, with other firefighters, waiting to see what information was available.

We are given our brief... 'Up to 23rd floor; people stuck in their flat go!'

The 23rd floor? I repeat it back, confirming the flat number to the Watch manager. I start up my BA set as the reality of how high we have to climb and have to do it on a single cylinder of compressed air! Weighed down carrying 30 kilograms of equipment, plus our fire kit and the weight of the BA on our backs we passed through entry control handing in our tallies and again confirming our brief. We made our way up a crowded stairwell struggling to make progress. At times we are unable to pass because of the amount of people on the stairs coming down. The stairwell is full of other firefighters in BA bringing people down all in various states and conditions.

The smoke grew thicker with each floor we climb. There are no proper floor numbers on the stairwell. There are two flights of stairs per floor. After about eight flights of stairs it was hard to know where you were. Someone before us had tried to write the floor numbers on the wall with a chinagraph pencil. This didn't last long as the greasy smoke was covering the walls with a film of blackness. Around the ninth floor we lose all visibility. The heat is rising. Still we continued up and up, through the blackness. We reached what we believed is 19/20th floor, but there was no way to tell? Here we find a couple desperately trying to find their way out. They are panicking. Choking and blinded by the thick toxic air. A quick pressure gauge check tells us that the amount of floors we'd climbed had taken its toll. We were getting low on air. There's no way we could make it up to the 23rd and back down 20 flights to the bridgehead. The couple were screaming at us, through all the coughing, trying to tell us there were five more people on the floor above!

I had awful decisions to make. Upsetting choices and a very short amount of time in which to make them. In what seems less than a minute these things go through my head. I will list a few of them for you. I needed to consider each one carefully before making my decision:

Now that we've stopped and lost our rhythm would we have enough air to leave this couple and try to reach the next floor?

Was the information we are getting from these people was correct? They are uncontrollably panicking as they choke and suffer from the heat?

If we let them carry on down the stairs unaided would they or could they find their own way out?

If we went up another floor would we actually find the five people?

If we found them what state would they be in? Could the two of us get that many out especially one or more are unconscious and who would we decided to take?

Do we have enough air to make it back down to safety ourselves from where we are?

Should I be considering asking my BA partner, a 'new mother', to risk even more than she already has…?

Can I accept/live with the thought that saving two lives is better than taking the risk to go up and potentially saving no one?

Aargh! Come on think! Am I doing enough? Can I give more? Am I forgetting any of my training? Stop---Breathe---Think. Think what? Why haven't we seen another crew for so long? Will another crew find them? Are we really where we think we are? The communication equipment, our radios, are playing up!

Have we missed an important message? Have the other crews been pulled out? Is the 'Tower' still safe?

I am arguing with myself in my head. Come on make a decision, and make it quick. These people are choking. OK, OK, OK! The decision's made! I do a double check. I ask my partner if it is the right decision. I'm already doubting myself. Come on get on with it… Right! Make the call. I try to radio down to our entry control.

'Alpha Control Priority!' No response.

'Alpha Control Priority!' Still no response.

Where are they… what's going on?

'Alpha Control Priority!' Did they answer? It's hard to tell. The signal is all broken. I think I can just about hear something.

'Alpha Control Priority!'

Alpha control responds… 'Go ahead with priority over.'

Are they talking to me? I can't hear my call sign. I pass the message. 'Alpha control. Two casualties found approx. 20th floor, crew escorting them down. Request another BA team be committed to reach flat on 23rd floor. Further traffic… five casualties are reported apparently trying to make their way out on the floor above. Over.' Alpha control: 'Message received.'

Were they talking to me? It broke up again. We really need to get out. Let's go! Grab my arm. Each taking a casualty we set off back down. Two floors down our casualties push us down a flight of stairs. They are screaming that they can't breathe. We try to reassure them.

'Stay with me! We are going to get you out. Please stay with me!'

Down and down we go, flight after flight. Then I hear a shout from behind me. It's from my partner. Her female casualty has collapsed unconscious. My partner is having to drag her down the stairs on her own. I can't help her. Two more floors down we find another crew making their way out. One firefighter is carrying a little girl. I hand my casualty to another firefighter who has a free pair of hands.

'Please take him out' I shout. 'We'll be right behind you.'

I turn to go but he hands me something, a firefighter's helmet! This can't be good. Why does he have this? Where is the firefighter it belongs to? I turn round and go back up one flight and see him. He's missing his helmet but he's with my BA partner. Not only does he not have a helmet but he has no BA either. Are you OK? Where's your BA set? He had given it to a casualty he tells us. He's coughing with the smoke, delirious from the heat and near exhaustion. Yet still he tries to help carry the casualty! Helping others is still his first thought. I shout at him.

'Get down those stairs. Get down to the bridgehead!'

I take the casualty's arms, my BA partner has her legs. We start down again. Round and round we go. Hearing the noise of crews working hard around us. Crews still going up pass us.

My BA pre-alarm starts to sound. This means my air is running low. Similar sounds are all around me. Turning a corner we see a white fire helmet. It's a watch manager in the stairwell. We've reached the bridgehead. My partner takes the firefighter without BA into the lobby to get him oxygen. The watch manager takes the casualty's legs from her. Walking backwards down another six flights and I'm on the ground floor. I hand the casualty over. Now I'm off back up those stairs. Reaching the entry control I shut down my BA set down and remove my facemask. I hope for a breath of fresh air. No hope, it's not clean air in here. I suck in lungful of light smoke. It makes me cough and retch, but it is better than the air higher up the Tower.

With my BA tally collected I find my partner. She's still with the helmetless firefighter and administering him oxygen. We go and take him down with us. As we walk outside we are desperate for a drink of water. We collapse onto the grassed area by the leisure centre. Someone see us and throws us some bottled water. I drink it down but it barely touches the thirst I have. As I look about me colleagues surround us, their tunics off, their T-shirts soaked through with sweat.

No one's really able to say a word. We all sit there looking up at the building we've just come out of. It's worse now! Fire is everywhere and it's fierce! It's hard to comprehend we were just in there. We see a man at a high window, trapped in his flat. We can hear urgent messages on the fire-ground radios.

They know he's up there but no one can get to him. Other crews are working hard trying to reach him. He's there for a long time before disappearing and then coming back.

Slowly we catch our breath. We service our BA sets, fit replacement full air cylinders and we are ready to go in again. Recovering, I go to find some more water. At a police cordon a woman stops me. She is crying and, pushing her phone at me, pleads she has her friend on the line. Her friend and baby are trapped on the 11th floor. It throws me. I struggle to reply. I look across to a police officer. I point at him and tell her he will take her to the people who will take her friend's information and pass it on to the crews inside. I say to her,

'Stay on the phone with her. Tell her not to give up. We are still coming. We are still getting to people I promise.'

No time to stop, don't get distracted. I've got to get a drink and get back in. Time passes quickly, some people are given jobs while others have to wait to be tasked with going back inside. Some time later, I couldn't say how long, we are all grouped together waiting for news. A senior officer is telling us he knows we've already broken all the safety policies we have. He knows the risks we've taken but that's not enough, we are going to have to take more! There are still more people in there who need us. He says he's going ask us to do things that would normally be unimaginable. To put our lives at risk even more than we already have. Everyone is looking round at each other listening to this officer who is trying to motivate us into action again. He didn't need to. We are ready. It is what we train for, colleagues who a little while ago were collapsed on the grass, are back up ready. Stood in their kit they're waiting for the orders to go in again.

Lots of things happened during the time I was waiting outside. Some people were rescued alive, others weren't. Some jumped. A mother threw her baby from a high floor. It was caught by a complete stranger. A mother saving her child from the fire. All this time, hour after hour, my colleagues were pushing themselves above and beyond what you'd think was humanly possible.

With the dawn, and time, we learn that pumps were made 40,

plus ten fire rescue units were urgently requested. Something that had never been done before! Now 20 relief fire engines have been ordered. As they arrive, with fresh crews, those of us that were here early start to be swapped over. We are told to find our crews and attend a de-brief. But no one wants to leave. Each and every one willing to give more. However, eventually we all have to leave the scene.

19 hours after starting our night shift Red Watch firefighters arrive back to our fire station. It's time to try and get some rest as in four hours we are back on duty again. We hand the station over to the oncoming Blue Watch. We tell them what equipment we know is missing. I change over my dirty fire gear so I'm ready for the start of the next shift at 8 p.m. I'm covered in sweat and dirt and although I shower the smell of smoke won't go away. I shower three times and give up. I'm beyond tired, but I can't sleep as there's too much going on in my head. I need a drink!

I head to the local pub with my colleagues. I order a shandy as I'm back on duty soon. As we sit with our drinks we don't really talk. In fact we sit in almost complete silence, lost in our thoughts and trying to begin to process everything that's happened. Yet we are aware of all the people around us. They're laughing and joking with friends, enjoying their drinks in the sun. They are oblivious to what we've seen. Unaware of what we've been doing all night.

I've no appetite, but I know I need to eat. We go and get some food but it's hard to concentrate. We go back to the fire station, there's no time to get home. I find a bed in the dorm room and eventually manage 45 minutes sleep before I wake. I wash my face and get dressed. I'm ready to report for roll call. I am ready to do it all again."

The Public Inquiry into the Grenfell Tower fire was formally launched in September 2017. It began hearing evidence in public in May 2018. The Chairman, Sir Martin Moore-Bick, said the fire was "the city's greatest tragedy since World War Two" and described it as "an event of unimaginable horror". It is anticipated that an interim report, with recommendations, will be issued in early 2019.

It has been suggested the full, final, report into the Grenfell fire will follow 12 months later.

As this book headed off to the printers the Grenfell Inquiry had broken up for the summer recess. As it did so some of the nation's 'quality' newspapers provided a critique of the Inquiries progress. When the Inquiry reconvenes in early September 2018 the London Fire Brigade's evidence will, once again, be the focus of its attention.

The *Guardian's* lead paragraph reported:

"It took just 36 minutes for a fourth-floor kitchen fire to sweep 20 storeys up to the top of Grenfell Tower in the early hours of 14 June 2017. The public inquiry into the disaster, which went on to claim 72 lives, is taking far longer. Barristers are now homing in on what happened second by second, with much of the evidence centring on the controversial refurbishment of the 1974 building, ordered in 2012 and completed in 2016 and the London Fire Brigade's fire survival guidance policy."

In an article covering the Grenfell Inquiry evidence, *The Times* headline read: "Grenfell: bravery, chaos and failings".

The Inquiry, to date (August 2018), has shone a harsh spotlight on some of the practices and policies of the London Fire Brigade but it has also highlighted the heroism, courage and the sheer tenacity of those willing to risk their lives to save trapped residents in fire conditions unprecedented since London's blitz during World War II.

The Inquiry has been presented with much expert evidence. Witnesses who have concluded that Grenfell Tower was riddled with faults that accelerated the fire and made survival harder. One such expert, Dr Barbara Lane, a technical expert, suggested a "culture of non-compliance." It meant more than one hundred fire doors failed fire regulations. The building's mechanical smoke ventilation system broke eight days before the fire, according to Mr Martin Booth, the managing director of PSB, which made the system. The Counsel to the Inquiry, Mr Richard Millett QC, warned organisations involved in the refurbishment evidence not to "indulge in a merry-go-round of buck-passing".

The London Fire Brigade had previously sent a letter to some

London councils warning of "external fire spread on high-rise residential buildings as a result of being clad in combustible panels that presented a generic health and safety issue". However, in evidence its firefighters knew very little of such risks. Michael Dowden, the first incident commander, agreed his knowledge was "as good as the person in the street".

The fire spread with such rapidity and ferocity that the fire survival guidance, or 'stay put' strategy (advising residents to remain in their flats rather than enter potentially hazardous communal areas) failed, according to Dr Lane. The London Fire Brigade, she contended, kept the policy in place for too long and when 107 people remained inside. BA-wearing firefighters were sent in to rescue some people while fire control staff were telling others to stay put. A total of 65 individuals were either carried or assisted out by fire crews. The LFB asked if evacuation was feasible with only one staircase, no fire alarm and no way to communicate a general evacuation alert.

Grenfell Tower only had a dry riser main, rather than a wet riser, which is mandatory for buildings more than 50 metres high. This meant high-pressure water could not get to the top of the building.

Failing fire brigade fire-ground radio communications meant information from 999 calls were ferried into the building on survival guidance forms, and occasionally pieces of paper, by firefighters acting as 'runners'. For a period there were not enough firefighters in extended-duration BA sets to try to rescue people on the higher floors. Some firefighters even gave up their own BA sets to escaping residents whilst others connected spare facemasks to their BA sets to assist trapped children to escape to safety.

During the hearings hardened firefighters needed regular breaks. They rarely shed tears but their faces sometimes went blank as if some overwhelming thought or feeling had suddenly overwhelmed them. The strain of providing frequently harrowing evidence was not just restricted to the firefighters and their officers, fire control staff also found recounting that night's ordeal challenging. Watch Commander Glyn Williams, from Fulham, and who co-ordinated much of fire survival guidance information at the base of the tower, said the fire had had "a massive emotional impact".

During the first month of London's firefighters and officers giving evidence the Inquiry heard how training specific to high-rise buildings and the dangers of flammable building cladding was inadequate. What follows are personal accounts presented to the Inquiry. One is from a control officer, the other a firefighter. Between them they had less than 18 months' service when a small kitchen fire, on the fourth floor of Grenfell Tower, started a catastrophic chain of events. It stands as the UK's worst fatal fire.

Sarah Russell is a Control Room Officer. Her statement was read into the Grenfell Inquiry evidence on 19 July 2018. This is an abridged version of her story from that fateful night.

"I am a Control Room Officer (CRO) and have been in post, on the 'Watch' for the past nine months. I enjoy my job because it is very varied and no day is the same. Before working on the Watch I had to complete a nine week training programme. I began my training on September 12th, 2016. Every week we learned a new element before being assessed at the end. We had to pass each assessment before moving on to the next stage. Training also covered how to handle mobilising calls, when or when not to mobilise. For example, advising callers regarding fire alarms when cooking and explaining why we would not be attending.

The process of call handing is centred on trying to find out information quickly. Essentially we want to know the address and type of incident so we know what, where and how to deploy to the situation. We have to quickly find out the problem and then decide whether or not to deploy. If we deploy we check the address using our systems and then mobilise appliances using specific codes dependent on the call and then communicate the information to the nearest stations via a teleprinter which advises the crews of the call they will be attending. There are no set questions that a CRO asks; however, there is specific information that needs to be obtained. How we obtain the information is down to the individual CRO, but speed is essential. Therefore addresses and type of incident are paramount; names less so. Names would only be particularly necessary if we needed to call other emergency services such as the LAS or the police and we would pass on basic information.

Each call is handled on its own merit and dealt with specifically. It is standard practice that if a caller is calling from a landline regarding a fire in their property we will tell them to leave straight away. However, if they call via a mobile it affords us greater communication and we can continue to speak to them and offer reassurance whilst they make their way out. Typically, calls should last for about a minute and a half; however, it very much depends on the call and the caller. We will always try to keep the caller calm and safe until the crews arrive with them but at the same time we have to be flexible depending on the number of calls coming through and the available time we have.

Standard practice for most fire calls would be to advise the caller to leave, saying that fire crews would be making their way, who would attend, contain and deal with the fire. The vast majority of the time, that is the safest place to be and safest piece of advice to give. If they are unable to leave we need to probe further and ascertain why they cannot leave, whether it be for fire, smoke or heat. In the event that the situation changes and they tell us they cannot leave, this becomes a Fire Survival Guidance (FSG) call.

A FSG becomes active at the point the caller says that they cannot get out of their property and they are affected by smoke. If they are in a flat above or below a fire and not affected by smoke it will not be a FSG. In the event of a FSG our advice centres on trying to make the caller as safe as possible until fire crews can get to them. We would advise the covering of gaps in doors with whatever can be used to keep smoke out. Ideally to keep windows open to let fresh air in, but if smoke comes in we advise they shut them and move to a room that is furthest away from the fire. There is a reference information file (RIF) for guidance in the event that anything is forgotten. FSG calls are very much lead by the caller, we can only advise.

Every call that comes in to the LFB is logged, regardless whether anyone is deployed to it. The incident will generate a number and the numbers then work sequentially. The numbers continue to go up and will only reset at the end of every year at midnight on New Year's Eve. Currently our number in

2017 is around 132,000 I believe. Each call that a CRO deals with will have their initials next to the log number so that we are able to access the individual incidents that we have dealt with. Routinely, each CRO can look up any call they have dealt within the last three months using their own ID codes.

As of June 14th, 2017 I had been on the Watch for six months and had recently completed my probation. We were working a night shift and based from Stratford, our fall-back centre, because of routine maintenance at Merton. Stratford is a smaller Control Room than Merton. I was the radio operator monitoring channel 2 (south London). CRO Sharon Derby was operating channel 4 (North London). The first part of the night ticked over as a normal shift but after midnight I became aware of a call to a 4th floor block of flats. Initially nothing out of the ordinary, but then we started to become inundated with calls to the same block. Soon, all call handlers were busy with calls and I could see on the computer screens, a red button flashing which means there are emergency calls waiting to be answered.

The number of calls began stacking up and up. I asked Sharon if she would mind combining both channel 2 and channel 4 on the radio. My channel was silent so I thought I could help better by answering calls. I did not want to sit doing nothing when everyone else was busy.

Sharon agreed so I moved back to call handling. The first call I took was about an hour long. I think it was about 1.15 a.m. when I answered and it was a young girl inside Grenfell Tower. I tried to find out basic information from her, such as the flat number, floor number and how many people were inside with her. She told me that she lived on the 20th floor but had gone higher to the 22nd. Once I had received the basic information and due to the influx of calls I thought about ending the call so that I could move on to take others. But then I thought again. I was talking to a twelve year-old girl who was very scared, so I decided to stay with her. She told me that she had already been affected by the smoke and had tried to leave several times but was unable to go. I told her to go to the room least affected and to shut the windows, stay low to the floor and cover her mouth.

When she said that the flames were outside the window it did not make any sense. The fire was on the 4th floor, so how could she be seeing flames on the 22nd?

I then started to hear calls coming from the 14th floor and it started to make sense. The fire had moved, very quickly. I asked the girl what her name was and she told me it was Jessica. I asked Jessica if she was calling from her phone and I think she said she was. I asked to speak to someone a bit older to try and get some more information from them, but she did not hand it over. I do not know why. Perhaps she did not want to. I felt I needed stay with her and that she needed me. I asked her if she wanted me to stay and she said 'Yes.' I am glad I did, even if it was only to offer her a little support.

The fact that she did not hand the phone to anyone else showed to me that she needed it. I stayed with her for the entire call which I think was about an hour. All I could do was offer support, to keep asking questions in the hope that her situation might improve, tell her the fire engines were there, fighting the fire and try and prevent panic. After about an hour I could not get anymore response from her, only rasping sounds, then nothing.

I stayed on the line a little while longer with my hand hovered over the call termination button. I was torn as what best to do. I eventually ended the call when the line fell silent. Reflecting on that call, I felt completely helpless. When people are pleading with you, saying 'I do not want to die' and I cannot physically do anything to help them it is very hard. I can pass on all the information but I cannot actually do anything. That is very tough.

Not long after the call finished I became aware that the advice we were giving callers to stay where they were had changed to try and make attempts to leave via the stairwell. I think this was about an hour or two into the incident. I was told by Joanne [Smith], the Control Room Senior Operations Manager. I am not sure if it was a decision made in Control or if it had come from the crews on the ground.

FSC information about flats was being written up onto white boards at the back of the control room and anything new we had to have passed to them. I have no idea how many calls I took. The time went very quickly. There was still a stack of calls that needed to be answered and we began telling them the new advice. We were able to tell on our screens, from the numbers, if the caller had called previously. There were quite a few that I spoke to on more than one occasion. It was relentless, call after call after call. I do not remember ringing anyone back or even having the chance, just updating the callers with the new advice.

We kept asking them that if their situation changed, to keep calling us back which a number of them did. There was no time to look at names or any particular individuals, only the numbers. We gave the advice and then moved on time and time again. The calls got a lot quicker as a result, but on a number of occasions I was torn as to whether to stay with them or move on. The vast majority of time I gave the advice and moved on to another call. There simply was no time to offer comfort. By this time, the incident had become a 40-pump fire. An unprecedented level. Every single call was a FSG call. One after another, after another, after another. With no time to stay with them I got the details and where they were and moved on trying not to get too emotional. Normally with a FSG call a supervisor will listen to make sure we are giving the right advice and pass on any messages to the radio operators for the crews on the ground.

At 5 a.m. there seemed to be a lull in the number of calls. It went eerily quiet and a little creepy. I remember someone saying, 'I wish they'd call again.' That way we would have known that they were still alive. The Control Room was completely drained and a number were very upset. I remember someone having a look on their phone at images when it went quiet. We had no TV on the Control Room so I had a look on the phone and then saw the extent of the blaze. I remember someone saying, 'Oh my God! How is anyone still calling us?!' The whole building was on fire.

After 5 a.m. there were a few calls but nothing in the realm of what we had dealt with before. A lot of the calls were from family members calling about relatives that lived in Grenfell

Tower. I answered a couple but then moved back to my role as radio operator. I remember messages coming from the police helicopter about a man on an upper floor who could not get out but who could be seen at the window. I am not sure what happened to him.

We were told that we had to speak to the counsellor before leaving. It was obvious that some people did not want to talk yet so they were told to expect contact at a later date. I think I left about 8 a.m. I think it hit me when I was driving home. It was all over the news and the radio. That's when I got upset.

Harry Bettinson was a probationary firefighter at the time of the Grenfell fire. He is stationed at Paddington Fire Station on the Red Watch. Harry undertook his outsourced 'Babcock' recruit fire-fighter training course in February 2016. During his 11 weeks basic training he received only one document on high rise fire procedure and had practised 'High Rise' bridgehead procedures but received no practical high-rise training and no input on the dangers of flam-mable cladding on high-rise buildings. When asked by the Inquiry Counsel if he was aware of the problems of metabolic heat stress, its signs and symptoms, Harry confirmed he was and sighted the bene-fits of his 'real' fire training. On 14 June 2017 Harry was in his ninth month of operational service.

Harry was one of five riding Paddington's pump when they were ordered to the "six-pump fire at Grenfell Tower" at 1.15 a.m. In his evidence Harry thought that he was attending a 'normal' high rise fire when, wearing BA, he and his crew mates reported to the second floor bridgehead. Briefed, they were ordered to the sixth floor where they found the smoke was worsening and everyday shapes lost their definition. Whilst evacuating the sixth-floor flats they came across a family of five. One of Paddington's crew managers and two of the firefighters provided urgent assistance and guided the family down to the lower floors. Meanwhile Harry and crew manager Guy Tillotson (a 24-year-service Paddington firefighter) ran towards the tenth floor banging and knocking on all the flat doors on the seventh, eighth and ninth floors. When they reached the tenth floor there was a noticeable rise in the heat levels and the smoke was down to the floor. Without any breathing apparatus 'Barrie' communications they were unable to let the bridgehead know of the conditions above, so returning to the ninth floor they were preparing to set their hose line into the 'dry' rising main and attack any fire on the tenth when suddenly dense smoke completely filled the ninth floor stairwell.

This was when firefighter Jim Wolfinden and crew manager Ben Gallagher discovered a family at the door of Flat 65, a mother and her young daughter. It was believed that after taking the other family down from the sixth floor the pair followed Harry's and Guy's footsteps back up! Harry explained to the Inquiry Counsel, "We now had two jobs. We had a family to get out and a fire to fight on the tenth floor." Flat 65 was located in the right hand corner of the ninth floor's enclosed lobby.

With Harry and Guy Tillotson standing in the lobby, by the dry riser, and Jim Wolfinden standing at the door of flat 65, talking to the family, in the space of ten to fifteen seconds thick black smoke filled the whole lobby area. They all retreated into the flat to work out what to do. With it rapidly getting hotter and the smoke conditions worsening outside they couldn't fight the fire as the priority now was getting the mother and daughter to safety. They would tell other crews to fight the fire on the floor above and get others to continue checking all the flats from the tenth floor up.

But there was no way to get the mother and daughter out without a supplemented air supply. The heat was too much and the smoke too toxic for them. Luckily the flat wasn't affected by the smoke or fire as yet so it was relatively safe for now. However, they could see the fire outside and burning bits of the Tower falling past the flat windows. It was decided that the two crew managers Tillotson and Gallagher, plus a firefighter from Brixton called Ben (who was standing by for the night at Paddington) would go down to get spare BA sets. Ben was already very low on air and his alarm was sounding.

Harry and Jim Wolfinden stayed with the mother and daughter. Knowing they had to conserve air, and it's difficult to speak through their BA masks, the pair turned off their BA sets and removed their facemasks. Harry informed the Inquiry, "This is not the done thing. It's against our proper procedure. You are not meant to come off air until you get back down to the bridgehead, but normally you wouldn't be staying in the building like this."

As Harry secured the front door with a duvet and other items to prevent the smoke seeping into the flat, Jim Wolfinden concentrated on speaking to the mother and daughter to keep them calm. All the while they could all see flames and burning debris falling down past the windows. "It was like fireballs and flaming arrows coming down," Harry reported.

The mother and daughter stayed remarkably calm the whole time. They did not panic but just sat listening, and talking to Jim Wolfinden who was reassuring them. The young girl, who was about four or five years old, never made a fuss. Harry had to shut the flat windows as smoke was starting to enter the room. (At this point Harry was still unaware just how big or serious the fire was, but realised they were running out of time.) Going back out into the lobby Harry monitored the situation and checked if the others were coming back up yet. He found the whole lobby was compromised: totally full of thick, black, hot smoke. He stopped briefly to look through the letterbox of an adjoining flat and saw that the whole thing looked to be on fire. Returning to the flat Harry called his Paddington guvnor, Watch Manager Steve Collins, on his fire-ground radio. Harry told the Inquiry Counsel, "We were thinking whether they could get the turntable ladder up to us to get us out." But Steve Collins told him there was no chance it could get anywhere near them due to the amount, and size, of the debris falling down.

The four of them waited in the flat for what seemed a very long fifteen to twenty minutes. Suddenly there was banging on the front door. Harry opened it, and much to the surprise of the fire-fighting BA crew, they asked Harry what the hell he was doing and why was he in the flat with no facemask on? Harry explained the situation and what they were doing. Told of the family inside and anticipating his crew mates returning with spare BA sets, so as to get the family out, the crew continued with their search and rescue role. As Harry shut and resealed the door, the mother and daughter remained calmly sitting in the flat.

Ben Gallagher and Guy Tillotson returned to the flat carrying two spare BA sets. As they entered the flat they too took off their facemasks. A short discussion followed as to just how they were going to get everyone out safely. But Guy was virtually out of air, others were very low on air. Putting one of the new BA sets on the mother, a spare facemask was connected to Harry's set so the little girl could share his air. Once again she made no fuss not even when the face mask was placed over her face. Guy attached his facemask to the other spare BA set and carried it.

With Harry holding the child against his chest they needed to get down as fast as possible. The whole place was being consumed by the smoke. Ben Gallagher led, clearing obstacles out of the way as he went, Harry followed, and the mother was behind him with Jim Wolfinden assisting her down. Guy Tillotson was at the rear carrying the spare BA. As soon as they left the flat they couldn't see a thing. On the stairwell the smoke was so thick that their BA torches could only penetrate about 150 mm (6 inches). There was no other lighting, but even if there was the black smoke totally obscured it. They had nine floors to get down.

The stairwell was, in parts, congested. There were extended duration breathing apparatus crews heading up the Tower. Getting past them was a real struggle due to the increased size of their BA sets. They were having to protect the mother in case she was barged into. Harry shielded the child who never made a fuss. The stairwell seemed even narrower than it had going up. Lengths of hose and other equipment littered the stairwell.

Ben was guiding Harry and child down as he cleared the way. It was getting hotter the further down they got. The heat was now uncomfortable through their firefighter's protective clothing and they all knew the mother and child never had that degree of protection. As they reached the third floor visibility improved. The bridgehead had now moved down to the ground floor lobby area. When they arrived the Watch Manager at the bridgehead took the little girl from Harry as he removed her facemask. They left the pair with the Watch Manager. Both the mother and child seemed OK despite their nightmare ordeal.

When Paddington's crew had gone to Grenfell it was an 8-pump fire. When they entered the tower, under air, it was a 25-pump fire. Now, coming out, it was a 40-pump fire. In evidence Harry said:

"This was unreal, it's nothing you could ever expect. As a

351

crew of four we collected our tallies and we left the tower out through the main entrance. All of our ADSU alarms had been going mad, none of us had air left. We needed to go and get our face masks and kits cleaned off, get new air cylinders and complete an A-Test with the BA sets so that we were ready to go in again."

In an uncustomary remark by the Inquiry Chairman, Sir Martin Moore-Bick, he praised the young firefighter when Harry finished giving his evidence. In Sir Martin's view, "You played a very important part in the Grenfell incident. Well done."

Footnote

When the Inquiry reconvenes in September 2018 the spotlight will inevitably turn onto the Brigade's principal officers and its Commissioner, Dany Cotton, as London Fire Brigade's responses to the Grenfell Tower fire are placed under continued Counsel scrutiny. Harsh lessons will, no doubt, be learned. Some changes to LFB policy and procedures appear inescapable. Improvements to certain aspects of training, to station personnel gathering pre-planning information and more reliable radio communications are unavoidable. The probability of recommending the introduction of fire escape hoods for those trapped by smoke in burning buildings, and carried by firefighters, seems highly likely.

However, one clear conclusion remains a certainty. Throughout this unprecedented fire the bravery, courage and dedicated commitment of the crews attending it will not go unnoticed by either the Inquiry or the wider public at large.

(Fact)

What Is a Firefighter?

"What is a firefighter?
They are the person next door... .
They are like you and me with warts and worries and unfulfilled
  dreams.
Yet they stand taller than most of us.
They are firefighters...
A firefighter is at once the most fortunate and the least fortunate of
  people.
They save lives because they have seen too much death.
They are gentle because they have seen the awesome power of violence
  out of control.
They are responsive to a child's laughter because their arms have held
  too many small bodies that will never laugh again... .
They don't preach brother and sisterhood.
They live it."

Author Unknown

Glossary

ACO: Assistant Chief Officer, the third most senior rank in the London Fire Brigade when it had ranks. Today the Brigade has 'roles' and the equivalent rank is Assistant Commissioner.

ADO: Assistant Divisional Officer; the rank above a Station Officer. Subsequently re-designated Station Manager.

Aerial: Fire engines capable of reaching the upper floor (maximum height eight floors) of buildings i.e. Turntable ladders, Hydraulic Platforms and Aerial Ladder Platforms.

AFA: Automatic fire alarms, a term used to describe a variety of automatic heat and smoke detectors that when activated set off a fire alarm and may connect to distant AFA control centres or fire control rooms.

BA: Collective name for breathing apparatus sets which enable a firefighter to enter an irrespirable atmosphere and work. Historically, oxygen cylinders were used with BA but now only compressed air is used. Currently in the London Fire Brigade most fire engines carry standard duration BA sets, with selected special appliances carrying extended duration BA sets.

Barrie: An intrinsically safe radio communications set worn in conjunction with BA sets.

Branch: The outlet connected to the end of a length of hose which enables either a jet of water or a spray to be directed onto a fire or an incident.

Bridgehead: A forward command position, normally in high-rise buildings, two or more floors below the fire floor, and where firefighters are briefed and deployed to deal with an incident.

CEAG A spark proof, battery lamp worn with the Proto (oxygen) BA sets. (Stands for Certified Electrically Against Gas.)

CFO: Former title of the Chief Fire Officer of the Brigade, now referred to as Fire Commissioner.

CMC: Former Command and Mobilising, which replaced the three Area control rooms; Stratford, Wembley and Croydon. Now termed Brigade Control it is an outsourced facility operation based at Merton, handling all the Brigade's mobilising across the Greater London area.

Conflagration: a fire of such intensity that jets of water have virtually no effect on it.

DC: Divisional Commander. Senior officer in the former London Fire Brigade and in the charge of a Divisional area. Discontinued as a term in 1986.

DO: Senior ranking fire officer, now termed a Borough Commander of Group Manager.

Dry Riser: if the building has a floor level higher than 18 metres but less than 50 metres or has floors more than 10 metres below ground it is constructed with a 'rising main'. Firefighters attach charged lengths of hose at the ground floor, then carry hose to any floor and are supplied with water. When a building is more than 50 metres high the rising main has to be a 'wet riser' and is permanently charged with pressurised water.

Donning and stating up: The putting on of a BA set and turning it on.

Fire: The rapid oxidisation of gaseous, liquid of solid fuel in atmospheric air.

Fire Rescue Unit: A generic term for London's fire appliances that carry out a 'heavy' or 'specialist' rescue role. Its equipment depends on where it is deployed. An FRU may carry heavy-duty cutting equipment for use at road traffic collisions or other transport incidents (e.g. rail). Line rescue equipment is carried on selected Units but all FRUs carry extended duration breathing apparatus sets. It forerunners were called Emergency Tenders and were once the only specialist rescue fire engines in the Brigade.

Firefighter: The entry level role in the UK fire service.

Goer: A fireman's term for a fire that is burning fiercely or 'going well' when the crews arrive.

Guvnor: A term of address used by firemen/firefighters to describe a watch Station Officer or Watch Manager.

Hydrant: A fixed water supply point on a water main found in nearly every street and located under the surface of the pavement and marked by a yellow descriptive marker plate indicating the size of the main and the distance from the marker.

Hydraulics: The science of the flow of liquids, and particularly the firefighter's science of the movement of water from one point to another by whatever mechanical means.

Jet: A fitting on the end of a hose which allows pressurised water to be directed onto a fire or another incident.

Job: A term used to describe a working incident, normally a fire that is serious upon arrival and may be protracted.

Junior buck ('JB'): The newest firefighter, male or female, to join a fire station watch. Normally from their recruit training and called probationers, they keep the tag 'JB' until the next 'newest' firefighter joins the watch.

Knock-off: Turning off the water supply from a fire engine pump or a hydrant.

Knots and lines: A drill where firefighters practise their skills a tying different fire service knots and use the different lines carried on fire engines.

Lines: Rope cut to a specific length and used for rescue or general purpose tasks.

Make up: A term used to describe an incident when more than the initial attendance is required to deal with a fire or other incident. A request for more resources/urgent assistance is deemed as a priority message and sent as "Make pumps", followed by the number of appliances/specials required – i.e. "Make pumps eight."

Multiple calls: An incident where the fire service control room receives more than four or five separate calls to an occurrence in a short space of time, indicating the incident is genuine or serious.

Nominal roll board: A roll board of all the individuals riding a particular fire engine or fire service vehicle. It is handed to the control pump/unit upon arrival at any make up incident to facilitate a roll-call in the event of an evacuation of fire service personnel.

On-the-bell: A term used to describe that a fire engine is en route to an incident. Originates from when fire engines only had a hand bell to warn and clear its passage through traffic.

On-the-run: A term used to describe that a fire engine or item of fire service equipment is operationally available and ready for use.

Ordering: A mobilising message for a fire crew/crews or senior officer(s) and given by control officers by teleprinter, radio or telephone directing firefighters to an incident. Origin of the phrase comes from when firemen were dispatched via telephone and the message started: 'You are ordered to...'

Persons reported: An urgent 'priority' message sent from an incident to indicate that person are involved or trapped by a fire. An ambulance is ordered to a fire immediately this message is received.

Pump-escape (PE): A duel-purpose fire engine, now no longer in use. It carried a 50-foot wheeled escape ladder in addition to two hook ladders. It was considered the 'rescue' appliance of the Brigade and every London fire station had one.

Pump-ladder: The dual purpose pumping appliance that replaced the pump-escape. The appliance is essentially the same but carries a 13.5 metre alloy ladder which replaced the wheeled escape.

Proto: A BA set that uses oxygen and which air is supplied to firemen via a re-breather bag and with a nominal duration of one hour.

Riders: Members of a watch on duty at fire station and allocated to a fire engine.

Running call: A verbal emergency call made directly to a fire station or a fire engine crew by a member of the public in person.

Seat of fire: The fire's point of origin; the firefighters' efforts are directed to attack the seat of a fire whenever possible.

Shout: A firefighter's term to describe an emergency call.

Smoke eater: A term used to describe firemen who frowned on the use of breathing apparatus and who could, seemingly, endure endless smoky conditions whilst fighting a fire in a building.

Smoke issuing: a fire brigade term used when smoke is seen emanating from a building or structure.

Tally:

1. A name tally that is attached to a breathing apparatus set and must be handed to the BA control officer by the wearer prior to firefighter entering an incident requiring BA.

2. A tally is attached to every pump outlet and indicates the station number and the delivery outlet number. At incidents the tally is removed and attached to the branch being fed by that specific pump outlet. It lets the crew know which pump is supplying their water at large incidents and allows the pump operator to react to and follow the crews' instructions.

Watchroom: A room designated at every fire station as the communications centre and where emergency calls are directed by the mobilising control. In times gone by it was the room where firemen kept watch 24 hours a day.